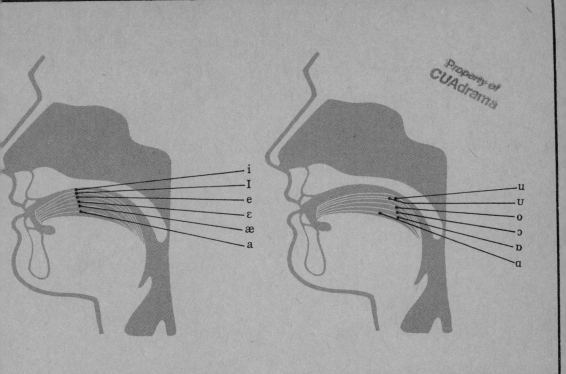

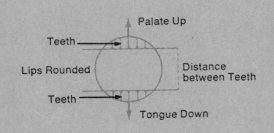

Palate Up

Teeth

Lips Rounded — Distance between Teeth

Teeth

Tongue Down

Your Speech and Voice

The Vowels and Diphthongs of American English

Symbol	Example	Symbol	Example
i	seat*	o	soap*
ɪ	sit	ʊ	foot
e	safe*	u	food*
ɛ	set	ə	alone**
æ	sat	ɝ	third §
a	half†	ʌ	shut**
ɑ	calm	aɪ	sigh
ɒ	odd‡	aʊ	now
ɔ	sought	ɔɪ	toy §§

*Normally diphthongal forms, [ɪ i, e ɪ, o ʊ, ʊ u].

**Unstressed vowel only.

†As in ENE; /æ / for most others; /ɑ/ for some.

‡As in ENE; /ɑ/ for others.

§For "r-less" speakers.

§§Other diphthongal, complex vowel forms are detailed in Chapter 12.

The Consonants of American English

Symbol	Example	Symbol	Example
p	pen	r	red
b	bend	s	said
m	men	ʃ	shed
w	win	ʒ	measure
			chump
			jump
			yes
			call
			Gaul
			sing
n	no	h	home
l	low		

your **speech** *and* **voice**

your **speech** *and* **voice**

Arthur J. Bronstein & Beatrice F. Jacoby
Queens College of The City University of New York

RANDOM HOUSE | *New York*

Preface

THERE IS NO DEARTH of texts available for use in voice and diction classes. Another is needed only if it presents the student and instructor with materials and treatment not readily available elsewhere. The authors of this text believe they have provided such a source, for the following reasons:

1. This text reflects the reported results of recent research on the physiology of phonation and on speech production generally. It has drawn freely from the expanding literature in descriptive linguistics and experimental phonetics.

2. This text not only presents the student with pertinent and extensive drill-practice material, but also provides detailed treatment of the subject matter necessary for an understanding of the characteristics of speech and voice used by educated American English speakers.

3. The treatment of such aspects as stress, juncture (pause), pitch, and melody patterns of American English does not reflect the treatment common to other texts in voice and diction. Rather, this text makes considerable use of the observations of such linguists and phoneticians, both here and abroad, as Kenneth L. Pike, George L. Trager, Henry Lee Smith, Jr., Dwight L. Bolinger, Lee S. Hultzén, G. F. Arnold, and J. D. O'Connor.

4. The recommended pronunciations are based on recent reports of scholars in American dialectology, especially those by Hans Kurath and Raven I. McDavid, Jr., through their publications based on the findings of the *Linguistic Atlas of the United States and Canada*; by Charles Kenneth Thomas, whose extensive recordings of American

v

speech provided source materials for his publications; and by others whose area studies are reported in such sources as *American Speech* and the publications of the American Dialect Society and the Speech Association of America.

This text is written for the student who is motivated to make his voice and all other aspects of his speech reflect the norms of cultivated American English, that is, those patterns used by educated speakers. The normative or standardizing entries that appear in this book are derived from the findings of current scholarship. The judgments expressed are thus general judgments, which do not always agree with the personal preferences of the authors.

Much of the practice material can be used by the student in self-teaching sessions. The authors know that no student can improve his speech and voice alone. He needs the expert guidance of the teacher who can explain, demonstrate, and help develop listening criteria. Once the student has learned to discriminate between similar and different forms, qualities, and patterns, he can apply these criteria himself, using the practice material.

The authors have reviewed each other's contributions and have tried to make a unified presentation. Each does, however, assume responsibility for his separate contributions. Dr. Bronstein contributed the sections on prosodic features and the sounds of the system (Parts Two and Four and Chapter 6), plus the pertinent introductory chapter (Chapter 1). Dr. Jacoby contributed the sections on speech mechanisms (Chapter 5) and voice (Part Five), plus the pertinent introductory chapter (Chapter 2).

We add a special note of gratitude to our colleagues in the City University of New York and elsewhere who, over the years, have discussed with us different aspects of this text—in our offices and at local, regional, and national conventions. We are especially indebted to the following colleagues, who took the trouble to correspond and consult with us on certain special problems of symbolization: Dr. William G. Moulton of Princeton University; Dr. Claude E. Kantner of Ohio University; Dr. Harold B. Allen of the University of Minnesota; Dr. E. Gene Ritter of the University of Hawaii; Dr. Max Nelson of California State College at Fullerton; Dr. Audrey Duckert of the University of Massachusetts; Dr. John W. Black and Dr. Ruth B. Irwin of The Ohio State University; Dr. Charlotte G. Wells of the University of Missouri; Dr. John B. Newman of Queens College; Dr. Dwight Freshley of the University of Georgia; Dr. Lee S. Hultzén,

Professor Emeritus, the University of Illinois; Dr. Cj Stevens of Hunter College; Dr. Arthur S. Abramson of Haskins Laboratories and Queens College; Dr. Marshall D. Berger and Professor Robert Sonkin of the City College of New York; and Dr. Alan C. Nichols of San Diego State College. Dr. Elizabeth B. Carr of the University of Hawaii read the two chapters on stress and melody; Dr. Eleanor M. Luse of the University of Vermont read all the chapters dealing with voice; and the late Dr. Claude M. Wise, Professor Emeritus, Louisiana State University, read the entire manuscript. We are deeply grateful to them for their careful reading, incisive comments, and suggestions for improvement. And, of course, we are most indebted to our students, whose questions and reactions over the years have strongly influenced our treatment of the material. Their prodding, added to that of our colleagues, to find better ways to teach speech and voice has provided, of course, our chief reason for writing this book. We hope we shall not disappoint them.

We are most grateful to the staff of Random House, Inc., and especially to Leonore Hauck, Managing Editor, for her patience and encouragement and to Jeannine Ciliotta for her discriminating editing.

We are grateful to Elsa Bronstein, who typed the drafts of Chapters 1 and 6 and Part Four and who designed all the drawings and charts in those sections; to Mary Zalkind, who typed the remainder of the manuscript; and to Jeannette Nadelberg, who did all the illustrations for Chapter 5 and Part Five.

Finally, we wish to thank Elsa, Nancy, and Nab Bronstein, Charles Perinchief, and Dr. Martha Schon, each of whom helped make it possible for us to complete the text.

A.J.B.

B.F.J.

To the memory of CLAUDE MERTON WISE—*teacher, scholar, critic*
(1887–1966)

contents

part five   **the voice**

figures

an outline of the book

part one | **introduction**

chapter 1 *The Speech and Voice We Use*

NO PERSON, no matter what language he speaks, sounds exactly like any other person. It is rare to mistake one person for another, unless both are complete strangers—strange in looks, sound, and ways. If we are not very well acquainted with Chinese people, we may mistake two young Chinese boys for the same person if we see them at different times. If all male Javanese adults look alike to the average American, as do perhaps all male adult leopards, it is because he has not learned to distinguish their differences. The Javanese parent has no such difficulty distinguishing his children from one another, of course. And, as obviously, the zookeeper has no difficulty distinguishing his two leopards from each other. "Similarity" and "difference" are relative terms.

It is obvious that an awareness of the differences between any two people is a very early step we take in understanding them. No one person is the same as another person, nor do we ever really confuse two people once we are really aware of each. Each of us differs from all others in too many ways to list. Two such differences are heard in the voice and speech we use.

Vast as are the differences among people, there are many similarities that are quite obvious to any of us when we stop to notice. Philippine children are more like one another than they are like Danish or Turkish children. And members of the James Abercrombie family in Aberdeen, Scotland, are surely more like one another than they are like members of the Giovanni Mazzeo family in Naples, Italy, or those of the Wu Chin family of Peking, China. It is such similarities that permit us to notice characteristics that help to

3

identify groups. The voices and speech patterns we use are also like those used by the neighbors in our community. Despite the differences among them, these basic similarities permit us to communicate with one another with considerable ease.

Our purpose is to analyze the similarities and differences between ourselves and others as speaking persons. The voice and speech patterns we use, once we analyze and understand them, become easily identifiable. What "belongs" makes us belong. What does not "fit," makes us conspicuous in the group.

To accomplish this purpose, it is necessary to analyze what makes us sound as we do. We shall need to be aware of the physiological, environmental, and cultural influences that have helped make us what we are. Our adjustments to these influences or our reactions to them can be noted in the ways we talk, walk, dress, and behave, in the voice quality we use, in the melody patterns we adopt, in the vowels and consonants we produce, even in the facial expressions and gestures we attach to our language as we speak to one another. Our concern in this book is to note those aspects of our language (the voice and speech) that are used by educated speakers of American English in urban areas of the United States. These are the patterns of voice and speech used by such members of our community as the teachers in our educational institutions, the writers and editors of our papers and journals, the officers of our banks, the political, business, and social leaders in our community who serve as elected representatives to local, state, and national legislative bodies, the professional people who minister to our needs when we require medical and legal help, and their friends. They are the patterns of voice and speech taught in our colleges and universities and used by those who communicate effectively in all situations, whose voice and speech are appropriate for them and for the particular occasion. These patterns, detailed in later chapters, can and do vary; the criteria of effectiveness and appropriateness do not. It is these criteria to which the reader is directed.

Once we know these aspects of speech and voice and can compare them with our own, we shall be able to note the similarities and differences. The choice, for us, will then be easy to make.

1.1. Determinants of Speech Patterns

The problem of whether or not to change how you sound is a difficult one to face. The motivation must be your own, for no change will have any lasting effect if accompanied by annoyance, hesitancy, regret, or doubt. Certainly how you sound is your business—you have made it such your entire life. All aspects of your speech and voice, except those bounded by the anatomical and physiological limitations of the speaking mechanism, have been either consciously or, perhaps to an even greater extent, unconsciously adopted by you. We sound as we do because of what we are, where we live, with whom we speak, and the effect we desire to create. Normally, the need to communicate makes us sound like others with whom we talk. As *they* speak, so do *we*. The language-learning process starts with the first sounds we hear in a never-ending continuum. Our own usages reflect those we hear. The residents of Bergen and Oslo speak Norwegian as those in Algiers and Rheims speak French, as those in Dallas and Ottawa speak English. Although it seems that willful choice is not an essential factor in the language-learning situation, it is hardly reasonable to assume that the environment provides us with no real choices.

Speakers *do* make choices whenever they speak: which word? how to place it with other words? with what expression, gesture, or facial accompaniment? with what intensity of voice? how loud or soft, how fast or slow? And a good part of the decision is dependent on the listener. For we hardly voice the same thoughts to different people in the same way! We do not speak with very young, strange children exactly as we do with familiar grown-ups—using the same polysyllables, the same melody changes, the identical vocal qualities, the same rates of speed, the same complex expressions.

Other choices in the use of our language may be more difficult to grasp, yet they are no less part of the decisions we must and do make. They are not choices of which language we speak or even of which regional dialect of that language we shall use. They are choices of the variety or style of that regional dialect we shall use, as well as of certain attributes of voice that permit us to communicate in the most acceptable and desired manner. We use those aspects of voice and speech that call the least attention to themselves—the voices that best fit ourselves and our environments, and the speech styles that are as much part of those environments as is the clothing we wear and the manner we assume. We do not choose to walk barefooted and tieless into the office of the principal of a high school, the president of a university, the chairman of the board of the major local industry. Nor do we, when admitted, scratch our backs, shout, squeak, or whine at him or speak with that variety of our language containing "deses," "doses," "ain'ts," "nuttin's," and "yeahs." Speakers with whom such expressions and dress are normal at all other times may find themselves at a disadvantage when dealing with the persons mentioned, for such behavior does not "belong" in the offices of such people.

The society in which we live has many varieties of dress, as well as of language. Different forms of our language may be expected on certain occasions and at certain social levels. If we are capable of making choices, we normally make those that reflect our understanding of situations and our desire to participate in them with the least amount of difficulty. If putting on a tie and brushing the hair is the "expected norm" in a social situation, we normally do so. If wearing long black tights and bulky sweaters is the norm in another situation, would we not do so too? If using a hoarse or nasal voice, an excessively rapid style, and special pronunciations for certain words sets us apart from the others, would we not choose to change if we could? Not doing so puts us at a disadvantage, one we consciously avoid if we can.

1.2. Language and "Correctness"

Let us pursue the matter of "correctness" a bit further. Is there a "best dialect" of English? Is one American-English regional dialect preferable to another? Should all well-educated Americans sound alike? These provocative questions are often raised. But they presuppose that there is one "correct" style or one "best dialect" clearly distinguishable from less acceptable ones. The answers to these queries must recognize that no one regional dialect is any "better" than another or that any one style of speaking is preferable to another for all people on all occasions. Should Bostonians sound like Michiganites? Do we expect to speak to others in identical fashion on different social occasions—some formal, some casual, some intimate? Such questions, once we understand what language is and how it functions, sound foolish, for they overlook the very nature and purpose of language.

Language use is the result of a social process. Language exists only within a social system. Once we recognize the social nature of language, we cannot assume that any one dialect or variety of that language is "better than" or "preferable to" another, except as it manages to accomplish the social functions demanded of it. If we speak to one another and accomplish the purpose of communicating our thoughts and desires effectively, expeditiously, efficiently, the variety of language we use is "good" for us and our listeners. Children on the playground may speak to one another differently from the way they might speak to an approaching teacher, or to a group of parents assembled at a parent-teacher association conference. A public-relations man will write his material differently when he prepares copy for a nationally circulated, high-priced weekly magazine and when he submits copy for a local daily newspaper. And when he talks about his firm's product during a weekend afternoon with his friends and neighbors, the form or variety of his speech is different again. These differences result from the recognition that different ways of speaking belong in different situations. Answering the question "What is right?" is not as simple as it seems. At the least, perhaps we might change the query to "Does it fit?" or "Is it appropriate to . . .?" or "Is it understood with ease?" or "Is it efficient?"

1.3. Labeling Usages

Once we recognize that there are different varieties or forms of the language we use, we avoid too quickly labeling different usages "correct" or "incorrect" merely because they are different. We can then proceed to analyze the different forms that do reflect the complexity of the social situations in which we speak. Many labels have been proposed for the many varieties of language usage. It is useful to look at some that are commonly employed.

One writer[1] has found it useful to recognize at least three different approaches: one dependent on the medium of expression—for example, newspaper English, radio and television English, and stage English; one dependent on the background of the speaker—provincial English, popular English, or vulgate English; and one that designates a situation—formal, informal, literary, or academic English or "trade talk." The editors of the *Linguistic Atlas of the United States and Canada* have found it useful to categorize all expressions tested and analyzed as *cultivated speech* (characteristic of educated, urban, middle- and upper-class people), *folk speech* (characteristic of isolated rural people of little prestige), or *common speech*, a convenient label for the wide range of expressions and pronunciations between the two others.[2] Still another author finds it useful to categorize these varieties as parts of a continuous stream of differences, reflecting the individual's interactions with his audiences.[3] Freidson attempts to "inquire into

[1] Paul Roberts, *Understanding Grammar* (New York: Harper & Row, Publishers, 1954), p. 14.
[2] Hans Kurath and Raven I. McDavid, Jr., *The Pronunciation of English in the Atlantic States* (Ann Arbor: University of Michigan Press, 1961).
[3] Eliot Freidson, "The Varieties of Individual Speech," *Quarterly Journal of Speech*, 42 (December 1956), 355–62.

the varieties of the individual's speech and see if it is possible to discern generalities of variation that may apply to all individuals."[4] He sees one variety as a highly elaborate system of grammatical speech signals that is impersonal, eminently public: perhaps that of a scientist speaking to other scientists at a conference. A second variety is characteristic of the same scientist's speech to his friends, wife, and family. It has a smaller vocabulary, with somewhat truncated grammatical usage, "without reliance on the elaborate possibilities of American English grammar."[5] Freidson believes that all educated individuals fluctuate between two such extremes: one characterized by careful, precise forms, the other by simple ones. He recognizes that the essential factor underlying the variations the speaker uses is sociological, not psychological. The speech fits the situation: formal, impersonal, and public versus informal, intimate, and private; from the most highly articulate speech to the most simplified. He sees these variations occurring along a continuum from speaking to a large audience, to speaking to a small audience of strangers, to speaking face-to-face with oneself (speech showing systematic variations that relate to the character of the audience).

A similar approach appears in a provocative essay called "The Five Clocks,"[6] in which the author distinguishes five styles or usage differences we command as native speakers of English. The reader is referred to Joos's discussion of details and his explanation of the differences among styles that can be called *intimate* (characterized by the coded expressions used by intimately related people, normally to remind the listeners of inner feelings through expressions known only to them); *casual* (the style we use with friends and acquaintances or with strangers whom we make "insiders" by treating them as such; *consultative* (in which the speaker supplies background information and the listener participates continuously—"our norm for coming to terms with strangers—people who speak our language but whose personal stock of information may be different"); *formal* (the style in which conversation begins between strangers—detached yet cohesive); and *frozen* (the style for print and declamation or "for people who are to remain social strangers"). Joos notes that "there is no law requiring a speaker to confine himself to a single style, perhaps even within the sentence. But normally, only two neighboring styles are

[4] *Ibid.*, p. 357.
[5] *Ibid.*, p. 358.
[6] Martin Joos, "The Five Clocks," Publication No. 22, Indiana University Research Center in Anthropology, Folklore, and Linguistics (April 1962).

used alternately and it is anti-social to shift two or more steps in a single jump, for instance from casual to formal."[7]

Behind all these approaches is the recognition that clear dividing lines between adjacent varieties or styles are impossible and that the speech we use is notably flexible; that it is not random; that it adjusts its very type or style in interaction with an audience and is therefore thoroughly social. All these varieties of individual speech, subtly or obviously different as they may be, are of concern to us.

The reader who expects to find proscriptions upon all those forms that do not fall into the category of "modern niceties" will be disappointed. He should not assume that fine discriminations can be easily made between formal and less formal varieties of educated speech or between certain less-educated forms (or sometimes even mild obscenities) and the language used by members of the social elite in their "less precise moments." Distinctions are often hard to draw, and boundary lines do not always satisfy those who have not themselves drawn them.[8] Drawing lines among the educated varieties is foolhardy and, with present evidence, in most instances unjustifiable. In some instances, distinctions are possible, even though hazy, between cultivated and less cultivated forms. When they seem clear, we shall draw them. When they do not, we shall be hesitant to do so. Any other approach should elicit stringent criticism.

It is perhaps necessary to state that although all the details are not known to anyone, enough is known to enable us to arrive at fairly accurate conclusions about the cultivated patterns of American English. Systematic studies of the current grammar, vocabulary, and pronunciation habits of American English speakers have been pursued at least since the 1930s—by individual scholars in universities throughout the country and in at least one major survey, begun in 1931.[9] Published findings are available for study,[10] and others continue to appear

---

[7] *Ibid.*, p. 17.

[8] Look up, for example, some heavy verbal "battles," keenly fought, upon the publication in 1961 of Merriam-Webster's *Third New International Dictionary*. Many pieces written during this controversy have been collected by James Sledd and Wilma R. Ebbitt in *Dictionaries and That Dictionary* (Fair Lawn, N.J.: Scott, Foresman & Co., 1962).

[9] Known as the *Linguistic Atlas of the United States and Canada*, this survey is sponsored by the American Council of Learned Societies. Three summary volumes of its findings have already appeared (in addition to many articles in scholarly journals, based on the collections assembled by the *Atlas* staff): Hans Kurath, *Word Geography of the Eastern United States* (Ann Arbor: University of Michigan Press, 1949); E. Bagby Atwood, *Survey of Verb Forms in the Eastern United States* (Ann Arbor: University of Michigan Press, 1953); and Kurath and McDavid, *op. cit.*

[10] Among the published reports on Southern speech are C. M. Wise, "Southern American Dialect," *American Speech*, 8 (1933); K. E. Wheatley, "Southern Standards,"

in scholarly periodicals. Decisions on language usage are not made at the whim of an author or the personal preference of any scholar. The available evidence can and should be sifted. There appears in these pages only what can be substantiated by the research evidence. The prejudices of the authors are put aside—as yours must be if you care to understand the nature and details of the language you speak. "Likes" and "dislikes" have no place here. Evidence does.

1.4. Standard and Nonstandard Forms

The overlapping of what is represented by these labels should not surprise us. Even apparently discrete standard-versus-nonstandard

American Speech, 9 (1934); W. C. Greet, "Southern Speech," in W. T. Couch, ed., Culture in the South (Chapel Hill, N.C., 1934); R. I. McDavid, Jr., "Low-Back Vowels in the South Carolina Piedmont," American Speech, 15 (1940); McDavid, "Postvocalic /r/ in South Carolina: A Social Analysis," American Speech, 23 (1948). On the speech of New York, see A. F. Hubbell, "Curl and Coil in New York City," American Speech, 15 (1940); C. K. Thomas, "Pronunciation in Downstate New York," American Speech, 17 (1942); Thomas, "The Place of New York City in American Linguistic Geography," Quarterly Journal of Speech, 32 (1947); Thomas, "Pronunciation in Upstate New York," American Speech, 10 (1935), 11 (1936), and 12 (1937); A. J. Bronstein, "Let's Take Another Look at New York City Speech," American Speech, 37 (1962). On Texas speech, see O. T. Stanley, "The Speech of East Texas," American Speech, 11 (1936); T. Z. Lawrence, "An Analysis of the Speech of Twenty Students at Texas Christian University," unpublished M.A. thesis, Texas Christian University, 1963; K. Wheatley and O. Stanley, "Three Generations of Texas Speech," American Speech, 34 (1959). On New England speech, see V. R. Miller, "Present-day Use of the Broad A in Eastern Massachusetts," Speech Monographs, 20 (1953); C. K. Thomas, "The Phonology of New England English," Speech Monographs, 28 (1961); W. Labov, "The Social Motivation of a Sound Change," Word, 19 (1963). On the speech of the Central and Western states, see H. B. Allen, "Aspects of the Linguistic Geography of the Upper Midwest," Studies in Languages and Linguistics in Honor of Charles C. Fries (Ann Arbor: The English Language Institute, 1964); Allen, "The Linguistic Atlas of the Upper Midwest of the United States," Orbis, 1 (1952); A. H. Marckwardt, "Principal and Subsidiary Dialect Areas in the North Central States," Publications of the American Dialect Society, 27 (1957); C. E. Reed, "The Pronunciation of English in the State of Washington," American Speech, 27 (1952); M. M. Kimmerle, R. I. McDavid, Jr., and V. Glenn, "Problems of Linguistic Geography in the Rocky Mountain Area," Western Humanities Review, 5 (1951); D. DeCamp, "The Pronunciation of English in San Francisco," Orbis, 7 (1958), and 8 (1959). On the speech of Hawaii, see J. Reinecke and A. Tokimasa, "The English Dialect of Hawaii," American Speech, 9 (1934); W. Wilson, "Speech Problems in Hawaii," Quarterly Journal of Speech, 23 (1937); E. Carr, "A Recent Chapter in the Story of the English Language in Hawaii," Social Process in Hawaii (Honolulu: University of Hawaii, 24, 1960).

Other reports can be found in the journals cited and in most issues of the Publications of the American Dialect Society. An overall view is available in chapter 9, "The Dialects of American English," by R. I. McDavid, Jr., in W. N. Francis, ed., The Structure of American English (New York: The Ronald Press Co., 1958); and in chapter VII, section 4, "Dialects," in H. L. Mencken, The American Language, 4th edition and the two Supplements abridged by R. I. McDavid, Jr. (New York: Alfred A. Knopf, 1963).

groups (or, to call them by more obvious labels, "cultivated and educated forms" versus "uncultivated and uneducated forms") have usages in common. A large part of the vocabulary of poorly educated speakers contains the very same forms found in the speech of the highly trained and well educated. Most of us use the same labels (words) for everyday expressions ("hello," "goodbye," "really?"), events, and things ("day," "night," "books," "house," "sky"). There are, however, usages, expressions, and pronunciations that are not common to both standard and nonstandard forms: "We din't never do it"; "Dis is my brudder"; "The baby drinked the miuk." These expressions are hardly common to speakers of cultivated English in any region of the country. They are associated with uncultivated, nonstandard speech. In all situations in which readers of this book find themselves, using these expressions would place speakers in socially disadvantageous positions. We do not mean that these expressions would be misunderstood or that they would not communicate intelligible messages to other speakers of English. They do. But such expressions are avoided by us because they carry with them messages that we do not intend to convey. Educated speakers of the language avoid such expressions simply because they are not part of the common, expected communicative process among those who, like themselves, might be labeled "cultivated." The result is that users of such expressions and pronunciations court the disapproval of speakers of the cultivated variety of the language. We cannot separate "standard" from "nonstandard" forms on the basis of personal preference or of the remembrance of things long past. Language, like other social customs, changes. The usages of any one period of time cannot be applied to another, unless the language is no longer in use. Such a language is "dead"; it is no longer subject to change. Nonstandard usages are not to be confused with older forms of the language. The latter are the current language's history. Our purpose here is to look at our language *synchronically*, that is, during a specific period of time: now. We are interested in the language in use by cultivated, living speakers.

It is useful to repeat and detail in somewhat different form some of our earlier points about the varieties of standard speech, for these varieties are the foundation of this text. All of us use at least two public varieties or styles of our language, one variously labeled "formal English" or "choice spoken English," the other as "general spoken English," "the common speech," "colloquial English," or "informal English." Mature speakers of cultivated American English typically possess superior educational backgrounds, usually four or more years of college. Characteristic of the middle and upper segments of urban communities, cultivated English has been called the variety ". . . taught, with various degrees of success in the schools; it is used on the radio and generally carries high prestige."[11]

A. *Formal English*

The "choice" or "formal" variety is the language style we use in formal, serious address. For most of us, this "formal English" is limited to solemn or formal occasions. It is more readily identified in its written form and is found in textbooks, scholarly essays, reference books, and magazines read by limited numbers of the highly educated. When spoken or written, it avoids contractions ("didn't," "wouldn't," "I'm") and employs very few ellipses ("I shall go either by car or [shall go] by boat"; "He eats cooked carrots, not raw [carrots]"). Spoken formal English uses very few extremes of intonation for dramatic effect, the range remaining within the confines of low to high, rather than from low to very high. And the pitch, loudness, and quality of the voice and the rate of speaking all reflect similar appropriateness to the formal occasion.

B. *Informal English*

The more common variety used by educated speakers is the "colloquial-informal" one, the language style of normal conversation, in less formal, less solemn social situations. In this style, the speech patterns range from the almost formal to the quite casual utterances we make in our daily activities: making our livings, speaking with members of our families, doing the marketing, discussing our affairs with our doctors or lawyers. At one end of the scale, this style closely approximates the written formal style; at the other, it tends to incorporate "folk usages."

When spoken or written, informal educated English does not avoid contractions and ellipses. Personal references, uncommon in formal English, are present, and popular expressions are not uncommon ("Her date was handsome"; "It's me"). Melodic levels are more extensive, ranging from low to very high. This variety of speech may be energetic and intense, as need dictates. It more closely reflects the attitudes and emotions of everyday living. It includes newer forms of speech that are perhaps avoided in more formal circumstances. It is the language of the radio and television salesman, the stockbroker and his customer, the librarian and the college student.

[11] H. A. Gleason, Jr., *An Introduction to Descriptive Linguistics*, rev. ed. (New York: Holt, Rinehart & Winston, Inc., 1961), p. 405.

The usages of such speakers and of others like them are reflected in our current standard dictionaries, in the dictionaries of contemporary usage,[12] in the special collections of vocabulary and pronunciation forms,[13] and in the scholarly essays written for journals concerned with such matters. It is not necessary to guess or presume too much about "cultivated usages." Even though all the facts of such usage are not known to anyone, a large body of evidence *is* available, and pronouncements about acceptability can be checked against such collected evidence.

1.5. Conclusion

These varieties of speech and aspects of voice are detailed in the remainder of this book. They are available not only for your investigation and study but also, once understood, for your use. Certain assumptions have been made. They include possession of normal hearing; of ability to discriminate between meaningful language forms and other common noises; and of normal structures for the initiation and projection of vocal tones and for the articulation of the many sounds of the language we speak. Finally, we assume that we are (and shall remain) part of that social segment we call "cultivated" or "educated," which uses what has been labeled "cultivated American English speech."

[12] See, for example, Bergen Evans and Cornelia Evans, *A Dictionary of Contemporary American Usage* (New York: Random House, Inc., 1957); and Margaret M. Bryant, *Current American Usage* (New York: Funk & Wagnalls Co., Inc., 1962).

[13] See, for example, the summary volumes of the *Linguistic Atlas* cited in footnote 9, p. 9.

chapter 2 *Your Voice and You*

SPEECH IS A FORM OF LANGUAGE that consists of sounds produced by utilizing the flow of air exhaled from the lungs. A long tradition of viewing these sounds in terms of *voice* and *diction* seems to imply that voice is one thing and diction another. Actually, the two are inseparable: Voice quality is affected by articulation, and diction in turn is affected by voice quality. Both the voice and the speech sounds you articulate are learned, and, as noted in the previous chapter, both reflect the society around you.

2.1. The Origins of Sound Quality

To a large extent, the way we sound is due to chance and to unconscious learning. Of course, our individual anatomical structures set the limits for the sounds we can produce, but the gamut of sounds available to us within these limits is prodigious. It is this range we wish to emphasize. Our speech includes a wide variety of consonances and dissonances, any one of which may be elicited by chance and then reinforced by environmental circumstances. What we learn to produce automatically out of the total welter of sounds depends upon the language habits of the people around us and the language habits they consider acceptable. Our speech can therefore be said to reflect both our individual personal structures and the social structure of which we are part.

That we use some sounds habitually, selecting certain ones again and again and neglecting certain others, does not imply that the ones we do use are any better or any worse than those we might have uttered.

14

Nor does it imply that our choices are immutable. It merely shows that a selection has been made. We shall refer to that particular kind of selection as "happenstance." Recognizing the accidental quality in our speech development can lead to an appreciation of how we can alter our vocal patterns.

2.2. The Development of Speech

A. *Early Voluntary and Involuntary Responses*

Although we cannot retrace each specific event in the process of our learning to talk, we can describe a general pattern in the development of our linguistic skills. The very first sounds uttered by a newborn baby give notice to the doctor that the infant is alive. It matters not at all at what pitch the baby announces his presence or whether the cry is nasal or shrill. The stimulus for the cry is a slap on the rump, and the result a reflex gasping inhalation that sets the vocal cords vibrating. It appears that the first sound uttered is not a learned response but occurs involuntarily in all live newborn babies.

For the first few weeks after birth the infant resorts to crying whenever he is hungry or in pain. Cries or vocal responses to pain are regarded as unpleasant *noises*. When the baby is happy or contented, he frequently makes softer, less piercing sounds, which we call "coos." Note that the stimuli for these vocal responses are pain or pleasure and that the infant responds muscularly whether he can hear or not.

B. *Learning and Environment*

A primary factor in the development of our vocal habits was the response made by the adults in our household when we cried or cooed and *had become aware of what we were doing*. When this awareness occurred is uncertain, but it probably took place long before we began uttering words. To attract adults' attention we made noises until someone came into view. After a while we knew which sounds caused certain effects and we produced them at will. We had learned to use certain voice qualities voluntarily. We had begun learning how to manipulate our environment to get what we wanted. The important thing to remember is that we *learned* to use a particular voice quality before we had learned to use a set of words designed to influence the behavior of people around us.

We learned so well, in fact, that even after we no longer needed the qualitative tonal patterns to elicit responses, we continued to retain many of the early vocal habits because we thought they were the "true us."

c. *Physiological Factors*

Although the gamut of sounds that we produced as infants was considerable, it was far less than our adult range. The physical attributes of the body that produced the sounds limited the potential number of different sounds we could emit. The basic sound producers were small. Within the range of that small vocal mechanism we had access to a number of pitches, each of which could be sounded at different loudness levels. Variations of quality could also be achieved by letting the air out through the nose, by increasing the mouth opening, by moving the tongue in some special way, or by any combination of these movements.

The size of the vocal structure, the amount of breath pressure available, and the shapes of the nasal and oral tract set limits to the sounds at our disposal. A fourth physical factor was change in the condition of the mucous membrane lining our vocal tracts. When, as sometimes happened, no response (or an unwanted one) was forthcoming from adults, the infant reaction was frustration followed by anger. The loud cries were accompanied by the congestion of tissue resulting from that frustration and anger. At that point the quality of the sounds changed. The earlier ones were temporarily discontinued.

d. *The Repertoire of Sounds*

Of the entire array of sounds at our disposal, we tended to use most often those that were most effective in getting results. *The habits of those about us were thus as important as any attributes of our own in determining what portion of our repertoire was to be repeated.* Such reciprocal patterning we have called "happenstance." Because learning played such a significant part in our sounding the way we do today, we must emphasize its effects: Had the circumstances around us been different, we might very well have come to use an entirely different set of sounds.

As we grew older, the physical structure of the vocal mechanism enlarged, and so did the repertoire of sounds. Today we have at our command language which we use to persuade people to behave in ways that please us. No longer do we need to rely on the quality of our voice alone to inform Mother that we are in pain or happy. That earlier whiny, shrill, raucous, or thin voice is no more natural to us at this age than is babbling or cooing—we have outgrown the need for it.

E. *The "Language Set"*

The reciprocal environmental patterning mentioned earlier was influenced by the fact that the adults around us used a particular group of sounds to symbolize thoughts, objects, events, hopes, and feelings. They spoke English or Swedish or German or Italian or Spanish or Japanese or Russian or one of any of a thousand languages. They had selected an arbitrary set of muscular modifications to produce a particular set of sounds to signify their ideas. The "language set" affected the range of vocal qualities indulged in continuously. We gradually learned to imitate these sounds, to associate them with meanings, and to give up the production of sounds that did not belong to the "set" of our native language. The particular modifications we use habitually were dictated by chance—the dialect of the geographic area or household into which we were born.

If we were born in the United States of English-speaking parents, the first sounds we uttered that were akin to English vowels and words filled the people around us with joy. They communicated their happiness to us. There were probably few other occasions when our accomplishments were as heartily cheered. We were encouraged to repeat them, and we did so with no effort whatever. Whether we said "mama" or "baby" or "up" or "light" or "out" or "more," whether we spoke with a whiny or a nasal voice, mattered not at all. The important fact was that we had voiced an English word and were therefore well on the way to becoming a member of a civilized linguistic community.

F. *The Melody Pattern*

Our voice qualities were reinforced from the time we were infants of two months or so. Our phonetic patterns were probably formed by the time we were two years old. During the interval we were sensitive to and used the melody pattern of speakers around us. The melody pattern is the variation in pitch that accompanies any language set. Before we became phonetically proficient, we were probably well able to reproduce the melody pattern. This ability helped people to understand us even though our articulation was not yet precise.

G. *Summary*

The qualitative variations of the sound patterns we uttered as children were determined partly by chance and partly by our physique. They were not necessarily pleasant, nor were they necessarily efficient. Indeed, they were not necessarily any more "natural" or comfortable for us than were any other sounds within our range. Our early vocal responses—voice quality, melody pattern, and phonetic patterns—were destined to become habitual because every time we produced them we were rewarded. Our ears grew accustomed to our own voices. We soon began to think that that voice was our only voice, and in time we came to feel that that voice and ourselves were inseparable. We then found it difficult to produce other voice qualities. Our hearing initiated strong censorship on our voices; it acted as controller of the vocal mechanism and refused to tolerate the production of unfamiliar patterns. Even when we are interested in altering our vocal habits, our ears may continue to challenge our wills. We are then likely to attribute our voice qualities to necessity rather than to admit that the choices reflect our personal preferences.

2.3. Psychological Factors and Voice Quality

In this text, we do not intend to analyze the subtleties of emotional responses experienced by human beings, nor do we intend to explore the psychological correlates associated with abnormal vocal behavior. Such explorations would be at best only speculative. Although they might further our insight into changing our own voices, they might also provide us with excuses to avoid the dull, prosaic, but important task of recognizing how we sound, which is a preliminary step in learning to use our muscles with more precision and grace and our hearing with more discrimination.

If our emotional problems are such that they restrict our actions and prevent us from achieving our intellectual or social potential, we would be well advised to seek expert help before we embark on any program of vocal re-education.

A. *The Link Between Vocal and Emotional Behavior*

The presence of a particular voice quality offers, by itself, no significant clue to the personality structure of an individual. Personality structure and vocal behavior are both learned. They may be learned simultaneously and may be causally related to similar events and experiences, but they are not causally related to each other. You can have an outgoing, friendly personality and still be plagued by a thin, nasal, high-pitched voice that you acquired long ago. If you decide to give up that voice in favor of a low-pitched, resonant, oral one, you will still remain an outgoing, friendly human being. The erroneous assumption that voice quality is inextricably tied to, or is the product of, personality has been a major block to voice improvement. The voice we use *is* a part of the total impression we make on others. Each of us can, however, modify his voice without upsetting or interfering with other aspects of behavior or with emotional integration.

B. *The Need to Communicate*

The strength of the desire to influence behavior is a psychological factor that may have a direct effect on the voice qualities we use. There are times when we feel very strongly about the need to communicate effectively, that is, to control the actions of others. In such instances we tend to expend considerable effort to achieve our ends and are most particularly in need of vocal skill. It is in these instances that our inefficiencies are likely to be most obvious. The greater the zeal to persuade others to our point of view and the more verbal we are, the more likely we are to abuse our voices. We must learn to listen to ourselves with a "third ear" to discover whether or not our voices impose restrictions that keep us from achieving our purposes. Just as we do not win an argument by talking loudly, neither do we win it by talking softly. The most effective combination is the right voice plus the right words.

2.4. Social Status and Voice Quality

Very little published research exists concerning voice quality as it relates to social status, although the problem received attention in a recent study by Harms[1] and was explored at great length by T. H. Pear[2] in England thirty years earlier. There appears to be widespread acceptance of the idea that a correlation exists between certain attributes of voice and social levels, but the details of the characteristics of a cultivated voice are not yet available in any useful form. The ambiguity of the vocabulary we use to describe voice and the lack of symbols to record the subtle shifts of pitch and loudness are, perhaps, two reasons why there have been so few studies to date. Because of the recent advances made in the development of high-fidelity recording and the interest linguists are now taking in these aspects of speech, there will probably be an increase in such investigations.

[1] L. S. Harms, "Listener Judgements of Status Cues in Speech," *Quarterly Journal of Speech*, XLVII (April 1961), 164.

[2] T. H. Pear, *Voice and Personality* (New York: John Wiley & Sons, Inc., 1931).

2.5. Vocal Efficiency

Meanwhile, although we agree that there are voices we can label as "cultured" or "cultivated" or as "raucous" or "vulgar," we shall treat voice from a functional point of view, in terms of the speaker's skill in meeting the vocal demands of the communicative situation. The labels of "efficiency" or "inefficiency" include appropriateness to the age and sex of the speaker, adequacy of carrying power, effectiveness in supplying clues to subtle shades of meaning, and, most important, vocalization that is not potentially harmful to the speaker. Vocal abuse may be observed at all levels of our society. Its consequences are well known to the medical profession and are now under investigation by speech scientists.[3]

Many vocal qualities appropriate to particular circumstances are available to each of us. It will be our task to evaluate them and to learn to have more of them at our command, as well as to use some habitually and more consistently than others.

We shall strive for voices that shift automatically in response to an ever-changing speaker-listener environment. The new voice patterns must be learned so well that they become automatic. If the responses remain on a self-conscious, voluntary level, the result is artificial and socially unacceptable.

A. *Situational Factors*

Aside from the limitations imposed on voice by individual anatomy and personality and by the influence of articulatory practices, situations arise that make considerable demands on vocal skill. In respect to loudness, for example, the distance between speaker and listener determines the amount of energy we use. The obligation is to be heard. Talking to someone seated three feet away, in quiet surroundings, we have to adjust the intensity of voice so as not to offend the ears of the listener. Conversely, in the presence of such high levels of background noise as that encountered near a jet plane take-off or in an industrial plant, we need so much energy that we might do well to avoid using our voices at all. In an auditorium or large lecture room without an amplifying system, we must use greater amounts of energy. On the other hand, in front of a microphone we must limit both the amounts

---

[3] See, for example, Henry J. Rubin and Irwin Lehrhoff, "Pathogenesis and Treatment of Vocal Nodules," *Journal of Speech and Hearing Disorders,* XXVII (May 1962), 152; and Hans von Leden and G. Paul Moore, *Larynx and Voice: Physiology of the Larynx Under Daily Stress* (Chicago: Gould Foundation, Laryngeal Research Lab., 1958), a motion picture.

of energy and the variability of pressure. The intensity changes must remain within a narrow range because of the characteristics of the amplifying system.

The content of the message, the familiarity of the listener with the vocabulary, and the receptiveness of the audience plus the need to persuade affect the pitch pattern, intensity, quality, and rate we use in a given situation.

B. *The "Right" Voice*

The question "What is the right voice?" must be answered in terms of the specific situation and the individual speaker or listener. From the listener's point of view, the minimal requirements of a good voice are audibility and appropriateness. From the speaker's point of view, the minimal requirements are economy of effort and expression of intent. As a general standard, the voice should have a pitch range appropriate to age and sex, pitch patterns that reinforce the intended meaning, an intensity that ensures audibility, and a quality that is clear and carries no unintended messages, all of which should be produced with minimal effort.

In September, 1962, *The New York Times* carried the headline, "A Golden Voice Hunted in Britain." The news item reported that the General Post Office was holding a contest for employees of the telephone company. The winner of the competition for the perfect voice would receive $280 and would have his or her voice recorded for the speaking clock. The General Post Office was looking for a voice that was "impersonal, free from obtrusive accent and that had purity of tone and clarity of enunciation."

A voice scientist might well be appalled by this definition of the "perfect voice." A psychologist might wonder about the search for a voice that is "golden" and "impersonal." *We* wonder why the competition was not open to machines, as well as to the 50,000 employees. Synthetic speech can sound as mechanical as a clock. It can be impersonal and can represent an abstraction of the human voice without contamination by any one personality.

2.6. Vocal Terminology—A Semantic Problem

Some of the difficulties in defining vocal qualities arise because our language does not have single, unambiguous terms to apply to a host of voices that are within the range of acceptable, good, or pleasant. We seem to agree on what we do not want rather than on what we do.

For example, we recognize that a husky voice is a noisy one and therefore unpleasant, but we have no word other than "clear" to symbolize the type of voice we do prefer. But the word "clear" is too broad a term to be valuable in identifying particular, personal qualities of sound. We get the impression that we should all strive for the *same* clear voice. Nothing could be further from the truth.

As our oral style tends toward the use of adjectives rather than of restrictive or qualifying clauses, we often omit the information carried by the latter, expecting the listener to supply it. The phrase "a good voice" is an example. But the listener does not usually supply the missing information inherent in this phrase because the message it conveys is not at all precise. One major purpose of this text is to make explicit the implied contents of such terms as "good," "acceptable," "high," "low," "soft," and "loud." We shall not attempt to coin adjectives to symbolize the vocal sounds we should like you to produce, but we shall give frequent exposure to the entire clause or to all its significant content.

The variations that are encompassed by the phrase "good voice" are obvious when you consider the voices of others. The authors of this text, for example, have clear voices that are considered acceptable, pleasant, and good. You would have no difficulty in telling them apart or recognizing either of them separately. You would label one voice male, the other female, and recognize both as those of adults.

It is possible for both authors to simulate the voice of an eight-year-old-child of either sex. But when either author tries it in class, he is sure to get a response of laughter. Why? Because our students recognize that we are adults and that we do not look like eight-year-olds. In other words, listeners will not tolerate the wrong age voice. They are uninhibited in their responses because they know from past experience that we can talk differently. You might keep this point in mind when your instructor puts an unflattering label on your voice and you say, in justification, "Nobody else ever told me I sounded like an eight-year-old!" Whenever we talk about a good or a standard voice we ought therefore to specify "good for whom"—good for a child, good for a young woman, good for a young man, good for an old woman, or good for an old man.

2.7. The Need for Voice Training

Skills are developed through appropriate practice. We can learn about skills, but we become skillful only through actual repeated performance. No great dancer or athlete learns his skills through knowledge of anatomy and physiology. If you are a dancer or a horse-back rider, a golfer or a swimmer, you have learned how to move your feet, your body, your arms, and your head by actually performing the physical activities.

So it is with speech. The following chapters will provide a blueprint for the deliberate skilled use of the voice and instructions for reaching a level of proficiency that will enable you to be heard and understood easily without intruding competing noises or signals in the messages you communicate. Above all, the blueprint will enable you to achieve this proficiency without damaging the mechanism that produces the voice.

How many people do you know who need voice training? Listen to politicians, reporters, scientists, lawyers, and other people who take part in radio or television discussions. (We are not suggesting that you listen to the voices of announcers or actors because they are ex-pected to be vocally skillful.) Our guess is that perhaps 30 of 100 speakers you hear will do very well. Perhaps one out of a hundred will do so poorly that you notice the deviant vocal behavior and consider the individual to have a voice defect. As many as 70 per cent of those you hear might benefit from some sort of voice training. Listen to the voices of your friends and family. Are they comfortably audible, pleasant, and of appropriate pitch? What percentage of these voices is efficient and supplies you with additional, subtle clues to meaning? After we have studied the complexities of verbal spoken utterance, you may wish to revise your estimate.

part two | **the prosodic features**

chapter 3 *The Rhythm of English:*
Stresses in Words and Phrases

THIS SECTION of our study deals with the rhythmic and melodic nature of English: the stresses within the words and expressions we use and the nature of the patterns of pause, stress, and pitch in the phrases and sentences we speak. These features are added to the sounds of speech that make up the words and phrases that communicate our thoughts to others. Before analyzing the speech sounds, we should understand these features as they form the very special rhythms and melodies used by speakers of English. Stress and the rhythm of English are discussed in this chapter.

3.1. The Special Rhythm of English

The rhythmic stress with which we speak English results from the constant variation of syllables of strong stress with others of weaker stress in a continuing, if not completely regular, pattern. This stress feature of English is accompanied by a characteristic time feature, that is, the interval between the prominent syllables of the language is almost uniform, even though the number of syllables between prominences varies from few to many.[1] Comparing some similar

[1] A recent analysis has questioned this isochronic feature of English, first described in any detail by Kenneth L. Pike, *The Intonation of American English* (Ann Arbor: The University of Michigan Press, 1940), p. 34. See Yao Shen and Giles G. Peterson, "Isochronism in English," *Studies in Linguistics*, Occasional Papers No. 9, University of Buffalo, 1962.

sentences will soon demonstrate this point. Note that each sentence in each group seems to take about the same period of time to say aloud.

> The room is dark.
> The big room is very dark.
> This is the room that's much too dark.

> Ties for sale.
> These ties are for sale.
> These are the ties that are put on sale.

The rhythmic units of a long sentence, separated here by single bars, demonstrate the same isochronic feature. Note that the number of syllables within each rhythmic unit varies.

The other day / when I was coming home / I found it on the street.

The swimmers / trying very hard / managed to reach shore that evening.

Typing the essay / she became quite aware / of the many spelling errors on the page.

If we re-examine these sentences, some conclusions are evident:

1. There is a tendency to speak our language with fairly regular time or rhythmic units, each of which has strong prominence.

2. These rhythmic units may be composed of different numbers of syllables.

3. Syllables of longer units are spoken more rapidly than those of shorter units.

4. Such rapid speaking of long syllables results in weakening and unstressing of the less important syllables and changes in the sound values of the vowels of such syllables.

5. The pauses after rhythmic units may be increased or decreased. These shorter or longer pauses, when combined with the rapidity or slowness with which we speak our phrases, help make the isochronic nature of our language noticeable.

Not all languages possess the stress-time feature of English. Spanish, for example, is a "syllable-timed language," in which all syllables tend to occupy approximately the same period of time, so that different sentences possessing the same number of syllables are of the same length. Also, the number of stresses in English sentences will vary, and the prominent stresses may occur anywhere in the sentences. In French, on the contrary, these prominent stresses occur at the terminal point of the phrase, and, in Czech, at the beginning. Thus the position of stress in English words or phrases is

free and variable rather than fixed and fully predictable. Our rhythmic pattern is so constructed that rhythmic units, whether small or
large, are spoken with almost equal lapses of time.

As stresses in English sentences appear on the stressed syllables of
the words of these sentences and as the rhythmic patterns of our sentences are mirrored in the words we speak, we shall first identify and
demonstrate the stresses we find in words before examining stresses in
phrases.

3.2. Stress in English Words

Stress can be identified as the strong rather than the weak rhythmic beat in a phrase or polysyllabic word. We also identify strongly
stressed syllables as those spoken with greater force (or intensity).[2]
Words of one syllable, spoken in isolation, are always pronounced
with strong stress. Contrasts in stress are therefore noticeable only in
words of at least two syllables: *ăroúnd, bĕlów, dĕfér, cónsciĕnce, moúntaĭn,
fúnnў.* (The ⌣ ⌐ marks represent weak and strong stresses, respectively.) Words of three or more syllables may possess degrees of stress
intermediate between the two extremes noted. Thus the words
bícўclĕ and *rídĕr* are spoken with only strong and weak stresses, but
the compound word *bícўclĕ-rìdĕr* is spoken with still another degree.
The first and fourth syllables of this compound word have different
degrees of stress, with a strong stress on *bí-*, an intermediate stress on
rì-, and weak stresses on the remaining syllables. Similarly, the stress
on the last syllable of *window* is surely not the strong stress of the first
syllable of *dópester* or the weak stress of the second syllable of *indŏlent.*[3]

---

[2] Actually, there is sufficient experimental evidence demonstrating that we identify
changes in stress by noting differences in the length and pitch of a given syllable, as well
as changes in the force used on that syllable. Normally, strongly stressed syllables are
louder (of greater force), of longer duration, and higher in pitch than are weakly stressed
syllables. A change in the force or intensity of a syllable is really only one cue to the
perception of a change in stress, and it may not even be the predominant one. See, for
example, D. B. Fry, "Duration and Intensity as Physical Correlates of Linguistic Stress,"
Journal of the Acoustic Society of America, XXXII (1955), 765–69; D. B. Fry, "Experiments
in the Perception of Stress," *Language and Speech*, I (1958), 126–52; Philip Lieberman,
"Some Acoustic Correlates of Word Stress in American English," *Journal of the Acoustic
Society of America*, XXXII (1960), 451–54; and Philip Lieberman, "Perception of Intensity
by Linguists," *Word*, XXI (1965), 40–54.

[3] The use of four stresses for strong, secondary, tertiary, and weak, ⌐ ⌃ ⌵ ⌣ , permits
the marking of the four contrasting stresses we hear when we say certain compound words
and phrases. Thus, although the three stresses are sufficient to mark the distinctions
among the syllables in the words in this section, an additional stress is needed to account
for the differences we hear between *a blackbird* and *a black bird* or between *Long Island* and

Practice : The words in the following list contain three levels of stress: strong, intermediate, and weak. Only the first six in each column are marked. Pronounce them aloud and mark the remainder as you hear them, using ´ ` ˘ for strong, intermediate, and weak stresses, respectively.[4]

válùe	ĭnvént	prólògue	fálsĭfỳ
bóttlĕ	sŭbvért	Wínnĭpèg	fămíliăr
cárrỳ	dĕfíne	fánfàre	fámĭlỳ
mánỳ	ălóng	díctĭonàrỳ	fórtĭfỳ
súpĕr	ămóng	Jèffĕrsónĭăn	sŭggéstĭblĕ
vísĭt	ăbíde	nótĭcĭng	pĕcúliăr
tender	erect	bibliophile	peculiarity
ready	defend	construction	notoriety
money	defensive	relatively	inexpensive
scarcely	nonsensical	golf club	window-washer

The rhythm of stressed and unstressed syllables can be seen more readily if we look at the syllables that can appear both before and after the primarily stressed syllable of each word. Here you will note that English possesses many and varied patterns of less stressed syllables that appear before and after primary stresses. A French, Greek, Japanese, or Norwegian student of English will not be able to memorize a rule for just what strong or weak stresses may follow or precede each other. He will have to learn the stress patterns of the words as he learns the words themselves—a hard but certainly not impossible task.

Each of the following words has the major stress on the first syllable. Four slightly different stress patterns appear for the syllables that

---

a long island. These differences would be marked as follows:

ă bláckbìrd	versus	ă blâck bírd
Lòng Íslănd	versus	ă lông íslănd

The four stresses are used later in this chapter in the discussion of compounds and phrases (Section 3.3).

[4] A check of any of these words in a reliable, current dictionary is certainly in order. Be sure to note the stress system used. A word of caution: Dictionaries typically do not show the presence of secondary stresses in disyllables unless they are compound words, *e.g., wínesàp, lívestòck,* but *prólogue, vámpire.* Dictionary editors assume readers will understand that, since words like *prologue* and *vampire* are respelled with full vowels in the second syllables, readers will not mispronounce these syllables as weakly stressed rather than as secondarily stressed syllables. Thus *prologue* and *promise* appear in the dictionaries with only one indicated stress mark on the first syllable of each. So do *vampire* and *vapor.* We certainly do not pronounce the second syllables of these four words with the same degrees of stress. *Vapor* and *promise* are normally pronounced with ´ ˘ , whereas *prologue* and *vampire* are heard with ´ ` stresses. An excellent study of word stress appears in G. F. Arnold, *Stress in English Words* (Amsterdam: North Holland Publishing Company, 1957).

follow the ones given strongest stress. Note the rhythmic patterns of the language as the stresses are used.

ˊ ˇ	ˊ ˋ	ˊ ˇ ˋ	ˊ ˇ ˇ
reading	diphthong	suicide	ambulance
ready	statute	compensate	minister
rolling	subway	generate	quality
better		satisfy	comical
tonic		modify	president
major		hurricane	studious
hardly		advertise	specially
clothing		realize	interesting

We can now organize the word lists that follow according to the presence of different stress patterns as they appear following or preceding the syllables with the strongest stresses. The stress patterns of English are complex, but we can draw some general conclusions:

1. A least three degrees are necessary to identify the stress patterns of English words.[5]

2. As stress increases or decreases, the spoken vowels of the syllables lengthen or shorten. Sometimes syllables become so short that they may even disappear. Sometimes, the vowels of the unstressed syllables change not only in duration but also in quality. In such instances, the vowel of the weakly stressed syllable becomes a different vowel.[6] You will note these features in the remainder of this chapter.

A. *Words with Primary Stress on Initial Syllable*

TWO-SYLLABLE WORD PATTERNS

ˊ ˇ		ˊ ˋ	
comfort	pompous	footsore	Norwalk
able	pumpkin	penknife	topaz
Harry	breakfast	zero	thorax
monkey	orange	brimstone	rosebush
paper	walking	peacock	typhoid
stocking	sofa	quartile	pockmark
meager	silent	migraine	bureau

[5] See Section 3.3 for discussion of a possible fourth degree of stress.

[6] Compare the initial vowels of the two words *acquire* and *acquisition*. Note that the first syllable of *acquire* contains not only a shorter vowel (compared to that of *acquisition*) but also one that differs in quality. In other words, we use a different vowel to initiate *acquire* from the one we use to initiate *acquisition*. Weak and unstressed vowels are treated in detail in Chapter 14.

THREE-SYLLABLE WORD PATTERNS

´ ` ˘	´ ˘ ˘	´ ˘ `
wallpaper	singular	notify
bullfinches	tanager	demagogue
bookcases	miracle	embryo
wheelbarrow	vehemence	Hildebrand
sunbonnet	chivalrous	ionize
outfitted	vigilant	Hellespont
horsewoman	pedantry	palliate
grasshopper	interesting	Panama
grandchildren	palpable	telephone
pineapple	Sylvia	concentrate

FOUR- AND MORE SYLLABLE WORD PATTERNS

The stress patterns of the first few words are noted; mark the remainder with the appropriate stress marks. Note the different rhythmic patterns.

ménthŏlàtĕd	animism	credulously
clássĭcălìsm̆	caterpillar	Nottinghamshire
clássĭcìsm̆	pumpernickel	virtually
spírĭtŭălìsm̆	succulently	mischievously
monotheism	liberating	infamously
blameworthiness	sugariness	ultimately
Judaism	despotism	preferable
syllogism	kindergarten	desperately
accuracy	respiratory	architecture
pitifully	charitable	variable
reasonable	miniature	obstinacy
reasonableness		literature

B. *Words with Primary Stress on Second Syllable*

TWO-SYLLABLE WORD PATTERNS

˘ ´		` ´	
parade	suggest	partook	bamboo
among	subsist	northwest	genteel
before	advance	forgo	crochet
amend	confront	without	toupee
around		withstand	

Practice: In which group would you place the following? *support, corrupt, Nanking, confirm, Marseilles, against, monsoon.*

THREE-SYLLABLE WORD PATTERNS

˘ ˏ ˘	ˏ ˏ ˘	˘ ˏ ˏ
completely	unlikely	returnee
amusement	(also ˏˏ˘)	employee
supplanted	proceeding	(or ˏˏˏ)
afforded	(also ˏˏ˘)	peroxide
amended	forgoing (v.)	tomato
suggestion	transgressing	(or ˏˏ˘)
cadenza	chastising	tomorrow
Columbus	utensil	(or ˏˏ˘)
sustaining	prehensile	Tuxedo
absurdly	(also ˏˏ˘)	(or ˏˏˏ)
deposit	trochaic	contribute
petition	bubonic	impregnate

FOUR- AND MORE SYLLABLE WORD PATTERNS

Again note the different rhythmic patterns, varying from ˏˏˏˏ to ˏˏˏˏ to ˏˏˏˏ for the four-syllable words. The five- and six-syllable words normally show ˏˏˏˏˏ or ˏˏˏˏˏ and ˏˏˏˏˏˏ or ˏˏˏˏˏˏ.

Practice : Identify the patterns of each of the following words.

interminable	interminableness	disorganized
Lancastrian	encyclical	orthography
insipidly	dissatisfy	telephony
telegraphy	philosopher	oblivion
experiment	ingenuous	significantly
impossible	indigenous	responsible
investiture	invincible	invidious
suppository	uncomfortable	interpretative

c. *Words with Primary Stress on Third Syllable*

Most words with primary stress on the third syllable contain four or more syllables. Note that the rhythmic patterns are fairly consistent here. Alternating syllables seem to possess medial or strong stress in the four-syllable words, the pattern of ˏˏˏˏ, as in *sèntĭméntăl*, being the common form. There are not many three-syllable words with stress on the final syllable. Some of them are listed below; note that the rhythmic pattern is commonly ˏˏˏ for these three-syllable words.

THREE-SYLLABLE WORD PATTERNS

understand	hollandaise	recommend
appointee	guarantee	seventeen
acquiesce	afternoon	cigarette
personnel	magazine	financier
twenty-one	ascertain	picturesque
dilettante	entertain	tweedledee
(also 4 syllables)	counteract	negligee
Genovese	intertwine	(also ‿ ˘ ‿)

FOUR-SYLLABLE WORD PATTERNS

indecision	contemplation	microscopic
circulation	philosophic	elongation
soporific	coefficient	inquisition
incubation	Appomattox	Uruguayan
unaffected	Nicodemus	modulation
graduation	diapason	supposition
sentimental	Dionysian	humanistic
digitalis	(also 5 syllables)	idealistic

FIVE- AND MORE SYLLABLE WORD PATTERNS

probability	indeterminate	popularity
immortality	electricity	parsimonious
curiosity	egotistical	indigestible
immemorial	multiplicity	virtuosity
nonconformity	neurasthenia	solubility
ideography	(also 4 syllables)	incongruity
incombustible	participial	impresario
indescribable	ichthyology	Lithuania
periosteum	indestructible	importunity

D. *Words with Primary Stress on Fourth and Following Syllable*

These very long, uncommon words demonstrate rhythmic patterns similar to those noted earlier, in which stressed syllables appear on the first, second, or third syllables of words. They fall into the following forms (the primarily stressed syllables are italicized).

Number of Syllables	Pattern	Examples
4	‿ ˘ ‿ ˊ	misunder*stand*
		aquama*rine*
5	‿ ˋ ‿ ˊ ˘	configu*ra*tion
		assimi*la*tion

Number of Syllables	*Pattern*	*Examples*
5	ˋ˘˘ˊ˘	magnifi*ca*tion
		certifi*ca*tion
6	˘ˋ˘ˊ˘˘	inferi*or*ity
		exhausti*bil*ity
	ˋ˘˘ˊ˘˘ or	instrumen*tal*ity or
	ˋ˘ˋˊ˘˘	partheno*gen*esis
	˘ˋ˘˘ˊ˘	materia*lis*tic
		personifi*ca*tion
	ˋ˘ˋ˘ˊ˘	autobio*graph*ic
		interpene*tra*tion
7	˘ˋ˘˘ˊ˘˘	intolera*bil*ity
	ˋ˘ˋ˘ˊ˘˘	inadmissi*bil*ity
8	ˋ˘ˋ˘˘ˊ˘˘	incommensura*bil*ity

Practice: Arrange the following words according to rhythmic patterns.

representation	redistribution	investigation
municipality	coagulation	pronunciation
appreciation	ideographic	inconsequential
circumlocution	interdependence	characteristic
predestination	decomposition	inapplicability
inimitability	electrification	overestimation
transcontinental	undiplomatic	extemporaneous
bacteriologist	articulation	anticipation
humiliation	encephalitis	disorganization
declamatorily	meteorological	inadvisability

E. *Effects of Changes in Stress on Vowels*

A feature of our language closely associated with the presence or absence of stress relates to the effects stress has on the vowels of syllables. You have already noticed that the presence of stress affects the duration of a vowel. The same two vowels in the word *vacate* differ in length, as the less stressed *o* in *notation* differs from the fully stressed vowel of *note*. Fully stressed vowels are typically longer than weakly stressed ones. In addition, the vowels of weakly stressed syllables (or unstressed syllables) may be changed in quality. The third syllable of *centralize*, possessing medial stress, contains quite a different vowel when the same syllable loses stress in *centralization*. Or note the stressed *o* in the fourth syllable of *autobiography*, compared with the sound of that syllable in *autobiographic*. Certain vowels of our language appear in both fully stressed and less stressed syllables, perhaps with changed duration. Certain vowels, however, are replaced by other vowels when the pertinent syllables lose stress. And vowels in unstressed syllables may assume completely different forms when they are accorded stress. (Further discussion of unstressed syllables and the changes that occur will be found in Chapters 10, 11, 12, and 13. Chapter 14 deals entirely with unstressed vowels.)

Practice: In the following list of words, syllables containing stressed vowels are compared with the same syllables with less stressed or unstressed vowels. The pertinent syllables are italicized. Changes in vowel length are marked with an asterisk; changes in vowel length and quality are marked with a dagger. The first five are identified. Can you identify the rest?

liber*al*ity	liber*al*	†
curi*os*ity	curi*ous*	†
so*lid*ify	so*lid*	*
*in*valid (adj.)	*in*valid (n.)	*
sys*tem*ic	sys*tem*	†
aro*mat*ic	aro*ma*	
pro*test* (v.)	Pro*test*ant	
*en*ter	*en*tertain	
a*dapt*	a*dap*tation	
*mo*ment	*mo*mentous	
de*mo*cracy	de*mo*cratic	
mono*to*nous	mono*to*ne	
*Ro*man	*ro*mantic	
*pro*noun	*pro*nouncement	
*re*bel (n.)	*re*bel (v.)	
so*lem*nity	so*lemn*	
ad*verse*	ad*ver*sary	
contin*en*tal	contin*ent*	
*woods*man	Hay*wood's*	

WEAKENING OF VOWELS

The function words in English, for example, articles, prepositions, pronouns, auxiliary verbs, and conjunctions, contain obscure vowels (or are spoken without vowels, in some instances) as stress is weakened. As they are unimportant words in the sentence, they are rarely heard as "strong forms" in the normal stream of speech. Samples of these words appear below. Note your pronunciation as you speak them aloud in the phrases and sentences. A check of these words in any current, reputable dictionary will show that each word is given both "strong" and "weak" entries. The weak forms are, of course, the normal forms when the words are not important in the sentence or when they are not said alone.

Word	*Use*
and	He and I.
of	The top of the house.
in	She walked in the room all day.
on	Put it on her head, quickly.
him	Try him out for a week.
her	Take her out of the house, please.
the	The man in the red hat.
can	What can he do?
or	She or I.
them	Give the ball to them now, please.
are	Where are you going?
at	He was at the neighbors' house.
was	She was talking on the phone.
us	Send it to us next week.
would	He would answer each question correctly.

OBSCURATION AND LOSS OF SOUND

The obscuring of vowels as they lose stress is an extremely common phenomenon in English, resulting in the presence of a weak vowel, commonly known as the *schwa* vowel. This schwa vowel is transcribed [ə]. It is the most commonly spoken vowel in English and can be traced historically to the introduction of unstressed syllables very early in the development of the language. The use of unstressed vowels, as you will learn later in more detail, is normal and expected in English. Avoiding their use leads to stilted, if not affected, speech. The use of weak vowels in such words as *above, among, martial, circus, moment, bottom,* and *actor* is common to everyone.

The phenomenon of unstressing, then, leads to the obscuration of vowels, ranging in degree from the use of shorter vowels to actual changes in vowel quality. Unstressing may also result in the loss of vowel and consonant sounds and of weak syllables.

Practice: Describe the loss of sound or syllable due to unstressing in each of the following words. You will find it useful to check each of these words in a current dictionary. Note also the spelling form (a good indicator of an earlier pronunciation in some instances) and the variant current pronunciations listed.

evening	funnel	suggestion
carriage	Worcester	Wodehouse
national	model	Gloucester
coxswain	button	chocolate
separate (adj.)	hidden	general
interesting	fasten	diamond
forehead	bachelor	Greenwich
extraordinary	family	sovereign
literature	parliament	every
annihilate	vehicle	naturally

F. *Shifts of Stress within Words and Phrases*

Different stress patterns appear in many words or phrases in our language as the result of at least five factors, all of which are discussed in the following paragraphs.

ALTERNATIVE PRONUNCIATIONS

Alternative pronunciations for the same word, both current in the same or different regions of the country, for example, *ro*deo and ro*deo*, *fi*nance and fi*nance*, may cause a shift in stress.

Practice: Check each of the following words in a reliable dictionary. Indicate the alternative pronunciations.

address	quintuplets	Sofia	preparatory
detail	pianist	decadence	allies
defect	recess	decade	romance
hospitable	adult	kilometer	lamentable
exquisite	esophageal	despicable	Tolstoy
abdomen	inquiry	quinine	fakir
advertisement	acclimate	perfume	pariah
illustrate	chauffeur	sonorous	attaché
harass	gladiola	cabala	blasé

CHANGES IN FUNCTION

A change in the function of the word, because of its use as a noun or verb (for example, *con*vert and con*vert*) or as an adjective or verb (for example, *ab*sent and ab*sent*) may cause a shift in stress.

Practice: Check these forms in your dictionary, and note the different pronunciations. Indicate the differences by underlining the stressed syllables.

traverse (adj.)—traverse (v.)   permit (n.)*—permit (v.)
envelope (n.)—envelop (v.)   protest (n.)—protest (v.)

* Also spoken with alternative pronunciation as nouns.

August (n.)—august (adj.)	contract (n.)—contract (v.)
concert (n.)—concert (v.)	digest (n.)—digest (v.)
convict (n.)—convict (v.)	increase (n.)—increase (v.)
intimate (adj.)—intimate (v.)	suspect (n.)—suspect (v.)
produce (n.)—produce (v.)	deliberate (adj.)—deliberate (v.)
address (n.)*—address (v.)	associate (n.)—associate (v.)
moderate (adj.)—moderate (v.)	frequent (adj.)—frequent (v.)
estimate (n.)—estimate (v.)	project (n.)—project (v.)
export (n.)—export (v.)	extract (n.)—extract (v.)
conduct (n.)—conduct (n.)	survey (n.)—survey (v.)
attribute (n.)—attribute (v.)	desert (n.)—desert (v.)
progress (n.)—progress (v.)	compliment (n.)—compliment (v.)

* Also spoken with alternative pronunciations as nouns.

CONTRASTED WORDS

A desire on the speaker's part to heighten or contrast one word with another, for example, "geo*logic*," but "*ge*ologic, not *bi*ologic," may cause a shift in stress.

Practice: Examples of contrasted words appear in the following sentences. Can you suggest others?

Chi*nese*	but	"It's *Chi*nese, not *Jap*anese."
seven*teen*	but	"He's *sev*enteen, not *six*teen."
de*fense*	but	"He plays a *de*fensive, not an *off*ensive position."
ge*ology*	but	"He is majoring in *ge*ology, not *bi*ology."

CHANGES IN RHYTHMIC PATTERNS

A change in the rhythmic pattern of the phrase, for example, "He is four*teen*" and "There are *four*teen boys at his house," may cause a shift in stress.

Practice: Examples of changes in rhythm appear in the following sentences. Can you suggest others?

un*real*	He drew an *un*real *face*.
nine*teen*	He fell on the *nine*teenth *step*.
half*way*	They call it the "*Half*way *House*."
bam*boo*	They found fifteen *bam*boo *shoots*.
up*stairs*	She hid in the *up*stairs *clos*et.
down*stairs*	The chair was in the *down*stairs *room*.

CHANGES IN FUNCTION IN COMPOUNDS

The stress patterns of polysyllabic words appear in compound words too. Normally a single primary stress is preceded or followed by weakly or medially stressed syllables. They therefore do not need special attention, except as we desire to recognize certain special situations in which the normal stress pattern of the compound word changes.

Such changes do take place when the compound word, with full stress on a certain syllable, shows reduced stress before a noun, that is, in what is known as an attributive position in the phrase. Notice the position of the primary stress in the word *nòrthwést* or *nòrthwéstĕrn*. When a word is in an attributive position, the position of the stress changes: *Nôrthwèst Pássăge, nôrthwèstĕrn flíghts.*

Practice : Note the differences in the uses of compound words and these same forms in such phrases as those below. We can manage comfortably with a three-stress system for the contrasts in the compounds below, but we need a fourth stress to note the contrasts in the phrases. The four stresses are primary, secondary, tertiary, and weak (ˊ ˆ ˋ ˇ), with two intermediate stresses between (ˊ and ˇ) (see footnote 3). Some of the phrases are marked. Try marking the others.

míncemèat—mîncemèat píe	ill-natured—ill-natured boy
pòstgrádŭatĕ—pòstgrâdŭatĕ coúrse	overbearing—overbearing parent
wástepàpĕr—wâstepàpĕr báskĕt	tightfisted—tightfisted man
bàckstáge—bâckstàge roóm	hand-knit—hand-knit socks
bàck doór—bâck doórmàt,	handmade—handmade sweater
bâckdoòr scréen	ice-cold—ice-cold drink
píg-heàdĕd—pîg-heàdĕd bóy	

Note too the changes in the stress patterns of the compound words below when compared with the phrases containing similar words. The first few are marked. Mark the others. Can you suggest still more?

ă bláckbìrd (the species)	ă blâck bírd (a bird of black color)
ă móvĭngvàn (it may be standing still)	ă môvĭng ván (a van that is moving)
a greenhouse (for growing flowers)	a green house (painted green)
the White House (in Washington)	a white house (painted white)
a highchair (for baby)	a high chair (for a short person)
a bluefish (the species)	a blue fish (in the tropical fish collection)

3.3. Stress in Words versus Accent in Phrases

Until now, we have been dealing with the stress patterns of words, without special concern for what happens to stresses as we move words into phrases and sentences when we converse. Although stress remains our concern when we analyze words, the term *accent* is preferable when we attempt an analysis of the patterns of stress in the stream of speech. A number of preliminary statements can be made for our purposes.[7]

1. Accent is the prominence given a particular syllable in a phrase or sentence. It is therefore syntactical or phrasal stress, rather than word stress.

2. An accent can fall on any syllable of a word that normally takes primary stress. It cannot fall on an unstressed or weakly stressed syllable of a word.

3. Some change in pitch will occur as we place the accent on a particular syllable. Normally, this pitch change is upward, so that the accented syllable stands out above the others of the phrase. The syllables *boy-* and *hap-* receive the accents in the sentences below.

        boy
                    fec
The   cott was not ef   tive.

          ⌒
        (hap)
She is a most un   py child.

4. Notice that the syllable with the accent of the phrase typically possesses greater intensity and duration and is spoken on a higher pitch than are unaccented syllables.

5. Changes in accent signify changes in the speaker's intent.

        was   here.   not
She   here.   She was   She was   here.
            two.   can't
    come   two.
I can   at   I   come at

6. The speaker can convey information by his choice of accent

[7] Stress and accent analyses are complex problems, and scholars have varied points of view on the treatment of these phenomena. The approach taken here reflects the position held by many students of the English language. For some of the differences, see, for example, Marshall D. Berger, "Vowel Distribution and Accentual Prominence in Modern English," *Word*, XI (1955), 361–76; George L. Trager and Henry Lee Smith, Jr., *An Outline of English Structure*, Studies in Linguistics, Occasional Paper No. 3 (Norman, Okla.: Battenberg Press, 1951), especially pp. 35–39; and Dwight L. Bolinger, "Stress and Information," *American Speech*, XXXIII (February 1958), 5–20. A very good review of the relationship of stress (accent) and pitch and the different approaches used can be found in Lawrence Raphael, "The Study of American English Intonation: 1946–1961," unpublished M.A. thesis, Queens College of the City University of New York, May, 1965.

placement. These accents therefore appear only where choices are possible.[8]

7. Very special situations call for very special emphases. In such instances, the pitch prominence of the pertinent syllables is considerably higher than expected in normally accented syllables. (As accent cannot be dissociated from melody, much of this discussion will be more meaningful if studied in conjunction with the material on intonation in the next chapter.)

<blockquote>
"I think it will do."
</blockquote>

becomes

<blockquote>
think
"I   it will do."
</blockquote>

and changes to

<blockquote>
         not!"
think
"I
</blockquote>

8. When no special emphasis in the phrase or sentence is desired, the accent normally falls at the beginning and end of the phrase, with perhaps greater prominence at the end.

Practice: In the following sentences, mark the syllables of each word with the different degrees of stress as you hear them when spoken aloud. The accented syllable of each phrase is italicized. Keep in mind that the accentual indication is dependent upon the information the speaker desires to convey.

Dìd hĕ *cóme*?	Hê lòoks vèrў̆ *íll*.
Long Island is a *long* island.	She was a *house*keeper.
John is a *fine* young man.	She was a *light*house keeper.
Call me to*mor*row.	Was she a *good* lighthouse keeper?

In the following selections, mark the syllables and indicate the accents.

Psychology is a difficult subject to learn. It deals with a study of people and how they behave. Through a study of psychology, we can learn to understand the reasons for certain patterns of behavior. These behavior patterns can be grouped, analyzed, and detailed. They can be compared with other behavior patterns.

---

[8] As Lee S. Hultzén notes in his provocative article, "Information Points in Intonation," *Phonetica*, IV (1959), 113, ". . . there is information . . . if the speaker . . . might have said something different from what he did say."

Keola was married with Lehua, daughter of Kalamake, the wise man of Molokai, and he kept his dwelling with the father of his wife. There was no man more cunning than that prophet; he read the stars, he could divine by the bodies of the dead, and by means of evil creatures; he could go alone into the highest parts of the mountain, into the region of the hobgoblins, and there he would lay snares to entrap the spirits of ancient.

For this reason no man was more consulted in all the Kingdom of Hawaii. Prudent people bought, and sold, and married, and laid out their lives by his counsels; and the king had him twice to Kona to seek the treasures of Kamehameha. Neither was any man more feared: of his enemies, some had dwindled in sickness by virtue of his incantations, and some had been spirited away, the life and the clay both, so that folk looked in vain for so much as a bone of their bodies. It was rumored that he had the art or the gift of the old heroes. Men had seen him at night upon the mountains, stepping from one cliff to the next; they had seen him walking in the high forest, and his head and shoulders were above the trees.

Island Nights' Entertainments
—Robert Louis Stevenson

chapter 4 *The Melody of English : Pitches, Transitions, and Contours*

4.1. The Melodies of Speech and Song

With an understanding of the stress patterns of words and the use of accents in phrases and sentences, it is now easier to approach another feature of our language—the melodies we use when speaking. English is a most melodic language, if melody is defined as the successive changes or contours of pitch used over a given group of sounds. A major difference between the melody of speech and the melody of song is a difference in the sustaining of particular notes on given syllables of words. Singers sustain notes and smoothly change pitches on following syllables as the melodies dictate. The pitch changes from syllable to syllable are much less discrete in speaking. The pitches of speaking *are* present, but they are not sustained for any relatively extended length of time. And single syllables, when stressed, may be spoken with variations of pitch, whereas such syllables would normally be sung on single, sustained pitches. "Song melody" becomes "speech melody," then, when we shade the discrete pitches, sliding them with almost obvious abandon into other pitches as we go to other syllables of the sentence. The "speech melody" can be arrested at any given point in the utterance. If that pitch is sustained for a slightly longer period, it will then sound "sung."

4.2. Some Definitions of Terms

Before proceeding, it will be useful to explain certain terms that will arise in this chapter. The discussion in the previous chapter dealt with stress, defined as the prominence we give to the syllables of words. The contrasts range from strong to weak, with a middle area of intermediate stresses between these two extremes. *Intonation* is concerned with differences in pitch and the contours that result from pitch changes that follow one another in a phrase or clause. These pitch changes can be heard at three levels: low, middle, and high. An extra-high pitch level (a fourth) is associated with special clause or sentence accent, such as occurs when we desire to note contrast, express surprise, or voice the unexpected. In every spoken sentence, these different pitch levels start at certain points. Such points are known as *contour* or *pitch* points. The *contour*, or the clause or sentence melody, contains at least two different pitch levels. A contour is heard for every sense group. A *sense group* is a phrase or clause containing one or more words bounded by a pause or transition. Each sense group possesses one accent. The *terminal transitions* or *junctures* or *pauses* that bound our clauses are spoken with sustaining →, rising ↑, or falling ↓ pitches. Each contour then contains at least two pitch levels and one terminal. Like the stresses discussed in the previous chapter, the pitch differences we use at the different pitch levels are *relatively* different from one another. We recognize them when we hear one in contrast with the other. Different stresses are not necessarily associated with fixed measures of intensity and volume. Similarly, different pitch levels are not associated with absolute or fixed frequencies. It is important that we note that relative differences do exist and that the differences in the speech of every speaker of our language are sufficiently marked to become meaningful to us as listeners.

The following treatment of melody-pitch-intonation in English is based on the special contributions of phoneticians and linguistic scholars who have managed to clarify a most complex subject. Without their theorizing and testing, our discussion of these subjects would be vague and inconsequential. The study of melody in language is most provocative. Continued study will add much to our understanding of this complex field.[1]

[1] Among the many contributions to the study of melody in English, the following will prove of special interest to the student who desires to pursue this matter. Detailed bibliographies are available in the first two. Kenneth L. Pike, *The Intonation of American English* (Ann Arbor: The University of Michigan Press, 1946). Lawrence Raphael, "The

A single chapter cannot cover in detail the melodic patterns of American English as they are used in all the many different situations that occur. As pitch patterns are used to express and heighten meaning and to convey innumerable attitudinal and emotional overtones, a complete volume on this one aspect of how we use our language would be necessary. Instead, this chapter will attempt to isolate and describe the major or structurally significant "tunes" we use when we speak and some of the more common variations within these "tunes." Our discussion will begin by noting how clauses and sentences end. We shall then proceed to analyze the pitch levels that may precede these terminals, as well as the possible order of their appearance. The arrangement of these different pitch levels, the movements to and from each level, and the forms the endings take constitute the intonation patterns or contours we need to analyze.

Perhaps it is too obvious to say that no sentence or clause in English is spoken or heard without an intonation or melody contour. This statement is true even if the thought expressed is matter-of-fact, that is, expresses no special feeling of the speaker. Even "colorless speech" is spoken with these patterned melodies, although they are somewhat compressed. And, of course, changes in attitude are expressed by changes in melodic patterns. The study of English must

Study of American English Intonation: 1946–1961," unpublished M.A. thesis, Queens College of the City University of New York, 1965. Dwight L. Bolinger, "Intonation: Levels vs. Configurations," *Word*, 7 (1951), 199–210; "Stress and Information," *American Speech*, 33 (1958), 5–20; "A Theory of Pitch Accent," *Word*, 14 (1958), 109–49; "Around the Edge of Language: Intonation," *Harvard Educational Review*, 34 (1964), 282–96. Frantisek Danes, "Sentence Intonation from a Functional Point of View," *Word*, 16 (1960), 34–54. Peter Denes and J. Milton-Williams, "Further Studies in Intonation," *Language and Speech*, 5 (1962), 1–14. Eli Fisher-Jørgenson, "Kenneth L. Pikes's Analysis of American English Intonation," *Lingua*, 2 (1949), 3–13. Charles C. Fries, "On the Intonation of 'Yes-No' Questions in English," *In Honour of Daniel Jones* (London: Longmans, Green, 1964), pp. 255–65. Charles F. Hockett, *A Manual of Phonology* (Bloomington, Ind.: University Publications in Anthropology and Linguistics, No. 11, 1955). Lee S. Hultzén, "Communication in Intonation: General American," *Study of Sounds* (Tokyo: Phonetic Society of Japan, 1957), pp. 317–33; "Significant and Nonsignificant Intonation," *Proceedings of the Fourth International Congress of Phonetic Sciences*, 1961 (The Hague: Mouton & Co., N.V., Publishers, 1962), pp. 658–61. W. Jassem, *Intonation of Conversational English* (Wroclaw: Wroclawskiego Tow. Naukowego, 1952). Roger Kingdon, *The Groundwork of English Intonation* (London: Longmans, Green, 1958). W. R. Lee, *An English Intonation Reader* (London: Macmillan & Co., Ltd., 1960). George L. Trager, "The Intonation System of American English," *In Honour of Daniel Jones* (London: Longmans, Green, 1964), pp. 266–70. George L. Trager and Henry Lee Smith, Jr., *An Outline of English Structure*, Studies in Linguistics, Occasional Papers, No. 3 (Norman, Okla.: Battenberg Press, 1951). Rulon S. Wells, "The Pitch Phonemes of English," *Language*, 21 (1945), 27–39.

therefore include the melodies that help to convey the information the speaker desires to project. Their analysis is as essential as that of the sounds of speech, their arrangements into words, and the orders and styles in which we organize and speak these words. All these elements are part of what we call "language" or "speech."

4.3. The Terminals

We end clauses and sentences in one of three ways, as noted at the beginning of this chapter: rising ↑, falling ↓, and sustaining →. These terminals are the results of complexes affecting the loudness and pitch of the voice, as well as perhaps its quality. Let us see how:

1. Terminals are indicated most obviously by "pauses" or "breaks" in the stream of speech. These pauses may be long or short, giving the impression of final or tentative endings. Normally, long pauses or breaks are associated with finality, but there are instances in which tentative pauses may be as long or longer than adjacent final ones. For example, some of the tentative pauses in the following paragraph marked → might last longer than the final pauses marked ↓.

John→I don't know how to say this↓ Your work record is good→ but→your attitude is such→that we cannot retain you↓ I'm sorry↓ Pick up your check at the window→and→good luck↓

2. The tentative pauses at terminal points may also occur not as significant breaks or periods of silence between sounds, but as extensions of the sounds and syllables and of the pitches on which they are spoken. Or these tentative terminals may, though rarely, be noticed as abrupt endings of the previous syllables and melodic contours that change the normally expected lengths of the spoken phrases.

3. Terminals are also noticed by changes in the loudness and pitch in which the sentence or clause has been spoken to that point.

The loudness may diminish or fade into silence, as when the speaker indicates finality:

> I can't↓
> Lead the way, please↓
> Put it down right there↓
> I'll let you know↓

The pitch may rise or fall, and the sound may be cut off rather abruptly, as when the speaker asks certain questions:

> What did you see?↓
> Could I see it please?↑

Is it bigger than an apple?↑
Is it bigger than an apple?↓
Will you come tomorrow?↑
Why should I?↓

The pitch may remain sustained and the loudness fade slightly, as when the speaker indicates the nonfinal expression of a series or when he speaks hesitantly:

Women→children→and men→in that order please↓
Does the store stock ties→shirts→and socks→as well as suits↑
I think he'll have enough money→but can't be sure↓

4.4. Pitch Levels, Pitch Points, and the Construction of Contours

Four pitch levels and three pitch points are sufficient to identify practically all expressions we use in American English.[2]

A. *The Pitch Levels Identified*

As differences in pitch levels are relative to one another, it is necessary to emphasize that we are not identifying pitch differences by actual frequency designations. Levels are merely higher or lower than other levels.[3] Each speaker uses these relatively different pitch levels within his own pitch range. The listener automatically translates them into correspondingly relative levels within each speaker's range. There are no absolute levels.

The normal level for the end of the phrase "It's funny," "Please

---

[2] Some believe that four pitch levels and four or five pitch points are needed to explain all the possible variations we use. See for example, Trager and Smith *op. cit.*; and Trager, *op. cit.* For most purposes, only three pitch levels need be noted; the fourth level is reserved for contrast, surprise, or especially emphatic expressions, and thus some people believe it is a variant of pitch level three. There seems to be agreement that no more than four pitch points or positions can appear in any one intonation pattern, this fourth, where used, being reserved for either a secondarily stressed syllable following the primary one or a secondarily stressed syllable preceding the primary one. If these two types are considered separately, then a possible total of five pitch points can be designated.

One does hear a new pitch point between the initiation of the expression and the primary accent of the sentence, as in

↓   ↓   ↓ ↓
It's a long story

when *story* retains the accent or sense stress of the sentence. And one pitch point follows the center of the sentence, when that syllable has secondary stress, as in

↓ ↓   ↓ ↓
I'll look for you Monday

when *look* is the syllable with the sense stress, or accent, of the sentence.

[3] See Chapter 15 for a detailed discussion of pitch and voice.

call him," or "What time is it?" (See Figure 4.1) is the lowest pitch level we use. We can designate it as pitch level 1, on a scale of three, and can note that the centrally stressed syllable of each sentence (the accent) is high (or on pitch level 3) and that any initial part of the sentence before that accent is on pitch level 2. Each pattern noted in Figure 4.1 follows the contour 231, and each ends in a falling terminal.

Figure 4.1. Sample Sentences Showing the Contour 231↓ .

We write such expressions as 231↓ and indicate the intonation pattern through the sequence of pitch levels and the terminal. A still higher pitch can be used as a substitute for level 3 when the speaker desires to express surprise or to call special attention to something. "You wouldn't dare!" would probably be spoken as 241↓, as would the expression "What a beauty!" said by a horsetrainer about a horse, a lad about a movie actress, a horticulturist about a new rose. But no more than three levels are used in any one contour. Level 4 is really a specially accented level 3, reserved for very special occasions. All the expressions we use are spoken with the three (or four) pitch levels mentioned.

These levels, followed by different terminals, can be arranged in different orders; when they are so arranged, they are our means of making statements, asking questions, commanding, requesting, or indicating boredom, surprise, and delight. We shall explore in detail only the most commonly used contours.

B. *The Pitch Points Identified*

Pitch points are the places at which identifiable pitch levels are initiated. They normally occur

    a. On the initial syllable of the phrase: "Please
    b. On the syllable with the primary
        accent of the clause or sentence: call
    c. On the final syllable of the clause
        or sentence: him."

In special circumstances, as noted in footnote 2, pitch points may also occur on secondarily stressed syllables between the initial syllables and the accents or on secondarily stressed syllables following the accents and before the final pitch points.

Two pitch points may actually fall on a single syllable, as in "I'm going home now"

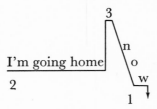

when the accent is on a single syllable or when the single syllable is the entire sentence or clause, as when we call "John!"

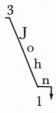

c. *Pitch Variations within Levels*

It is necessary to keep in mind that we speak with variations of pitch between pitch points. For example, take the following sentences, each of which possesses three pitch points and two or three pitch levels. The accents appear at pitch level 3.

Take him ⌐ home ⌐ please.   2(2)31

Where is ⌐ Char ⌐ lie?   231

Is ⌐ Anne coming?   23

Actually, we do not retain the identical pitch for each syllable throughout "Anne coming" in sentence three nor in the "take him" and "where is" parts of sentences one and two. There are noticeable changes of pitch within these pitch levels that can be represented by relatively higher or lower dots between two lines. Using larger dots for stressed syllables and smaller dots for unstressed syllables, we might represent these three sentences as follows (the number of the pitch level appears above each syllable):

	2	2	3	1
Take him home please.	●	·	●	·

	2	2	3	1
Where is Charlie?	●	·	●	·

	2	3	3	3
Is Anne coming?	·	●	●	·

Practice: Indicate the pitch differences you hear in each of the following sentences. Use the dot system.

Take me home now.	I think so.
Hello Harvey.	See that horse go!
Find another seat please.	Hi, John!
Be careful.	One more, please.
Let's eat here.	I can't see that far.

Notice that the pitch glides while the stream of voice continues, or the voice may jump to another pitch when it breaks. Some of these differences in pitch are significant to the listener, signaling the speaker's estimate of what is important and what is less important. These significant pitch differences are the means we use to identify different parts of the sentence—the part before the accent, the accented syllable, the part following the accent. Pitch changes within each level may take place, but they are insignificant changes. In the same way that we use different *t* sounds in *steam* and *team* yet know them both as the sounds of /t/,[4] the differences within pitch levels may exist as insignificant differences—all parts of the entities we call pitch levels 2, 3, and 1.

[4] See Chapter 7.

D. *Intonation Contours*

When we place appropriate pitch levels in succession and follow them with terminals, we achieve partial or complete utterances with intonation contours. All our speaking consists of sounds combined into words, spoken with different pitch-level configurations separated from one another by pauses or terminals. No speaking takes place without these levels and terminals. The speaker, reader, or actor cannot convey any thoughts to a listener through speech without the use of intonation contours. And, unless he conveys the expected contours (at the expected pitch points and with the expected pitch levels and terminals), he will not convey the desired meanings to others. The major contours of our language will be identified below, and each will be illustrated by appropriate examples.

4.5. The Contours of Complete or Final Utterances

There are three kinds of utterance that normally end in low pitch levels: statements, commands, and "information questions."[5] The contour proceeds to pitch level 1 from a higher 3 or 2, and the level 1, in turn, glides to the terminal ↓. The accented syllable of the clause or sentence is commonly spoken at the highest pitch level and with the greatest intensity. Preceding expressions, if any, are spoken at the normal level, 2. The fall to the 1 level occurs immediately after the 3 or 2 level, with ↓ as the terminal. This intonation contour is known as a (2)31↓ or (2)21↓, the parenthetical (2) indicating that the utterance may contain only the latter two levels. A variation of the (2)31↓, the (2)41↓, occurs when we place very special emphasis on a certain syllable for effect. Such an accent (perhaps in an expression of surprise or anger or contrast) could appear on the *not* of "You'd better not!" or on the first syllable of "Never!" or at the initiation of "Wow!"

Additional pitch points may occur in this contour of finality, so that one may hear a 2231↓ or 2331↓, as in

2   2   3   1   2   3   3   1

"It's not funny" or "It's a long book"

In some expressions only the 31↓ will be heard, as in

3   1   3   1

"Try it" or "Johnny"

[5] Information questions begin with such words as *how, when, why, where,* and *what* and are not answerable by single words like *yes, no, perhaps, maybe.* "Yes-no questions" are discussed later in this chapter.

Pitch changes within pitch levels do occur. As noted briefly in the previous section, a means of representing such changes is to place a dot for each syllable (large for a stressed and small for an unstressed syllable) between two lines of a staff. This system gives a slightly different contour picture to the eye.[6] Both the level numbers and the dot system are useful notational devices and are used in the following exercise sentences.

A. *Diagraming the Contours*

Levels and terminals   *Dots and lines*

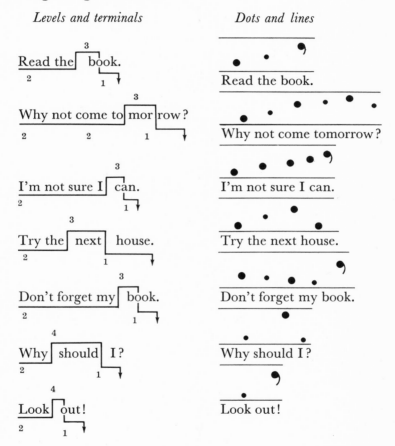

Practice: Try marking the melody of each of the following short sentences according to either system. Note that each is a statement with a

---

[6] See, for example, A. C. Gimson, *An Introduction to the Pronunciation of English* (London: Edward Arnold Ltd., 1962), chap. 10, pp. 234–54.

low ending—that each is uttered with a contour of completeness or finality.

What a nuisance he is!	Have another cup.
He's a very bright boy.	Why don't you keep quiet?
Drive slowly.	It happened at 3:00 P.M.
Be careful of that rock!	Don't go in there!
These shoes don't fit.	Sally is due tomorrow.
That horse wins every race.	Come on in. The water's fine.
He was out at second base.	Sure! I'll call at ten.
That view is certainly beautiful.	No. He couldn't.
I think I'll go tomorrow.	Yes. I did.
He speaks much too quickly.	Nonsense!

B. *Stress and Melody Markings*

There is a certain usefulness in combining stress markings and the indications of intonation, so that we may see how interrelated they are. As mentioned in the previous chapter, the stressed syllables of the sentence may receive the accent of the sentence. Before attempting the practice sentences on pp. 55–57, note the following points:

1. The highest part of the contour will fall on the primarily stressed syllable, the one that receives the accent of the clause or sentence. For example, pitch level 3 will appear on the word *grass* in the sentence, "Walk on the *grass*, please."

2. Other stressed syllables before the accent of the clause normally maintain pitch level heights above 1. For example, in the same sample sentence, the word *walk* will be spoken at pitch level 2. The contour will look like this:

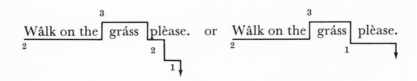

On certain special occasions, stressed syllables may be spoken above the accented syllable. For example, in the sentence below, the accent is placed on *dare*, the word conveying the special point of information. As spoken with the feeling, duration, and intensity expected from one who has just learned that another young lady plans to "steal" her special boy friend, the contour might look like this:

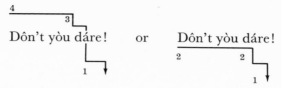

Dôn't yòu dáre!   or   Dôn't yòu dáre!

3. An intonation contour can contain a single syllable or word, but it will always possess at least two pitch levels and a terminal. The single-word sentences below contain a 41↓ and a 31↓ contour.

No!   Nev er!

4. Every sense group or clause will have its own contour, each with its own accent, levels, and terminal.

5. One accent will appear in each sense group. It will be marked with a primary stress mark. Other stressed syllables of the clause will be less stressed.

6. The accent of the clause does not fall on unstressed or less stressed syllables. If such a normally less stressed syllable *is* to receive the accent of the clause or sentence, it will be elevated to primary stress in order to convey the information demanded. For example, compare the sentence "He walked in the *snow*" with "He walked *in*, not *on*, the snow." The word *in* is elevated from an unstressed syllable in the first sentence to a primarily stressed syllable in the second sentence.

Practice: The following sentences should be marked for both stress and melody. All are spoken with finality and therefore end in pitch level 1 followed by ↓. Syllables spoken with the accents of the clauses are shown in capital letters. Three of the sentences are marked by both the pitch-level system and the dot system. Mark the others. Special meanings of the first ten sentences appear in parentheses.

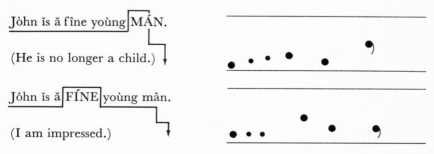

Jòhn is ă fîne yoùng MÁN.

(He is no longer a child.)

Jôhn is ă FÍNE yoùng mân.

(I am impressed.)

Why did HÉ còme?

(I never expected HIM.)

Why did he COME?
(—if he's so bored?)

The elevator operator is ILL
  today.
(Matter-of-fact statement.)

The elevator OPerator is ill today.
(Not the starter.)

Long Island is a LONG island.
(Matter-of-fact statement.)

Long Island is a LONG island.
(I had no idea it was 125 miles
  long!)

She is our HOUSEkeeper.
(Matter-of-fact statement.)

She is OUR housekeeper.
(She doesn't work for you!)

Say the sentences below as marked. Change the accent and contour of each sentence in order to convey a different meaning.

Take Tommy HOME please.	My ears are HURTing.
Why can't HE drive?	WHO'S taking the dog out?
My coat is on the CHAIR.	Why SHOULD he?
DON'T push me.	Don't touch that COAT.
Carrots ARE healthy for you.	Take it EAsy.
How ARE you?	English IS easy.
Chew it CAREfully.	Chemistry is a DIFficult subject.
The weather's getting COLD.	The story was exCITing.
No NONsense, please.	Famous people are NEVer boring.
Let's eat CHInese food tonight.	Silly people ARE boring.

Surfboarding is a THRILling sport.	I find her FAScinating.
They hired a new PRINcipal.	When did HE find out?

4.6. The Contours of Incomplete or Nonfinal Utterances

We tend to speak in short phrases or clauses, each followed by a sign of melodic incompleteness to notify that more is on the way, until we have finished the utterance. If you will read the preceding sentence aloud, you will hear yourself use such nonfinal signals. You will use the falling clause terminal ↓ only once—after *utterance*. You will use at least two or three nonfinal clause terminals, however. Depending on your mood, rate of speaking, audience, and situation, you may have spoken this sentence with → or ↑ in any of these places:

We tend to speak→in short phrases→or clauses→each followed by a sign→of melodic incompleteness→to notify↑ that more is on the way→until we have finished the utterance↓

We signify incompleteness in two ways: The pitch level remains at the higher 2 or 3, not falling to the low level 1, and the clause terminal remains sustained (→) or rises (↑) so that, though the intensity may fade, the pitch of the voice remains up.

Among the expressions with contours ending in pitch level 2 or 3 plus rising or level terminals are: addresses by names or titles (salutations), incomplete parts of full sentences, the nonfinal expressions in series, the earlier parts of alternatives, and expressions of hesitation or doubt. Our system of writing indicates this nonfinality with commas, semicolons, colons, dashes, and series of dots for terminal signals, but it cannot show the intonation contours preceding such signals.

Practice: Many such expressions are marked here as they might be spoken by an individual. Variations can appear if the speaker's intent calls for a change in the placement of the accent. Say each aloud, and note the appropriate contour. See how the meanings change if you change the contours, and note especially what occurs if you complete the contours with the falling terminal ↓. At such times, incongruous expressions may result.

Only parts of some contours are marked. Enter the contours for the unmarked utterances.

Addresses

Mr. Roberts, may I present . . .

Mr. Chairman, members of the Board . . .

Mr. Jones, how are you?

Thanks John. I'll see for myself.

Hel lo Jane. Nice of you to come.

Mr. Mayor, we represent . . .

Look out, Jim, he's dangerous.

I don't know, Betty, if I can.

Parts of sentences

If she calls, . . .

Should that snow slide, . . .

When the mail comes, . . .

Whenever she acts like that, . . .

If the pressure falls, . . .

Insects, which are necessary for the
pollination process, . . .

The movie was fine, but . . .

He came back very late, and . . .

Earlier parts of series

Buy two pounds of tomatoes one pound of stringbeans five pounds of

apples and three watermelons.

Try coloring it green blue yellow or red before you decide.

I have no such reaction—neither good bad pleasant nor distressed.

I need some ties, shirts, socks, and shoes.

He speaks four languages: French, English, Chinese, and Dutch.

He should take courses in philosophy, anthropology, comparative literature, and physics before leaving school.

One, two, three, four, five.

Earlier parts of alternatives

Will you come to day or tomorrow?

Can you drive quickly as well as safely?

Do you want white, gray or blue?

Let's go by boat or plane.

Do you take sugar or lemon in your tea?

Either swim or sink!

Try harder or not at all!

Are you a student, member of the staff, or guest?

Is it hard or soft?

I can't tell if it's black or white.

Expressions of doubt or hesitancy

I sup pose he could.   (I'm not really sure though.)

I'm not sure about it.   (Though I wish I were.)

I wish I knew how bad it is.   (But it's too early.)

I couldn't tell.   (Maybe you can.)

She may manage fine.   (I have my doubts though.)

Maybe I'll call at nine.   (Can't be sure though.)

4.7. The Contours of General Questions

A. *Questions with Rising Contours*

Questions that require "yes" or "no" answers may be considered utterances of nonfinality, spoken with contours that rise to the 3 level and end with rising terminals (↑). Note that each of the following questions takes a possible "yes" or "no" answer (or "perhaps" or "maybe" or "I don't know" in place of the "yes" or "no").

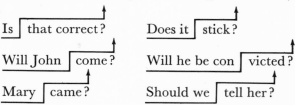

To each of these, the finality occurs with the answer "yes" or "no." The rising terminals at the end of these questions seek completeness in the responses to be made. In each instance, the pitch rises and remains until the fading-rising clause terminal.

B. *Questions with Falling Contours*

At least two exceptions to the typical question pattern are common. One is the question of alternatives, in which the terminal falls:

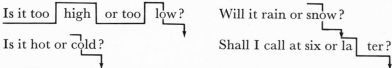

The second exception is a variation of the question that takes a "yes" or "no" answer. For example, the following questions can be spoken as shown. Note that the different rising or falling contours are part of standard American English.

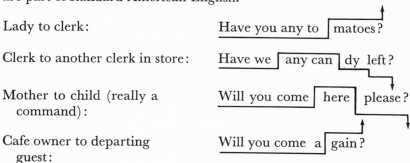

Lady to clerk:

Clerk to another clerk in store:

Mother to child (really a command):

Cafe owner to departing guest:

Trying to find out about a
certain restaurant:

Was the | ser | vice good?

Doctor to patient:

Are you | o | verweight?

Possible repeated question
in a two-person conversation:

Do you go to | school?

What did you say?

Do you go to | school?

Practice: Mark the following sentences.

Is he growing taller or fatter?	Should I call tomorrow?
Can you see the top?	Shall I call Monday or Tuesday?
Is the train late?	Do you admit students on grades
If she falls from that height, can	alone?
she live?	Are you hiring today?
Does chemistry bother you as it	If not, on what basis do you
does me?	admit students?

4.8. Other Intonation Contours

No textbook of the scope of this one can analyze the many variations within the melodies we use. Although the study of melody in English is not new, much is unknown about the interrelationships among melody, meaning, attitude of speaker, and nuances related to emotion. Detailed studies now going on will provide us with answers we do not yet have. Surprise, anger, boredom, adoration, fascination, hatred, and joy affect the way we speak. Speakers in pulpits, actors on the stage, politicians on raised platforms, and students in class can utter the same phrases with considerable variation in meaning. The mood of the speaker, his point of view, the situation of the moment, the state of the audience, and the previous climate of opinion all affect how he stresses, pauses, and inflects.

Practice: The following selections should be spoken aloud for listening practice. Mark each sentence for stress and intonation contour. Note that different contours and sense stresses appear as your intent changes. Practice in marking the stresses and in noting the intonation contours will prove helpful.

> I wandered lonely as a cloud
> That floats on high o'er vales and hills,
> When all at once I saw a crowd.

A host of golden daffodils,
Beside the lake, beneath the trees
Fluttering and dancing in the breeze.

Continuous as the stars that shine
And twinkle on the milky way,
They stretched in never-ending line
Along the margin of a bay:
Ten thousand saw I at a glance
Tossing their heads in sprightly dance.

"The Daffodils"
—William Wordsworth

There was a sound of revelry by night,
And Belgium's capital had gathered then
Her Beauty and her Chivalry, and bright
The lamps shone o'er fair women and brave men;
A thousand hearts beat happily; and when
Music arose with its voluptuous swell,
Soft eyes looked love to eyes which spake again,
And all went merry as a marriage bell;
But hush! hark! a deep sound strikes like a rising knell!

"Waterloo" from *Childe Harold's Pilgrimage*
—George Gordon, Lord Byron

The first ray of light which illumines the gloom, and converts into a dazzling brilliancy that obscurity in which the earlier history of the public career of the immortal Pickwick would appear to be involved, is derived from the perusal of the following entry in the Transactions of the Pickwick Club, which the editor of these papers feels the highest pleasure in laying before his readers, as a proof of the careful attention, indefatigable assiduity, and nice discrimination, with which his search among the multifarious documents confided to him has been conducted.

'May 12, 1827. Joseph Smiggers, Esq., P.V.P.M.P.C.,* presiding.'

* Perpetual Vice President—Member Pickwick Club.

The Pickwick Papers
—Charles Dickens

If by leaving a small pleasure one sees a great pleasure, let a wise man leave the small pleasure and look to the great.

He who, by causing pain to others, wishes to obtain pleasure for himself, he, entangled in the bonds of hatred, will never be free from hatred.

What ought to be done is neglected, what ought not to be done is done; the desires of unruly, thoughtless people are always increasing.

But they whose whole watchfulness is always directed to their body, who do not follow what ought not to be done, and who steadfastly do what ought to be done, the desires of such watchful and wise people will come to an end.

The Proverbs
The Buddhist Scriptures

part three | **the systems**

chapter 5 *The Speech Mechanisms*

ALTHOUGH WE commonly focus attention on the lips, the tongue, and the larynx when we talk about speech and voice the fact is that almost half the body is engaged in the production of speech sounds. This chapter describes very briefly the anatomical structures used actively when we speak. In addition, the movements of these structures as they operate in the production of speech are explained. Finally, you will be introduced to the terminology that is needed to study speech as an acoustic event.

The speech mechanism includes the auditory system, the respiratory apparatus, the oral portion of the digestive system, and a sizable portion of the central and peripheral nervous system. Specific centers in the brain enable us to inhibit involuntary responses like breathing in and breathing out at a steady pace and to substitute voluntary control of breathing that is more suited to speech requirements. The manner in which we control our breath for speech becomes habitual, and we do not think about it when we talk. Nevertheless, we can exert conscious control of it within the limits of the biological demands of the body. All speech acts are learned responses.

5.1. Sound

Speech consists of a series of discrete sounds, which are complex and which range in quality from tone to noise. The tones are composed of a group of vibrations numerically or proportionately related to one another. The slowest vibratory component of each tonal complex is referred to as the *fundamental frequency*. The remaining

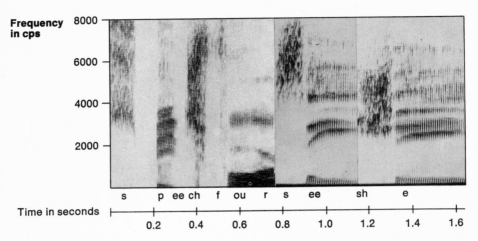

Figure 5.1. Spectrograms of the Words *Speech Four* As Spoken by B.F.J. and *See* and *She* As Spoken by A.J.B.

Note: Frequency analysis of spectrum up to 8,000 cps. Time is indicated on horizontal axis, frequency on vertical axis, and intensity by darkness.

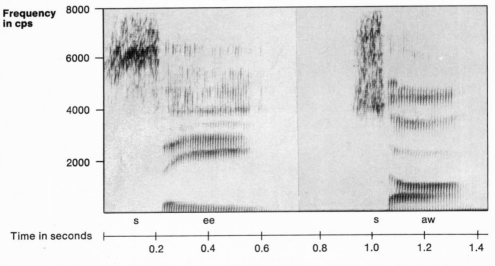

Figure 5.2. Spectrograms of the Words *See* and *Saw* As Spoken by A.J.B.

Note: Frequency analysis of spectrum up to 8,000 cps. Time is indicated on horizontal axis, frequency on vertical axis, and intensity by darkness.

components of the tone are more rapid vibratory segments that are integral multiples of the fundamental frequency. These rapid vibratory elements are harmonics, or overtones, whose frequencies are mathematically predictable if the sound is a tone. When the overtones consist of random frequencies that are not integrally related to one another, we have noise.

A. *The Tone-Noise Continuum*

Some speech sounds, like voiced fricatives and plosives (like /z, v, b, d/) are actually part tone and part noise. Voiceless fricatives and plosives (like /f, s, t, p/) are classified as noise. Their frequency components are unrelated to one another, and no fundamental frequencies are recognizable. Vowels, nasals, and /l/ and /r/ sounds are tones that have a musical quality. Most speech tones are vowels. In the sentence "I know Mary," all the sounds are voiced, and all are tones. In the sentence "I love Mary," all the sounds are voiced, but one sound (/v/) is part tone and part noise. In "I hate Lucy," five sounds are voiced tones, and three are the voiceless noises /h/, /t/, and /s/.

B. *Frequency Distribution*

The acoustic profile of each sound in our language is uniquely different from that of every other sound. This difference results from the particular frequencies present in the tonal complex of each sound, as well as from the relative intensity of each frequency. This specification of frequency and energy (intensity) distribution provides a description of each sound, which we recognize as its individual "quality." Speech sounds that are noises are identified by the ranges of frequency distribution. The sound of *s* in *see* on the spectrogram in Figure 5.1 demonstrates the presence of random frequencies that start at about 4,000 cycles and continue through 8,000 cycles. (We know that there are even higher frequencies present.) The amplitudes or intensities of the random frequencies are unevenly distributed throughout the band of frequencies. The qualitative uniqueness of *sh* is discernible through the presence of a wider frequency distribution than for that of *s*. It starts at about 2,000 cycles. The strongest intensities registered are between 2,500 and 3,000 cycles. When we compare the frequency characteristics of these two sounds, we say that *s* has higher frequencies than has *sh*. What we mean is that the lower limit of the range is higher for *s* than is the lower limit for *sh*. Both sounds have similar high frequencies. The relationship among frequency intensities remains fairly constant as we increase the amount of energy, which is another way of saying that a particular quality can be identified even when the loudness of the sound changes.

c. *Formants*

English vowels are qualitatively different from one another. They are distinguished by their harmonic or frequency structures (see Figures 5.1 and 5.2). Voice scientists often distinguish vowels according to the regions of prominent energy in the sound spectrum. The most intense frequencies are called formants. The first two formant areas (F_1 and F_2) are most significant in the recognition of vowels. The presence of formant 3 (F_3) increases the likelihood of identification, but it is not always included in the acoustic description. In Figure 5.2 you will note additional areas of prominence that are part of vocal quality.

5.2. The Auditory System

Through our hearing we are able to identify the various patterns of harmonic structure that distinguish speech sounds, as well as the patterns of individual voices. Not only is the ability to hear a primary requisite for the development of speech, but it is also a factor in the maintenance of speech patterns. Sometimes this factor even interferes with the acquisition of new speech habits.

The auditory system includes the ear (outer, middle, and inner), the eighth cranial nerve, and its links to the auditory centers of the brain. The outer and middle ear serve to conduct the vibrations of sound to the inner ear, which is embedded in the bony tissue of the skull (see Figure 5.3). Within the cochlea of the inner ear there is a fluid called "perilymph," which moves in response to the sound stimuli. A membranous canal within the fluid contains the specialized receptors that convert the mechanical energy into electrical impulses. The impact of the liquid on the sensory nerve endings within the central canal gives us information about four attributes of sound: duration, harmonic structure, fundamental frequency, and intensity. The information is transmitted via the eighth nerve to the brain, where the sound is perceived. The acoustic elements are identified as rhythm, quality, pitch, and loudness.

The sound must have sufficient energy to cause a reaction in the inner ear. The greater the intensity of a sound, the greater the number of sensory endings affected and, therefore, the louder the sound. The intensity needed for a sound to reach the ear of the listener depends upon the distance between the sound source and the listener and the presence of competing sounds that can block out the speech sounds. Both pitch and quality are recognized at particular places along the cochlea. High-frequency responses are mediated through receptors that are located near the entrance to the inner ear. Lower frequencies cause stimulation farther along.

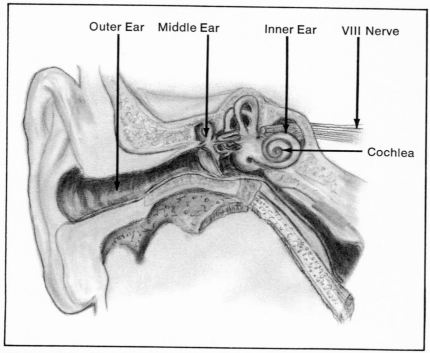

Figure 5.3. The Auditory Mechanism.

Sound from a speaker normally reaches a listener's ears through the movement of air in the outer ear. This movement is converted into mechanical energy by the action of the eardrum. It is then transmitted via the tiny bones in the middle ear to the inner ear. When sounds come to the ears in this way, one hears by air conduction. You hear your own speech in two ways: Not only does your speech reach your ears by air conduction, but the sounds also come to you directly by bone conduction. The vibrations are transmitted directly from the sound-producing mechanisms, by way of the bones of your skull, to the liquid in your inner ear. This double pathway accounts, in part, for your not hearing yourself exactly as others hear you. It also accounts for the fact that you cannot avoid hearing your own speech even if you completely close off the outer ear.

5.3. Breath

The essential source of speech is breath. The essential action of the speech mechanism is interference with or resistance to the breath streaming through the vocal tract. The breath we use for speaking is the air that we inhale into our lungs and from which we take oxygen to supply the needs of our bodies. The lungs rest on the diaphragm, a muscle that divides the torso into two cavities: the thorax, or chest cavity, and the abdomen.

A. *The Structure of the Thorax*

The bony structure of the thoracic cavity consists of the ribs, the vertebral column (backbone), the sternum (breast bone), the clavicles (collarbones) and the scapulae (shoulder blades). The bones are joined to one another in such a way that when they are moved by action of various muscles, the chest cavity is increased in size. Among the many muscles that surround the thorax we need mention only four: the external intercostals, the internal intercostals, the levatores costarum, and the diaphragm. Figure 5.4 shows the major muscles that are used for respiration. The intercostal muscles are to be found between the ribs. The external intercostals form an outer layer that covers the internal intercostals. The levatores costarum are short narrow bands of muscle fiber between the ribs and the vertebral column (not visible on drawing). The contraction of these three sets of muscles, assisted perhaps by others, causes the rib cage to swing outward and upward when the body breathes in. The diaphragm is a broad, double-dome-shaped muscle extending across the base of the thorax. Its fibers radiate toward a central tendon from the sternum in front, from the sixth and seventh ribs on the sides, and from the upper lumbar vertebrae in the back. When the diaphragm contracts during inhalation, the floor of the thoracic cavity is lowered, and the lung volume is further increased. Without the aid of a fluoroscope, the action of the diaphragm cannot be seen.

B. *The Structure of the Abdomen*

The bony framework of the abdomen, or lower half of the body, includes the vertebral (or spinal) column and the hip bones. The front wall of the abdomen consists of a strong, flexible muscle, the fibers of which stretch vertically, horizontally, and obliquely. The internal organs of the abdominal cavity, the viscera, can be pushed forward or compressed as the diaphragm contracts and moves down during inhalation. At the same time, the upper portion of the abdominal

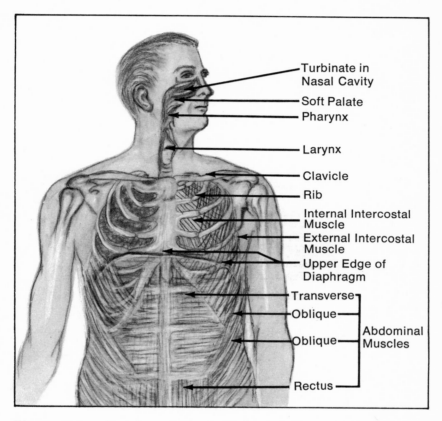

Figure 5.4. Drawing of Head, Neck, and Torso with Muscles of Respiration.

muscle relaxes. During the process of exhalation, the abdominal muscle contracts, and the viscera resume their previous positions as the diaphragm relaxes. Your control of the breath stream for speech depends upon your ability to move the ribs and the muscular wall of the abdomen. The specific muscles that are involved are of no import to you as a speaker, even though they are voluntarily controlled.

As a matter of fact, different speakers may use different muscles to assist in the voluntary expiratory act.

5.4. The Larynx

The air sacs in the lungs are the endmost portions of an extensive system of tubular branches that converge to form the bronchial tubes, the trachea, and the vocal tract. Speech sounds are produced by interference with the outgoing breath stream in different portions of

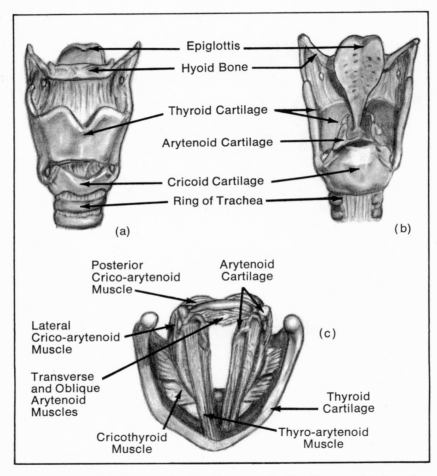

Epiglottis
Hyoid Bone
Thyroid Cartilage
Arytenoid Cartilage
Cricoid Cartilage
Ring of Trachea
(a)
(b)

Posterior Crico-arytenoid Muscle
Arytenoid Cartilage
Lateral Crico-arytenoid Muscle
(c)
Transverse and Oblique Arytenoid Muscles
Thyroid Cartilage
Cricothyroid Muscle
Thyro-arytenoid Muscle

Figure 5.5. Diagrams of the Laryngeal Cartilages: (*a*) Anterior aspect, (*b*) posterior aspect, (*c*) superior aspect.

the vocal tract. The first point at which the air flow can be impeded is in the larynx. The vertical dimension of this portion of the tract ranges from two to three inches in front and is considerably less in the rear. The larynx is situated in the upper part of the front of the neck just above the trachea. See Figure 5.5 for schematic views of the larynx. You will note that the larynx consists of four major cartilages that provide the supporting structure for the muscles that act to block the outgoing air. The cartilages are the thyroid, cricoid, and paired arytenoids. The cricoid is a circular cartilage, the diameter of which is approximately 3/4 in. The area of the vocal tract at the base of the cricoid is about the size of a one-cent piece. The thyroid cartilage forms a semicircular wall above the anterior portion of the cricoid. At the sides, the inferior cartilaginous processes of the thyroid rest on the cricoid. The arytenoid cartilages are shaped like pyramids. They are located on top of the back of the cricoid.

A. *The Vocal Folds*

From the lateral walls of the larynx, two folds of tissue of considerable thickness project inward (see Figure 5.6). The protruding folds contain a complex system of muscles that are essential for tone production. When the muscles of the vocal folds are at rest, the space between them, as viewed from above, appears with the apex in front. In the laryngeal mirror, the image is reflected so that the apex of the vocal folds is reversed.

B. *Laryngeal Tone*

The laryngeal cartilages are moved by the contraction of the intrinsic muscles. As a result of the motion of these cartilages, the vocal folds move to the midline and close the vocal tract (see Figure 5.7). This movement blocks the movement of air from the lungs. When enough pressure is exerted from below, the edges of the folds are forced apart, and air escapes in a series of puffs. The resultant vibration of the vocal folds produces laryngeal tone—a sound with a fundamental frequency and more than fifty harmonics, or overtones. The degree of contraction of the intrinsic laryngeal muscles and the force of the breath pressure determine the fundamental frequency as well as the intensity of the tone. The greater the sum of the tension in the intrinsic muscles, the greater is the resistance of the vocal folds to being separated. To overcome the increased tautness of the vocal folds, the air pressure must be increased. Each

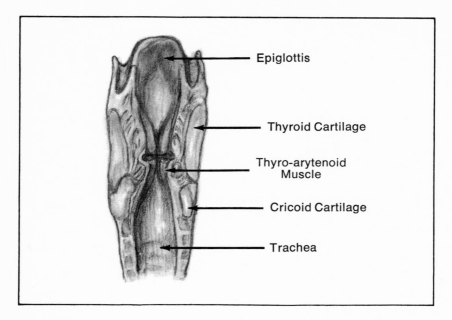

Epiglottis

Thyroid Cartilage

Thyro-arytenoid
Muscle

Cricoid Cartilage

Trachea

Figure 5.6. Inside View of the Larynx As Seen from the Back.

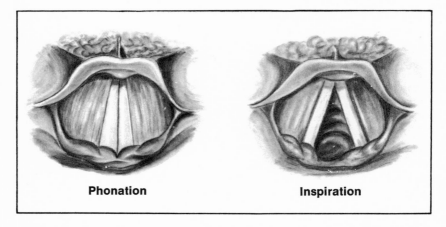

Phonation

Inspiration

Figure 5.7. Vocal Folds in Closed Position for Phonation and in Open Position for Quiet Inspiration.

open phase and breakthrough of air is followed by a period of closure when no air flows through and pressure is built up again. The complete cycle of opening and closing occurs quite rapidly. It is known as the *duty cycle* and may last for as much as 0.01 sec. or for as little as 0.004 sec.

5.5. The Pharynx

Just above the larynx, the vocal tract continues on into the pharynx, which is an irregularly shaped cavity approximately 5 in. long (see Figure 5.8). There are three sets of muscles embedded in the back and side walls of the pharynx. Their contraction diminishes the size of the vocal tract. The superior pharyngeal constrictor can act in conjunction with the soft palate to close off the nasopharynx. This prevents the outgoing air from entering the nasal cavities and diverts it through the mouth. Here we have the second point at which the air flow can be impeded in the vocal tract. As long as the soft palate is relaxed, the breath stream can move through the nasopharynx into the nasal cavities. The third point at which the air flow in the vocal tract can be impeded is at the juncture between the pharynx and the mouth. The back of the tongue is raised to the soft palate, diverting the outgoing air into the nasal passages.

5.6. Oral and Nasal Emission of Breath

The vocal tract has two arms that branch out from the pharynx in a forward direction. In English speech we try to use only one branch at a time—either the nose or the mouth. In recent years, some investigators have questioned the necessity for insisting on a single exit for all oral sounds. There is no doubt that many speakers do not maintain 100 per cent closure of the pharynx passage leading to the nasal cavities (velopharyngeal constriction) all the time. There is equally little doubt that most good speakers do maintain closure most of the time, except during nasal sounds. There is agreement among investigators that inability to achieve such closure results in unpleasant and perhaps unintelligible speech. You have probably heard extreme instances of such distortions in the speech of someone with a cleft palate or paralysis of the soft palate. Whether or not you actually achieve complete closure of the velopharyngeal valve is not so significant as is the knowledge that complete closure represents the ideal

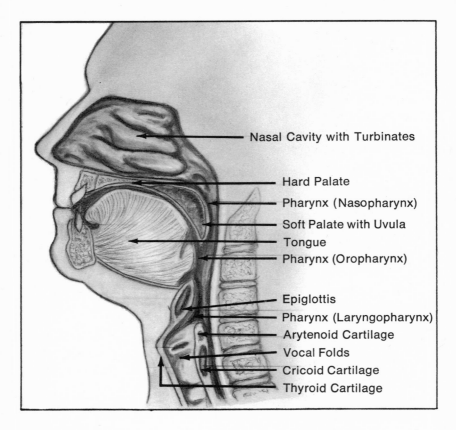

Nasal Cavity with Turbinates

Hard Palate

Pharynx (Nasopharynx)

Soft Palate with Uvula

Tongue

Pharynx (Oropharynx)

Epiglottis

Pharynx (Laryngopharynx)

Arytenoid Cartilage

Vocal Folds

Cricoid Cartilage

Thyroid Cartilage

Figure 5.8. Head and Neck with Vocal Tract.

toward which we aim. Further discussion of closure will be found in our discussions of pitch and quality (see Chapters 15 and 17).

A. *The Nasal Cavities*

The nasal cavities serve an important function in the production of the three English nasal consonants, those heard at the ends of the words *rum*, *run*, and *rung*. Each of the cavities is narrower than the pharynx and is therefore likely to add strength to some of the higher harmonics generated at the larynx and not filtered out or dampened by the passage through the pharynx. The inner surface of the nasal cavities contains bony projections from the lateral walls. The passage is further restricted by the presence of hair cells emerging from the mucous membrane (lining). Any swelling of the mucous membrane decreases the passage still more. Because the progress of air is retarded by its movement from a wide channel to two narrower passages, pressure must be increased if the air is to continue on and out through the nose. For some speakers, the bony structure of the nose acts as a sounding board or resonator to reinforce certain fundamental frequencies or low-frequency harmonics. For all people, the nose acts as a cavity resonator to amplify higher frequencies.

B. *The Oral Cavity*

The mouth is the oral outlet of the vocal tract. It is coupled to the vocal tract only when you lower your jaw or open it. When the mouth is in its resting position, the tongue fills the cavity, the velum is lowered, and the vocal tract is joined to the nasopharynx and nasal cavities. If the lower jaw is depressed, carrying the tongue along with it, the mouth cavity can be enlarged so that it becomes wider than the pharynx. By moving the tongue, an infinite number of shapes and volumes can be created in the oral cavity. The vast number of qualitative changes that may be produced is essentially due to the movements of the tongue and jaw. If you keep the free edges of the front of the tongue resting against the back of the lower front teeth, you can raise the front, middle, or back of the tongue a little above the floor of the mouth. You can also raise each of the three parts as high as the roof of the mouth to make contact with the hard and soft palates. Or you can raise the respective parts of the tongue to any height between the floor or the roof. The particular positions that the tongue and jaw assume determine the resonating characteristics of the oral cavity, thus affecting the emerging vowels and the ultimate quality of the voice. From this discussion, it should be clear that the air flow through the vocal tract can be impeded at any point in the mouth cavity.

5.7. Speech Skill

From our brief explanation of the speech mechanisms, it is obvious that speaking involves the coordination of a great many muscle actions. Speaking necessitates control of movements of structures that are used primarily for life-preserving activities. Learning to talk is more complex than learning to dance or to swim. Nevertheless, we have all learned to talk. Just as the dancer and the athlete learn to move their bodies smoothly, with grace and seemingly effortless power, so does the skillful speaker learn to move his lips, jaw, tongue, palate, vocal folds, and thorax with considerable efficiency. The speaker's task is more difficult, for he must be able both to tense and to relax certain muscles whose movements he cannot perceive directly.

Parts Three and Four of this text describe in detail the behavior, or movements, of the speech mechanisms for the production of clear and intelligible English speech.

chapter **6** *An Introduction to the Sounds of the System*

MUCH, IF NOT ALL, of the discussion in this brief chapter will be repeated in greater detail in the immediately following chapters on the sound segments of the language we speak. The purpose of this chapter is to present an overview of our sound system—the consonants, vowels, and sound clusters and their means of representation and identification. This chapter will introduce to you, for easy reference, most of the terms used later, and it will chart the sounds of our system too, in order to provide you with comparative reference points. The symbol system used throughout this text is given both here and on the inside cover of the text.

6.1. Terms

A. *Phonemes and Morphemes*

We are concerned with the identification and analysis not only of the significant sounds of our language but also of the major variants of these sounds as we speak them in different contexts and in the different dialects of the country. The significantly different sounds of any language are known as its *phonemes*. They are the sound blocks out of which words and expressions are built. The words *box* and *fox* differ in the initial phonemes as do the words *me* and *knee*. This phonemic difference results in different words.

Words and smaller units of sound that are parts of words are the

81

morphemes of the language, the smallest meaningful units of our linguistic structure. For example, note such words as *book, walking, advent,* and *players,* each of which consists of sounds that combine into meaningful entities as follows: the work *book* may be divided, according to the diacritical system of the *American College Dictionary,*[1] as the three sounds b-o͞o-k to make the morpheme {bo͞ok}, understood to be "a written or printed work of some length." This combination of sounds is not divisible into smaller meaningful units. *Book* contains three phonemes combined into a single morpheme. The words *walking* and *advent* each contain two morphemes. Using the diacritical system, these words are respelled as *wôkĭng* and *ădvĕnt.* Each is separable into two morphemic entities {wôk} and {ĭng} and {ăd} and {vĕnt}. And the word *players* contains three morphemes, separated as {plā}, {ər}, {z}, the concept of the plural form plus the concept of "one who" plus the concept of "play." The following words can be respelled according to a dictionary diacritical system and can each be separated into four morphemes.

Will you be home?	(wĭl yo͞o bē hōm)
	1 2 3 4
Tom's crying.	(tŏmz krī ĭng)
	1 2 3 4
Please don't come.	(plēz dōnt kŭm)
	1 2 3 4
Impoverishment	(ĭm povər ish mənt)
	1 2 3 4

B. *Allophones*

Each of the distinctive sounds (phonemes) of our language system may be spoken with variant forms in different contexts or by persons from other environments. These variants of phonemes are known as *allophones.* You can probably note, even at this stage of our study, that the two initial *k* sounds of *keep* and *cool* are formed a bit differently and sound somewhat different. But they are both heard and understood by us as /k/. Both are variants, or allophones, of the phoneme we know as /k/. (The convention is to use slants for phonemic forms, as here, and brackets for phonetic forms. The more forward /k/ of *keep* may be represented as [k˖], the diacritical mark indicating the position of the tongue.) Actually, we use allophones when we speak. We identify

[1] Copyright, 1965, by Random House, Inc.

these allophones by reference to the generalized phonemes that are the basic units of the sound system of our language.

Added to these sounds are the features of pitch, pause or break, and stress, the *suprasegmental* features discussed earlier in this text. These special features are our means of asking questions or making statements (by using certain combinations of pitch levels and terminals). They may be used to help us distinguish between similar-sounding utterances containing the same strings of sounds (*a name* vs. *an aim* or *night rate* vs. *nitrate*); a break appearing after the *a* or *an* or the /t/ of *night* causes certain phonetic features that would not appear otherwise. And the suprasegmental features noted, for example, in the sequence of ´ ˘ rather than ˘ ´ stresses, help us account for our understanding that the noun is spoken *óbjĕct* and the verb, *ŏbjéct*. These features have all been described in Chapters 3 and 4.

Still other features are part of the communication event. *Paralinguistic* features are concerned with special qualities of voice or special changes in the tempo or in the loudness or softness that may accompany our speaking. For example, a very loud utterance might well convey quite a different impression from that conveyed by the same utterance spoken very softly. Or a person may speak with great rapidity. The same words spoken very slowly would perhaps convey quite a different attitude or intent. We also usually add certain motions (or expressions) of the face and other parts of the body while speaking. These motions are known as *kinetic* features. An example is the accompaniment of an utterance by a wink of the eye or by a smile. The same utterance accompanied by a stare or a frown would convey quite a different impression to the listener.

The segmental, suprasegmental, paralinguistic, and kinetic features are all parts of the total event of speaking. The latter two, still under careful study and analysis, are not treated in this book.

6.2. Representation of Sound Segments

In order to identify phonemic and phonetic features of our speech we use the symbolization system developed by the International Phonetic Association. This system is commonly used in articles and books that treat the phonetic study of our language and in the only extant pronouncing dictionaries of American and British English.[2]

[2] John S. Kenyon and Thomas A. Knott, *The Pronouncing Dictionary of American English* (Springfield, Mass.: G. & C. Merriam Co., 2nd ed., 1949); and Daniel Jones, *English Pronouncing Dictionary* (London: J. M. Dent & Sons, Ltd, Publishers; and New York: E. P. Dutton & Co., Inc., 11th ed., 1956).

With this system we are able to represent each sound of the language by a single clear and precise symbol. This phonetic alphabet must be learned through practice. As all the discussions and practice material assume an acquaintance with this alphabet, you would be wise to learn it at once and to become skillful in transcribing with its symbols.

	Upper and Lower Lips	Lower Lip and Teeth	Tongue and Teeth	Tongue Tip and Teeth Ridge	Tongue Blade and Post–alveolar Area	Tongue Blade and Palate	Tongue Back and Velum	Glottal Area
Stops	p b			t d			k g	
Affricates					tʃ dʒ			
Fricatives		f v	θ ð	s z	ʃ ʒ			h
Nasals	m			n			ŋ	
Lateral				l				
Glides or semivowels	w				r	j		

The sounds of this alphabet are charted according to the articulatory positions of the tongue. Each sound (symbol) appears with a key word for identification. The details of the variant forms are discussed in the following chapters.

A. *The Consonants of American English*

Symbol	*Example*	*Symbol*	*Example*
p	*p*en	r	*r*ed
b	*b*end	s	*s*aid
m	*m*en	ʃ	*sh*ed
w	*w*in	ʒ	mea*s*ure
f	*f*ine	tʃ	*ch*ump
v	*v*ine	dʒ	*j*ump
θ	*th*in	j	*y*es
ð	*th*en	k	*c*all

Symbol	Example	Symbol	Example
t	*t*en	g	*G*aul
d	*d*en	ŋ	si*ng*
n	*n*o	h	*h*ome
l	*l*ow		

These consonants may be charted for easy identification by their manner and place of articulation, as in Figure 6.1. The voiceless consonants are the left-hand elements of the pairs; the voiced ones, the right-hand elements. Their articulatory areas are also noted in the schematic drawing in Figure 6.2, for greater assistance in identification.

The acoustic aspects that permit us to perceive and identify some of the consonant sounds of our language may be seen in the spectro-

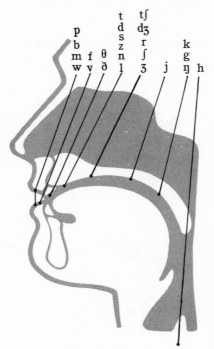

Figure 6.2. The Areas of Articulation for the Consonants of American English.

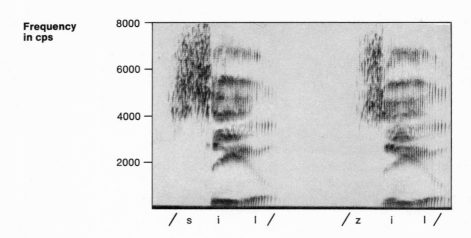

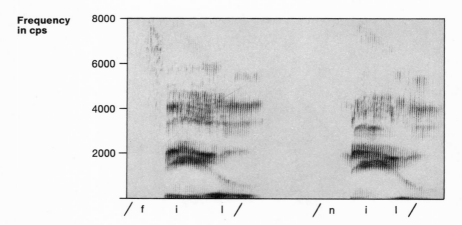

Figure 6.3. Broad-band Spectrograms of the Consonants /s, z, f, n/ Compared in Initial Positions.

graphic illustrations in Figure 6.3. These spectrograms show the resonance frequencies of the sounds and the transitions between sounds. The peaks or bands correspond to the basic frequencies of the vibrations in the vocal tract. The relatively large, dark regions are known as *formants*. They have already been discussed in Chapter 5.

B. *The Vowels and Diphthongs of American English*

Symbol	Example	Symbol	Example
i	s*ea*t*	o	s*oa*p*
ɪ	s*i*t	ʊ	f*oo*t
e	s*a*fe*	u	f*oo*d*
ɛ	s*e*t	ə	*a*lone**
æ	s*a*t	ɜ	th*ir*d §
a	h*a*lf†	ʌ	sh*u*t**
ɑ	c*a*lm	aɪ	s*igh*
ɒ	*o*dd‡	aʊ	n*ow*
ɔ	s*ough*t	ɔɪ	t*oy* §§

Acoustic aspects that permit us to perceive and identify the vowels may be seen in the spectrographic illustrations in Figure 6.5. Note the different frequency (formant) regions or bands. The vowels are in two sets of three, for comparison.

C. *Special Symbols To Indicate Variant Forms*

These diacritical markings or symbols are used whenever the phonetician desires to indicate special departures from the expected pronunciation. They are used here and there throughout this text and should be used by you whenever you desire to note special aspects of pronunciation. These sounds will have to be demonstrated as described. In some instances, you are referred to a pertinent part of the text.

* The vowels in the words *seat, safe, soap,* and *food* are normally diphtongal: [ɪi, eɪ, oʊ, ʊu]. These variants are discussed in detail in Chapters 10–13.

† This sound is that of *half* as it is spoken in eastern New England. The /æ/ and /ɑ/ are used by speakers in other areas for the sound in this word. See Chapters 10 and 11.

‡ This sound is that of *odd* as it is spoken in eastern New England. Speakers in other areas used /ɑ/ for the sound in this word. See Chapter 11.

** The /ə/ is used here as an unstressed vowel only. The stressed form of the sound in this word is similar to the /ʌ/ of *shut*. Many texts do transcribe the words *above* and *affront* as [əbɔ́v] and [əfrɔ́nt]. This text will transcribe these words as [əbʌv] and [əfrʌnt]. See Chapters 11 and 14.

§ This symbol is for the sound common to the "r-less" speakers in the South, New York City, and eastern New England. The presence of /r/ or of a constricted vowel in this word is variously symbolized in different texts, so that the word *third* may appear as [θɜrd], [θɔ́rd], or [θɝd]. See Chapter 12.

§§ Actually there are innumerable diphthongal or complex vowel forms in English. They are detailed throughout Chapters 10–13.

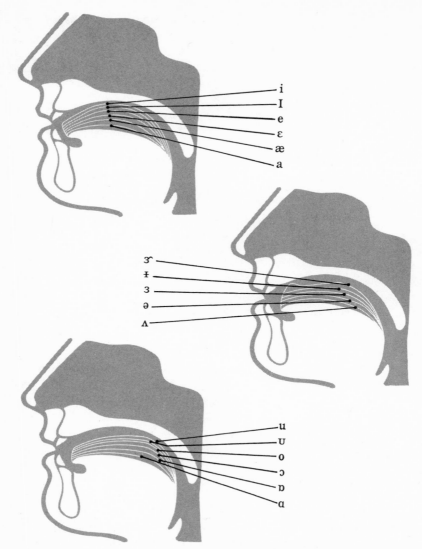

Figure 6.4. The Tongue Curves for the Vowel Positions of American English. (The differences in the resonance chambers of the mouth and pharynx during the formation and emission of the different vowel sounds are not demonstrated here. For those differences, see the figures in Chapters 10, 11, and 12.)

SOURCES: Adapted from Arthur J. Bronstein, *The Pronunciation of American English* (New York: Appleton-Century-Crofts, 1960), pp. 138–40; and Jon Eisenson, *Basic Speech* (New York: The Macmillan Company, 1950), pp. 83–85. By permission of the publishers.

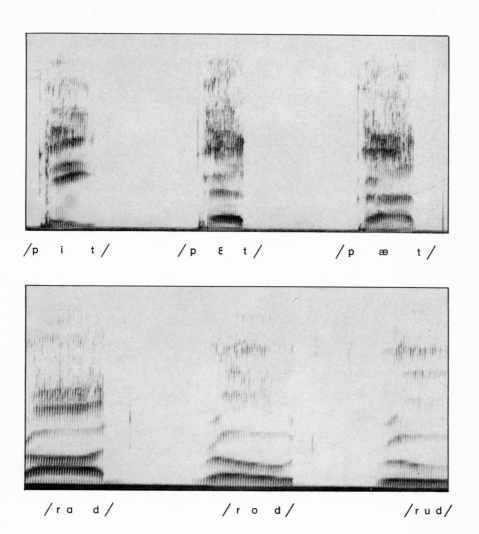

Figure 6.5. Broad-band Spectrograms of the Vowels /i, ɛ, æ, ɑ, o, u/.

Symbol	*As in*	*Transcribed*	*Described*
ʍ	when	[ʍɛn]	Voiceless /w/, variant of /hw/ (see Chapter 8).
ç	huge	[çudʒ]	Voiceless palatal, variant of /hj/ (see Chapter 8).
c	key	[ci]	Palatal stop, frontal variety of /k/ (see Chapter 7).
ɦ	ahoy	[əɦɔɪ]	Voiced /h/ (see Chapter 8).
ɨ	swim	[swɨm]	A high, central vowel used by some speakers instead of the [ɪ] that others are wont to use (see Chapter 10).
ʔ	oh	[ʔou]	Glottal stop (see Chapter 7).
¨	no	[nöu]	Centralized variety (see Chapter 12).
−	ship	[ʃɨp]	Centralization (see Chapter 10).
~	man	[mæ̃n]	Nasalization added to a sound.
ₒ	his son	[hɪz̥ sʌn]	Devoicing.
˯	butter	[bʌt̬ɚ]	Voicing (see Chapter 7).
┥ , ⊥	stone, city	[sto┥n, sɪ⊥ tɪ⊥]	Fronting, raising a sound.
⊤, ⊢	half, fall	[hæ⊢f, fɔ⊢l]	Lowering, backing a sound.
:	calm	[kɑ:m]	Lengthening a sound.
·	hot	[hɑ·t]	Half lengthening a sound.
˷	wealth	[wɛl̪θ]	Dentalizing a sound (see Chapter 9).
ḷ	funnel	[fʌnl̩]	Syllabifying a sound (see Chapter 9).
ʰ	pen	[pʰɛn]	Aspirated sound (see Chapter 7).
ᶜ	upper	[ʌpᶜɚ]	Weakly aspirated sound (see Chapter 7).
=	spend	[sp=ɛnd]	Unaspirated sound (see Chapter 7).
−	hip boot	[hɪp⁻ but]	Unreleased stop sound (see Chapter 7).

6.3. Special Terms

A number of special terms are used in the following portions of the text that analyze the sounds of our language. They are mentioned here, defined, and illustrated for quick reference. You will understand them only as you study the pertinent analyses that follow this chapter. They are used because they help us to describe with reasonable accuracy special features of the sounds we make.

A. *Tongue Positions for the Vowel Sounds*

Term	*Definition*	*Chapter*
Front vowel	A vowel made with the tongue arch relatively forward in the mouth.	10, 12
Centralized vowel	A vowel made with the tongue arch relatively centralized in the mouth.	11, 12, 14
Back vowel	A vowel made with the tongue arch relatively back in the mouth.	11, 12
High vowel	A vowel made with the tongue relatively high in the mouth; /i, ɪ, ʊ, u/ are high vowels.	10–14
Mid vowel	A vowel made with the tongue relatively midway between the positions for the high and low vowels; /e, ɛ, ɜ, o/ are mid vowels.	10–14
Low vowel	A vowel made with the tongue relatively low in the mouth; /æ, ɑ, ɒ, ɔ/ are low vowels.	10–14

B. *Consonant Positions in Syllables*

Term	*Definition*	*Chapter*
Prevocalic sound	A sound before a vowel; the /pr/ cluster in *pray* is prevocalic.	—
Intervocalic sound	A sound between two vowels; the /l/ of *follow* is intervocalic.	—
Postvocalic sound	A sound after a vowel; the /r/ of *four*, when pronounced, is known as "postvocalic r."	—

C. *Consonant and Vowel Modifications*

Term	Definition	Chapter
Palatalization	The elevation of the blade of the tongue toward the palatal area of the mouth; palatalization occurs when the /l/ of *will* changes to [lʲ] as in the pronunciation *will you* [wɪlʲ ju] and *William* [wɪlʲjəm].	9
Velarization	The retracting of the tongue toward the velum; *live* pronounced with a velarized /l/ may be transcribed [lʷɪv].	9
Dentalization	The placing of the tongue tip or blade on or against the teeth during the formation of a sound; the /θ/ of *thin* is dentalized, as is the /n/ of *month* [mʌn̪θ]; the /t/ of *tin* is not dentalized in English, but the /t/ of *eighth* is [eɪt̪θ].	9
Aspiration	The presence of emitted voiceless breath following a consonant, as in [pʰɛn, tʰɛn, kʰi].	7

D. *Vowel Forms*

Term	Definition	Chapter
Checked vowels	Vowels checked in their formation by consonant sounds that close the syllables; the vowels of *set*, *sit*, and *shut* are spoken as checked, not free, vowels in English.	10
Free vowels	Vowels that can exist as syllable finals; the final sounds of *see*, *say*, *sue*, *sir* are free vowels.	10

Term	Definition	Chapter
Complex vowel nucleus	A combination of vowels that serves as the nucleus of the syllable; *write* and *rout* both contain combinations of vowels that serve as such syllable nuclei [raɪt, raʊt] (see diphthongs).	13
Monophthong	The simple vowel of a syllable noted in each part of the disyllables *above* or *sitting* [əbʌv, sɪtɪŋ].	10 and 11
Diphthong	Two vowels spoken within the confines of a syllable, as in *sigh* [saɪ] or *sound* [saʊnd].	13
On-glide	The initiating position of a complex sound, as heard in [sᴵi, ʃᵁu], in which the [ᴵ, ᵁ] are the on-glides.	
Off-glide	The culminating part of a complex or clustered sound; in the pronunciations [puᵊ] and [soʊ], the [ə] and [ʊ] are the off-glide forms.	
Upgliding forms	The forms made by the gliding of the tongue toward a higher position in the mouth [ɪi, ʊu, ɛɪ, ɔʊ].	10–13
Ingliding forms	The forms made by the gliding of the tongue away from the back or front part of the mouth; other terms are "centralizing" or "centering" forms.	10–13
Centering glide forms	The forms made by the gliding of the tongue toward a central vowel from a less central position, as in [fɪᵊl] or [hwɪᵊp] for *fill* and *whip*.	10–13

Term	Definition	Chapter
Constricted vowel forms	Vowels made with the tongue muscle constricted and raised from a more relaxed position; the pronunciations of the word *turn* as [tɝn] and [tɘn] reflect constricted and unconstricted forms of the same vowel.	12

Practice: Try reading the following nonsense syllables.

mɪkt	fug	pɑbu
næst	mɛd	noʊgɪn
rɪn	nɛki	ruks
tɛp	fus	pʊst
slɛp	ridɛn	seɪθ
stit	lɪŋ	ðʌdʒ

Try reading the following phrases.

wi keɪm tɘdeɪ.   kʌt mi ɘ pis ɘv keɪk.
si ɪf hiz ɘt hoʊm.   kæn ʃi hændl ðæt bæt?
dɪd dʒɛf draɪv?   ðeɪ wɛnt tɘ ðɘ rɪŋk.

Try transcribing these sentences.

Take him home.   Just drive in.
Don't drink that milk.   What day is this?
He's in love with Sally. Welcome to our city.

Transcribe the first few lines of the preface to this text.

The following sentences contain some of the special symbols noted earlier. Refer to Section 6.2 if in doubt. A few stress and terminal marks appear. Add these marks to those sentences where they are omitted.

Next to each transcribed sentence is another for your transcription. Transcribe the sample sentences, using the diacritical phonetic symbols. "Narrow transcription" contains those modifying phonetic symbols used to identify certain special aspects of speech. "Broad transcription" includes the symbols without such detailed diacritical markers.

[ʍɛ̇n dɪd̯ ðíːz bɔ̀ɪẓ kʰʌm ↓]   Why did the men fight?
[sɨ ðæt⁼ mæn ↑ hi·z bɪfiaɪnd ðɘ   I wonder if the other people will
  lɪtˡ] st⁼æ̈nd̯ ↓]   try to cross that road?
[st⁼ápᶜ ìt⁻ ↓]   Keep out.

[tʰeɪk⁻ ðæt⁻ tʰæksi▾ pl̥iz̥]   Leave Tommy's playthings alone.

[ɪts ʔænə kʰɑn→dæd̥ ↓ rɪ⁼   Stop trying to find a more
  mɛmbɚ ʍaɪ ʃɨ lɛftᶜ ↑]   expensive toy.

[ʃi mærɪ˄d çu→ðæt fʌni▾ mæn   Who remembers that huge lake
  hu nü nʌθɪŋ ↓]   on the edge of that little town?

part four | **the sounds**

chapter 7 The Plosives

WE ARE NOW READY to apply ourselves to an analysis of these sounds in the context of speech. Except for certain descriptive generalizations, the comments that follow are not concerned with the sounds in isolation. We are not interested in *one* sound as it might be spelled or spoken, but with the forms that it takes in its various contexts, regardless of how it is spelled or pronounced when isolated from its environment.

As we are concerned with both the system of the sounds of our language and the details of utterance normal to most of us, we shall borrow freely from the researches of the phonemicists (those concerned primarily with identifying the systematic nature of the sounds we use), the phoneticians (those concerned with the physiological and acoustic details of the phonology), and the dialectologists (those who gather evidence of the actual functional varieties of usage and of the regional dialects we use at all social levels). Commonly, of course, research in the science of speech is all three kinds simultaneously, and the separate parts are not always easily kept distinct from one another. Evidence from research in any one of these areas affects conclusions and directions of thought in the others. But the methods or approaches do differ, as do the emphases. For us, all three have produced pertinent evidence that we cannot ignore. Therefore, the material presented for practice and the results desired by you and your teachers are discussed and described with these findings in mind.

7.1. The Plan of Presentation

Similar sounds are presented in groups for the easy identification of their contrasting aspects in context. You will find the following points included in the presentation of these sounds throughout this part of the text:

a. Sounds identified and briefly described

b. Sounds in the contexts of words and phrases, for the identification of similar and contrasting aspects

c. Brief notes about special words or regional variants

d. Notes about certain forms or usages not commonly found in the speech of the educated

e. Material for transcription and ear-training practice—phrases, sentences, and short selections

7.2. The Voiceless Plosives /p, t, k/

As noted in Chapter 6, these sounds, like their voiced counterparts /b, d, g/, begin with the closure of the two lips, the tongue tip to ridge, or the back of the tongue to the velum, respectively. The air pressure builds as the obstructing articulators remain in contact, while the sound is "stopped" or "held" momentarily. The sound is emitted

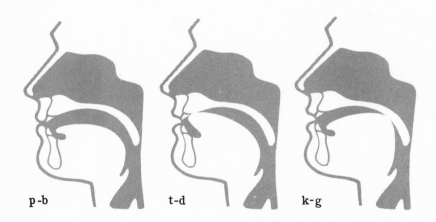

p-b   t-d   k-g

Figure 7.1. The Articulators that Form the Plosive Sounds.

SOURCE: Adapted from Arthur J. Bronstein, *The Pronunciation of American English* (New York: Appleton-Century-Crofts, 1960), Fig. 10, p. 68. By permission of the publisher.

explosively when the pressure behind the closure is released as the articulators forming the occlusion separate. The degree of aspiration emitted is dependent on the neighboring sounds, the nature of the stressed syllable in which the sound appears, and the position of the sound in the syllable. These three sounds are voiceless. They and their voiced counterparts /b, d, g/ are known as *stops* or *plosive* sounds. Their production is diagramed in Figure 7.1.

A. *Strongly Aspirated Plosives* [pʰ, tʰ, kʰ]

Note that these strongly aspirated sounds precede stressed vowels in each instance. /p, t, k/ are not so strongly aspirated when they do not precede stressed vowels.

Practice: Transcribe these words, phrases, and sentences as you say them aloud.

In initial positions in words

pea	tea	key	peel	teal	keel
pore	tore	core	poor	tour	courlan
pin	tin	kin	pale	tale	kale
purse	terse	curse	pine	thyme	kine
pick	tick	kick	pot	tot	cot
pack	tackle	cackle	pane	tame	cane
polled	told	cold	park	tart	cart

Toss the penny. Tom told Ted. Catch the cake. Terry caught the pot. Pa likes hot pie. I can't keep it. Put the peas in the pot. Keep that cook and you'll keep your customers. Kim kicked the cat, then tied it to a pole. She poured the coffee into the cups. Tania took history. Put Teddy's toy back. He turned pale as he told the horrible tale to his two pals. She served tea from a steaming pot, pouring it for each customer.

In medial positions in words

compare	contain	record (v.)	compose	contemn	accord
depend	deter	decay	appear	attire	recall
deposit	detach	decanter	report	attend	recast
depict	detect	decathlon	suppose	intoxicate	incorporate
saponify	satiric	sarcophagus	prepare	protect	incumbent
unpen	untied	unkempt	topography	totality	toccata

The accountant compared the figures. The Taconic Parkway had many detours. They unpenned the pigs by detaching the wires holding the gate. "Suppose they cannot attend," she complained. The pupils reported their findings to the detectives. Pearl appeared before the accountant with her accounts in order. She retired when the attending physician departed. It may be uncomfortable if you depend too strongly for protection on meager bank deposits.

B. *Weakly Aspirated Plosives* [p^c, t^c, k^c]

Before less stressed vowels

polarity	tonality	kinetic
polonaise	tonsorial	Korean
pintano	Tasmanian	Killarney
depot	rotate	catamaran

Before unstressed vowels

slipper	slighted	slicker
steeper	two-seater	seeker
happy	fatty	tacky
vapor	satyr	taker
pathetic	Toledo	conceive
parabola	telephony	conjunction

As final sounds [p^c, t^c, k^c], [p ⁻, t ⁻, k ⁻]

map	mat	knack
beep	beet	beak
sump	saint	sink
sloop	slate	slake
kelp	smelt	milk
crepe	Pete	crack
tape	slept	soak
mope	clout	sleek

When these sounds are not final in phrases, they behave as medial sounds, but if they precede stressed vowels in the phrases, they do not assume the fully aspirated quality of syllable-initial voiceless plosives. That is, the /t/ of *cat*, which would be pronounced [kæt ⁻] or [kæt^c] in the sentence "I took the cat," would probably appear as [kæt^c] in the phrase "He took the cat in." And the word *cat* in the latter sentence would normally not be pronounced with a final, strongly aspirated /t/ like the [t^h] we normally hear in *detain* [=t^{h}eɪn] or in *tin* [t^{h}ɪn]. Compare "Wash with soap" with "Put some soap on" with "The fat was saponified." This variation is perhaps better explained by the fact that there is a greater voice-onset lag between the voiceless plosive

/p/ and the vowel /ɑ/ of *saponify*, permitting an [ʰ] to be sounded ([səpʰɑnɪfaɪ]), than there is between the /p/ and /ɑ/ of "soap on." In the latter phrase the /p/ more closely approximates the kind of release associated with less forcibly exploded medial stops.[1]

c. *Unaspirated /p, t, k/ in Clusters with Preceding /s/* [sp⁼, st⁼, sk⁼]

Spain	stain	score
spore	astonish	askance
aspire	bestow	risky
bespeak	Constantinople	discuss
disparage	distort	Scotch
respell	steep	skinny
spurting	withstand	inscrutable
spendthrift	sturdy	reschedule

The voiceless plosives are not aspirated before stressed vowels when they cluster with /s/. Actually, they sound like the unaspirated /p, t, k/ sounds heard in Cantonese or French, when in this cluster position. Nor do they aspirate in final positions if clustered with preceding /s/ before the stressed vowel of a following word: Compare "Put the clasp on" with "Put the cap on," and "Is your rest over?" with "Bring your pet over."

Practice: The voiceless plosives are italicized in the following selection. Read the selection aloud, and note the special form each voiceless plosive takes. Can you describe each one?

The re*p*ort of his undeniable delirium a*t* sea was li*k*ewise *p*opularly ascribed *t*o a *k*indred *c*ause. And so *t*oo, all the added moodiness which always af*t*erwards, *t*o the very day of sailing in the *P*e*q*uod on the *p*resen*t* voyage, sa*t* brooding on his brow.

Moby Dick
—Herman Melville

Identify the voiceless plosives in the following selection.

Here, then, was this grey-headed, ungodly old man, chasing with curses a Job's whale round the world, at the head of a crew too, chiefly made up of mongrel renegades, and castaways, and cannibals—morally enfeebled also, by the incompetence of mere unaided virtue or right-mindedness in

[1] See Leigh Lisker and Arthur S. Abramson, "A Cross Language Study of Voicing in Initial Stops: Acoustical Measurements," *Word*, XX (December 1964), 384–422, for an excellent explanation of the relation of voice-onset time to aspiration of initial stops in English and other languages.

Starbuck, the invulnerable jollity of indifference and recklessness in Stub and the pervading mediocrity in Flask.

Moby Dick
—Herman Melville

7.3. The Voiced Plosives /b, g, d/

These sounds, formed like their voiceless counterparts /p, t, k/, retain fuller plosive force when they initiate stressed syllables, whereas they tend toward weaker sounds when they precede less stressed and unstressed vowels or when they are final. They are, of course, always unaspirated in English. When final in a phrase, such a sound anticipates the cessation of vocal cord vibration that will occur at the pause by becoming voiceless in the final part of the sound. Failure to do so would result in a slight vowel offglide; for example, "Here is the rug" [——— ðə rʌgᵊ], rather than [——— ðə rʌg̊]. Voiced plosives also assume voiceless forms when they precede the voiceless fricative sounds of a succeeding word in the same phrase (see following drill material).

The voiced plosives /b, d, g/ are not so forcibly exploded as are the voiceless /p, t, k/. The energy needed to form and emit the voiced plosive sound is used both for activating the vocal cords (phonation) and for the explosive force of the release. Less air (energy) is therefore used to build up the compression in the cavities above the vocal cords before the release of the voiced plosive. Normally, then, voiceless consonants are emitted with greater force or energy than are their voiced counterparts.

A. *Preceding Stressed Vowels*

beau	doe	go
abide	adept	begone
booty	do	goober
big	dig	gig
bust	dust	gust
abundance	indefinite	regarding

B. *Preceding Unstressed Vowels or Final in Syllable*

before	reader	eager
cabin	ridicule	struggle
able	beadle	soggy
rabbit	bidder	legacy
rub	red	vague
crib	cried	shrug

Practice: Devoiced plosives are final in phrases and precede voiceless fricative sounds in the same phrase: [-b̥, -d̥, -g̥]. Read aloud and transcribe:

Don't rub.	a good slide	in the bag
a good grab	Well read!	Hold Sue's dog.
Call a cab.	Eat your salad.	a slippery rug
a marble slab	Come outside.	He's big.
His name is "Abe."	Put it in the shed.	Catch that bug.
I heard Fan sob.	Watch that bird.	Watch him dig.
Grab flies.	yard thrush	frog swamp
Abe slept.	Slide safely.	big Sally
Gabe slipped.	Hide Shirley.	pig sty

7.4. Voiced and Voiceless Plosives in Similar Environments

A. *The /t-d/ Contrasts*

ten—den	writing—riding	bent—bend
time—dime	sighting—siding	front—frond
tore—door	bleating—bleeding	trite—tried
team—deem	beetle—beadle	plight—plied
tip—dip	hearty—hardy	sought—sawed

B. *The /p-b/ Contrasts*

pie—buy	napping—nabbing	lope—lobe
pore—bore	scrapple—scrabble	slop—slob
poor—boor	rapid—rabid	nap—nab
pike—bike	topper—robber	cup—cub
pried—bride	aping—baby	lap—lab

C. *The /k-g/ Contrasts*

cut—gut	bicker—bigger	slack—slag
croup—group	vicar—vigor	leak—league
cot—got	Becker—beggar	sack—sag
cull—gull	snicker—snigger	wrack—rag
crab—grab	lacking—lagging	pick—pig

Practice: Differences in the lengths of vowels occur before voiced and voiceless stops. Such differences are described in detail in the chapters on the vowels, but it is interesting to note this phenomenon here so that you can see how the voiced and voiceless plosives, instantaneous though they seem to be, do affect preceding vowels, just as other voiced and voiceless consonants do. Say each of the pairs of words aloud and note the differences in the lengths of the vowels as you do.

beet—bead	slap—slab	sick—Sig
slit—slid	cup—cub	flack—flag
heat—heed	mop—mob	picks—pigs
meet—mead	nap—nab	leak—league
cot—cod	rope—probe	smock—smog

7.5. Unintentional Plosives

Plosives may be inserted unintentionally between sounds as the articulators move through the plosive positions for following sounds. Most speakers are not able to distinguish between *dense* and *dents*, *bans* and *bands*. The inserted /t/ or /d/ is not normally noticed in these words. The sense of the sentence normally dictates which homophonous word has been used. These inserted sounds are sometimes called "excrescent plosives."

Inserted plosives

/p/	/b/	/t/	/d/	/k/
dreamt	hams	sense	sins	length
something	limbs	prince	fans	strength
Samson	psalms	once	lines	strengthen

Unintentionally inserted velar plosives are rare in English. The /k/ is sometimes heard as an excrescent in *length, lengthen, strength, strengthen*. Excrescent /g/, as in *sings* or *songs*, is not pronounced in English. The /g/ in words like *finger* or *mingle* is, of course, not excrescent. (See Chapter 9 on nasal sounds for a detailed discussion of the use of /ŋ/ in English.)

7.6. Plosive Clusters

A. *Addition of Endings*

Plural, possessive, and present-past morphemic endings /s, z, t, d/ are added to words ending in the plosive sounds. Voiceless /p, t, k/ are followed by *-s*, pronounced /s/, and voiced /b, d, g/ are followed by *-s*, pronounced /z/.

Added /s/			*Added /z/*		
rips	hits	takes	ribs	hides	leagues
slips	pots	ticks	mobs	cods	pigs
maps	mats	racks	throbs	slides	bags
sleeps	nuts	locks	Abe's	nods	logs

Voiceless /p, k/ are followed by -*ed*, pronounced /t/, and voiced /b, g/ are followed by -*ed*, pronounced /d/.

Added /t/		*Added* /d/	
rapped	leaked	crabbed	hogged
flipped	streaked	nabbed	flogged
slapped	cracked	robbed	shrugged
cupped	picked	throbbed	rigged
hoped	shrieked	ebbed	bagged
stopped	licked	rubbed	nagged

The /t-d/ endings do not follow words ending in /t, d/. Instead, the third-person singular past tense of the verb is [-ɪd] or [-əd]. *Pat, pad, seat, seed* become [pætɪ̆d, pædɪ̆d, sitɪ̆d, sidɪ̆d].

B. *Before Consonants*

Plosives, clustered before consonants, whether or not in the same syllables, are not strongly released sounds. An obvious lack of plosive release occurs when the following sound is homorganic with the preceding plosive, that is, when they are both formed by the same articulators, like /k/ and /g/, /b/ and /p/. A strong plosive burst does not occur, however, even when the following sound is not homorganic: /k/ and /d/, /b/ and /t/. When stop sounds cluster with following fricatives, in the same or adjacent syllables, the force of the plosive bursts seems to be absorbed into the formation of the following sounds. Compare "hit Don" with "get fresh" with "a tone." A forceful /t/ release occurs only on the last phrase, whereas the /t/ of the first phrase is unreleased and the burst of the /t/ of "get fresh" is absorbed.

Before homorganic consonants

Stop Barney.	hot dog	slick grease
top bureau	red topper	slick goose
Rub Pearl's head.	Beat Danny.	big Kate
Rope Bossy.	sad Therese	bug catcher
Bob pulled.	hate dinosaurs	big kite

Before other consonants

slipped	hot biscuit	act
rubbed	sad flower	sick tomcat
Sip soda.	wide porch	bagged
crib side	slight gentleman	Take good care.
Let Florence go.	Get Sally's shoes.	His dad fussed.
Bob shrugged.	I saw Meg sink.	He had bad vision.

C. *With Nasal and Lateral Sounds*

Plosives clustered with nasal or lateral sounds are released nasally (through the nose) or laterally (over the sides of the tongue) (see Chapter 9).

rip many	slight Nell	bottle	beadle	pickle	goggle
topmost	beaten	glottal	ladle	sickle	struggle
Rub my back.	hidden	pot luck	Ned lost.	crackle	gaggle

Some clusters with nasal plosions are common to quite informal, casual pronunciations, whereas the articulatory precision of more formal speech obviates such pronunciations. There is sufficient evidence of their inclusion in educated patterns of informal, casual, and intimate speech. The following syllabic forms are not part of careful, precise, formally educated speech:

cup and saucer	[kʌpm̩ ——]	wagon train	[wægŋ ——]
open the door	[oupm̩ ——]	bacon and eggs	[beɪkŋ ——]
it happens	[—— hæpm̩z]	dragon	[drægŋ]

7.7. The Intervocalic /t, d/

A variety of voiced intervocalic /t/, [ṭ], appears quite commonly in informal, casual educated speech. Precise speech or speech approximating the formal tends to avoid the voiced variety. The more formal variety of this sound is a flapped allophone of /t/, of weak intensity and voiceless. It does not possess the precision of an initial /t/ of a phrase or word. In more casual speech, it approaches the voiced allophone of medial /d/.

This allophone of /t/ is commonly heard before unstressed vowels, as in *city* and *butter*. It may also appear when before syllabic /l/, as in *kettle*; between nonsyllabic /l/ and an unstressed vowel, as in *salted*; between /n/ and an unstressed vowel, as in *painted*; and between two unstressed vowels, as in *when it is nice*.

Practice: For purposes of contrast, similar words and phrases are listed (read aloud and transcribe your pronunciations).

kitty	kiddy	beetle	beadle
Latin	laden	settle	saddle
writing	riding	pelted	melded
sorted	sordid	petal	pedal
coated	coded	twenty	Wendy

He was a hearty man.

He was a hardy man.

He climbed the latter (slope).

He climbed the ladder.

They were hurting the sheep.

They were herding the sheep.

The apples were crated.

The eggs were graded.

There were eight of them.

It was aid of a sort.

He bit a roll.

He bid a lot.

Mr. Ritter came home.

Mr. Kidder came home.

He heated the corn.

He heeded the warning.

It seemed fated to him.

It seemed faded to him.

They were writing slowly.

They were riding slowly.

"Great Aid" was the firm's name.

"Grade A" was the firm's name.

He was neater now.

He will need her now.

7.8. Effects of Adjacent Vowels on Stops

Although all sounds are affected by adjacent sounds in the context of words and phrases, the stops /k, g/ demonstrate such effects very noticeably. Typically made with the back of the tongue bunched up and in contact with the velum (as noted in *car* and *gone*), these sounds shift noticeably forward in the mouth, toward the high arch of the palate, or farther back, toward the velar valve, depending on the adjacent sounds. Compare your pronunciation of *keep*, *cop*, and *cool*, and you will note that the hump of the tongue shifts from the high palatal position in [kip] to a farther back position for [kɑp], and to a still farther back velar position for [kul].

Practice : Pronounce the following words and phrases, noting the effects of the different adjacent vowels on the /k/ and /g/ sounds.

keep	kip	coop	get	gate	got
ski	sky	score	lag	log	lug
skip	skate	scum	flag	flog	slug
hick	hook	hock	game	gone	goon
Nick	Mack	mock	gang	garter	goober
shake	shock	shook	gangrene	girdle	goat
skeet	scale	school	guilt	golf	gopher
Dickey	hockey	looking	guest	guide	goad
sticking	stacking	stocking	geese	guess	goose

7.9. The Glottal Stop

A seventh stop sound is part of our speech in certain special situations. This sound, known as a "glottal stop," "laryngeal click," or "glottal catch," is a voiceless unaspirated sound. It is pronounced when the laryngeal glottis is suddenly released from a closed position, the result of considerable breath pressure and excessive resistance at the glottis. It has no spelled form. Other languages like Arabic and German possess this sound as a normal part of the sound system. English does not.

The glottal stop appears typically in both the formal and informal styles of speech. It commonly precedes an initially stressed vowel as in "Oh!" [ʔóʊ] or "Ah!" [ʔɑ́:]. It may also be inserted as a boundary marker between two vowels, especially when the second syllable begins with a stressed vowel, as in *triumphant* [traɪʔʌ́mfənt], "I *am*" [aɪ ʔǽm], or "He *is* the tallest in the class" [hi ʔíz ——]. The glottal stop accompanies stress and is associated with tension of the larynx.

The substitution of a glottal stop before syllablic /n, l/, as in [mʌʔn̩] for *mutton* or [biʔl̩] for *beetle*, is not common in educated speech.

Practice: Note your pronunciation of the following words and phrases to see if you use a glottal catch. Can you avoid its use in any of them?

Oh!	triumphant
Ah!	mutton
Easy!	kitten
Arthur!	gotten
Oscar!	mountain
It isn't!	Hottentot
We *are*?	needle
Go up, not down!	pickle
aorta	knuckle

The stop sounds are italicized in the following selection. Transcribe these sentences as you say them, and describe each italicized sound. Listen to a friend's reading of this selection. Comment on any differences you perceive that he makes in the formation and emission of these stop sounds compared with those you make in the same contexts.

Now Morn, her rosy s*t*eps in th' eas*t*ern *c*lime
A*d*vancing, sowe*d* the earth with orien*t* *p*earl,
When A*d*am wa*k*ed, so *c*ustome*d*; for his slee*p*
Was aery ligh*t*, from *p*ure *d*igestion *b*red,
An*d* *t*em*p*era*t*e va*p*ours *b*land, which th' only soun*d*
Of leaves and fuming rills, Aurora's fan,
Ligh*t*ly dis*p*ersed, an*d* the shrill ma*t*in song
Of *b*irds on every *b*ough. So much the more
His won*d*er was *t*o fin*d* unwa*k*ened Eve,
With *t*resses dis*c*om*p*osed, and *g*lowing chee*k*,

As through unquiet rest. He, on his side
Leaning half raised, with looks of cordial love
Hung over her enamoured, and beheld
Beauty which whether waking or asleep,
Shot forth peculiar graces; then, with voice
Mild as when Zephyrus on Flora breathes,
Her hand soft touching, whispered thus:—Awake,
My fairest, my espoused, my latest found,
Heaven's last, best gift, my ever-new delight!

Paradise Lost, Book V
—John Milton

chapter **8** *The Fricatives*

FRICATIVES ARE NOISY SOUNDS. Two adjacent articulators act as a constrictive barrier through which the speaker forces the breath stream. The degree of friction is dependent on the force of the emitted stream and the proximity of the two articulators to each other.

Four pairs of fricative sounds and one unpaired fricative are part of the phonemic system of all English speakers. The voiceless-voiced pairs are /f-v, θ-ð, s-z, ʃ-ʒ/. The unpaired fricative is /h/.

Two other fricative sounds are also used in English. These two sounds [ʍ] and [ç] are the fricative allophones of /w/ and /j/, respectively, and should normally be discussed with those sounds in Chapter 9. Because of their fricative nature, however, they will be treated briefly in this chapter, immediately following the discussion and practice sections on /h/. We shall begin our discussion of the fricatives with /h/ and these two special sounds, followed by the sections on the paired voiceless and voiced fricative sounds.

8.1. The Fricative /h/

The /h/ is the glottal or laryngeal fricative sound. It is initiated in the glottal area as the breath stream is forced between the vocal cords. The articulators in the vocal tract are not specially set for this sound, however, but for the following vowel sound. For example, in the words *him, hen, here,* and *how,* the articulators are, from the beginning, positioned for the vowels following the /h/. If you say each of these words aloud, you will note that there is no real articulatory transition in the oral cavity between the /h/ and the following vowel.

The /h/ we hear in these words, then, is the result of the breath forced between the vocal bands and through the vocal tract already formed for the following vowel. The friction at the glottis (where the /h/ is initiated) plus the cavity friction that takes place in the pharynx and mouth already set for the following vowel create the sound we hear as the initiating /h/ of these words. There are, then, as many positional varieties of /h/ as there are vowels that may follow it.

A. *The Voiced Allophone* [ɦ]

A voiced allophone of /h/, transcribed [ɦ], may result when the /h/ appears between two voiced sounds. Thus the medial /h/ in *behind* and *behave* may be accompanied by vocal cord vibration, resulting in [bɪɦaɪnd, bɪɦeɪv]. Note that when it initiates the word and phrase, /h/ remains [h]. If it is medial and between voiced sounds, it may tend toward [ɦ].

who	who came?	Will whoever is there come out!
home	which home?	Whose home is that?
high	that high	He stood on a high hill.
hill	grass hill	the stone hill over there
honey	make honey	Make some honey today.
hoof	horse hoofs	He heard horses' hoofs.

Practice: Transcribe the following sentences. Do you use [h] or [ɦ] in these words?

I see his head ahead of us. Whenever we eat honey it hails. Some homes are higher than other homes. Take your horse over that small hill near that tall hunter. Hounds and horses are needed for the hunt. The hydrangeas were hybrid forms. Although "housewife" and "hussy" are historically related linguistically, they are not interchangeably used today. The hysterical hygienist was calmed by careful handling by the internist.

B. *Preceding Different Syllabics*

Note the changed position of the articulators as /h/ precedes different vowels. If you whisper any of these words, note that there is no change in the articulators as you move from /h/ to the following vowel, nor will you hear any transition from this consonant to the vowel. It is for this reason that some consider /h/ before a vowel, although it functions linguistically as a consonant, acoustically a voiceless vowel: *heel* [hil] or [i̥il].

Practice : Say and transcribe the following words.

he	him	hair	hand	hard	hat
hall	home	heat	hip	help	hoyden
hot	haul	honey	house	high	longhorn
hospital	horrid	horse	howl	ahoy	preheat
rehearsal	inhale	exhale	unheated	inhuman	heard
unhooked	prohibit	cohort	unheard	ahead	reheat
inhabit	overhaul	unhand	somehow	hook	Harry
Huxley	whose	humble	hyphen	behest	unhitch

c. *Certain Unstressed Forms*

The /h/ is often deleted in the unstressed forms of such words as *has*, *have*, *had*, *he*, *him*, *her*, and *his* in phrases like those that follow. The words containing the stressed syllables of each sentence are marked with ´ for primary and ˆ or ˋ for intermediate stresses. Weak stress is unmarked.

He has góne.
Whère has she góne?
Màny have léft.

Gíve him his bàll.
Ì sáw her.
Ìt's his ówn bôok.

Sòme had cóme.
Dìd he crý?
Ì'll sée him when he cômes.

He had nóne.
Whỳ had you góne?
Will he wálk?
Gíve it to him.

Tàke his cóat plêase.
Tòm has spóken.
We have cóme.
Yòu have thrée of them.

Ì sáw him.
Gíve it to her.
Í have her còat.
Gìve her míne.

Practice : The /h/ is irregularly deleted in the italicized words in this list. Do you pronounce all of them in these words?

Perhaps I shall. All *vehicles* for the *Philharmonic* concert are parked there. The *humble* man could not tolerate the *unhistorical* references. We *vehemently* denied the accusation. The troops *annihilated* the guerrillas. The *rehabilitation* code was used in all the centers. She attended the *exhibition*. The *inhalation* process is complex. By bowing their *foreheads*, they rendered appropriate *homage*.

8.2. The [ʍ] and [ç] Fricatives

Two other fricatives are used by many speakers of English. They result from the clustering of /h/ with the glides /w/ and /j/, resulting either in /hw/ or /hj/ forms or, as many phoneticians prefer to think of them, in voiceless fricatives resulting from the devoicing of the /w/

and /j/ forms. The voiceless bilabial fricative is represented as [ʍ]; the voiceless palatal fricative, as [ç].

These two fricatives are not part of the phonemic system of many speakers of English. They may vary with /w/ and /j/ in the same speaker's speech or in the speech of the same regional areas and the same social levels. Let us discuss them separately.

A. *The Voiceless Bilabial Fricative*

Many speakers never confuse such pairs as *weather-whether, wear-where, wine-whine*. Others pronounce them as homonyms. As in educated British speech, where an earlier [hw] or [ʍ] had merged with [w] by the late eighteenth century,[1] we find loss of /h/ in at least three large regional areas of the United States: the coastal Middle Atlantic; a narrow strip of coastal New England from the Kennebec to Boston; the coast of South Carolina and Georgia.[2] For speakers from these areas, a phonemic /ʍ/ (or /hw/) does not occur. For others, as contrasts do appear, a phonemic /ʍ/ is present. For the latter speakers, *hair-where-wear, hitch-which-witch*, and *heel-wheel-weal* begin with three clearly distinctive forms: a glottal fricative /h/, a voiceless bilabial fricative /ʍ/ or a clustered /hw/, and a frictionless glide /w/. Such speakers may be heard throughout the country at all social levels, although the evidence seems to point to the growing use of /w/ for these *wh-* forms, especially in urban areas.

Practice: Here are examples of the /h, ʍ, w/ in words and sentences for contrast. Do you use all three?

hind	whine	wine	hit	whit	wit
heel	wheel	weal	hack	whack	wagon
her	whirr	were	hot	what	watt
hail	whale	wail	heat	wheat	weed
hate	whey	wait	halt	wharf	warp
hen	when	Wendy	height	white	wight

Bind the hay. Curds and whey. Find the way. Show me where. Show me his hair. Show me your wares. Will Henry bring the whiting when Wendy comes? Whales do not wail in the hail. Meanwhile the weather

---

[1] See A. C. Gimson, *An Introduction to the Pronunciation of English* (London: Edward Arnold Ltd., 1962), p. 212.

[2] See Hans Kurath and Raven I. McDavid, Jr., *The Pronunciation of English in the Atlantic States* (Ann Arbor, Mich.: University of Michigan Press, 1961), p. 178 and maps 174, 175; and McDavid, "American English Dialects," in W. Nelson Francis, ed., *The Structure of American English* (New York: The Ronald Press Company, 1958), pp. 513–27.

became somewhat bearable. Everywhere he turned, he noticed gymnasts performing cartwheels. Whenever Harry breakfasted at the hotel, he ordered buckwheat cakes. He wheedled a wheelbarrow from Mr. Washington. Mr. Wheeler was wheeled around in a white wheelchair. He thought that white-collar workers earned higher wages than blue-collar workers. Higby was the only Whig whose wig didn't fit. The witch hitched her broom to whichever star was nearest.

B. *The Voiceless Palatal Fricative*

In such words as *huge* and *humor*, we may hear three possible forms: [hjudʒ, judʒ, çudʒ; hjumɚ, jumɚ, çumɚ]. When used, the [ç] results from the coalescence of the initial /h/ with the /j/, resulting in a voiceless palatal fricative sound. For most speakers, *who, you*, and *hue* initiate with three clearly different sounds: /h/, /j/, and /hj/. Many speakers, however, use no initial voiceless form in the *hu-* words, nor does the evidence permit a label of "uneducated or dialectal speech" for such pronunciations as [judʒ, jugo, jumɪd, jumən] for *huge, Hugo, humid*, and *human.*

In *The Pronunciation of English in the Atlantic States*, Hans Kurath and Raven I. McDavid, Jr., note that *humor* is prevalently pronounced [humɚ] or [jumə], the initial /h/ occurring only in New England and upstate New York.[3] Grant Fairbanks, in his widely used *Voice and Articulation Drillbook*,[4] says: "The number of American speakers who omit [h] before [hj] is sufficiently large that the status of the omission as an error is questionable." Perhaps the confusion will be even more manifest if we compare some recent dictionary entries for words with these initial forms. Compare your own pronunciations with the listed ones in the table on page 117.

Evidence does not warrant insistence on an initial /çu/, /hju/, or /ju/ for any of these words. If regional preference indicates use of initial /h/, as it seems to do in New England and upstate New York and perhaps elsewhere, the loss of /h/ is not indicative of any special variety or level of speech. Perhaps like /w/ for /ʍ/ or /hw/, the use of /ju/ for /çu/ or /hju/ is on the increase at all social and educational levels. Only further collected evidence can warrant a more decisive statement of preference for educated, informal speech.

[3] Kurath and McDavid, *op. cit.*, p. 178 and map 176.
[4] Grant Fairbanks, *Voice and Articulation Drillbook*, 2nd ed. (New York: Harper & Row, Publishers, 1960), p. 64.

Practice : Compare /hu/, /hju/, and /ju/ forms.

Who means it? You mean it. Hugh means it. It was the humane thing to do. If you desire, you may do it. Who may do it? Who, other than you, Morton, will come? I find your humor delightful. Will you go, Hugo? What did you mean when you analyzed Hume's use of "history"? Will you and Hugh check the humidity, please? "You're on the air," the announcer shouted to the Huron chief. Which human did Hugh mean? Humility is a human trait; humaneness should be.

	Kenyon and Knott Pronouncing Dictionary of American English (1953 *edition*)		The American College Dictionary (1965 *edition*)		Webster's Third International Dictionary (1961 *edition*)	
	/hju/	/ju/	/hju/	/ju/	/hju/	/ju/
huge	*	*	*	†	*	*
human	*	*	*	†	*	*
humane	*	*	*	†	*	*
humor	*	*	*	*	*	*
humorist	*	*	*	*	*	*
humorous	*	*	*	*	*	*
hue	*	†	*	†	*	†
Hugh	*	†	*	†	*	*
Hugo	*	†	*	†	*	*
Hume	*	†	*	†	*	†
humus	*	†	*	†	*	*
humerus	*	†	*	†	*	†
humid	*	†	*	†	*	*
humidity	*	†	*	†	*	*
humidify	*	†	*	†	*	*
humidor	*	†	*	†	*	*
humiliate	*	†	*	†	*	*
humility	*	†	*	†	*	*
Huron	*	†	*	†	*	*
humanity	*	†	*	†	*	*

* = entered.   † = not entered.

8.3. The Voiceless Fricatives

The four voiceless fricatives /f, θ, s, ʃ/, each of which possesses a voiced partner in English /v, ð, z, ʒ/, are emitted through slits created when lips and teeth, tongue tip and teeth, tongue blade and ridge, and tongue blade and hard palate are brought close together (see Figure 8.1).

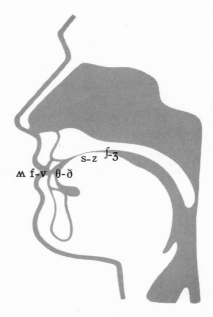

Figure 8.1. The Articulatory Positions of the Fricative Sounds.

SOURCE: Adapted from Arthur J. Bronstein, *The Pronunciation of American English* (New York: Appleton-Century-Crofts, 1960), Fig. 11, p. 84. By permission of the publisher.

Two pairs of these fricative sounds are also known as "sibilant sounds," a term used to identify the "s" family of sounds. The four sibilant sounds /s, z, ʃ, ʒ/ are easily identified by their comparatively high ranges of noise, acoustically somewhat unpleasant (see Chapter 5 for spectrographic representation of /s, ʃ/). The fricatives, along with the plosives and affricates, are the "noisy sounds" of the language, and the sibilants are the noisiest of them all.

A. *Initial Voiceless Fricatives*

In this list the voiceless fricatives are compared in initial positions in syllables preceding stressed vowels. Note the different articulatory position taken for each fricative sound and the different acoustic characteristics of each.

fin	thin	sin	shin
four	Thor	sore	shore
fie	thigh	sigh	shy
first	thirst	sir	shir
furred	third	surd	shirred
feat	Thea	seat	sheet
a furred fox	a third thought	a surd sound	a short shrub
a funny film	a thin thief	a sad sigh	a silent surf

B. *Before Unstressed Vowels in Prevocalic and Intervocalic Positions*

leafy	Cathy	fussy	pushy
laughing	nothing	passing	crushing
scaffold	Ethel	whistle	bushel
inference	Arthur	lesser	fisherman
information	enthymeme	insecure	hushaby

C. *Initiating Stressed Syllables in Phrases*

He de*f*erred to his *s*on. Don't *th*ank *F*anny or *Sh*aron. He's *c*ertainly *sh*y. She *s*ounds *s*ick. *Th*ink *sh*arp. *F*igs and *s*ausages might make an interesting *s*upper. *F*ind a *th*ankless task, and *th*ink twice be*f*ore doing it.

D. *In Final Positions in Words*

laugh	lath	lass	lash
if	myth	miss	fish
leaf	sheath	peace	leash
Lef	Beth	yes	mesh
Biff	pith	Swiss	swish
cough	wroth	sauce	wash

Practice: In the following sentences and phrases, the voiceless fricatives are italicized in the first two selections. Can you select all others? Transcribe as you speak these selections.

Try *s*aving a *suff*i*c*ient amount of ca*sh* be*f*ore *th*inking of a vaca*t*ion.

Four *s*core and *s*even years ago our *f*athers brought *forth* on thi*s* continent a new na*ti*on, con*c*eived in liberty and dedicated to the propo*si*tion that all men are created equal.

Gettysburg Address
—Abraham Lincoln

So it chanced one night: for I must say that a thief, under the pretext of being a goldsmith, had spied on me, and cast his eyes upon the precious stones, and made a plan to steal them. Well, then, this fellow broke into the shop, where he found a quantity of little things in gold and silver. He was engaged in bursting open certain boxes to get at the jewels he had noticed when my dog jumped upon him and put him to much trouble to defend himself with his sword.

The Autobiography of Benvenuto Cellini

E. *Clusters with Voiceless Fricatives*

The voiceless fricatives cluster with one another, with voiceless plosives, and with frictionless consonants. Examples of plosive clusters with /s/ and /ʃ/ follow:

caps	cusp	cats	cast	hacks	husk
maps	lisp	mats	mast	packs	brisk
hips	spy	fits	passed	six	scare
		washed			
		crushed			
		meshed			

Note that /ʃ/ does not cluster initially with the stop sounds, except in borrowed terms from foreign languages: *Przemysl* (a Polish city [pʃɛmɪʃl]), *Shkoder* (an Albanian city [ʃkɔdər]), and *Sturm und Drang* (German term meaning "storm and stress" [ʃturm unt drɑŋ]). The interjection *pshaw* is pronounced [ʃɔ]. The initial sound of *cheese*, /ʧ/, is an affricate sound. It is treated as a single sound, rather than as a cluster of two sounds. Affricates are discussed later in this chapter.

CLUSTERS WITH /s/

The /s/ sound may follow any voiceless consonant except another sibilant. These /s/ clusters form the plurals or possessives of nouns and the third person singulars of verbs. As no word ends in voiceless /h/, /s/ does not cluster with it.

lips	cats	creaks	scuffs	laths
pipes	hates	kicks	laughs	froths
lapse	lets	fox	coughs	faiths

INITIAL /s/ AND /ʃ/

Initial /s/ is clustered with the glide or semivowel consonants and the nasals /m/ and /n/. Initial /ʃ/ is clustered with /r/, but it is clustered with the other frictionless consonants only in pronunciations borrowed from other languages.

swim	slim	smear	snear	Shreveport	suit*
swine	slime	smite	snide	shrike	suicide
swag	slack	smack	snack	shrank	suiter
sway	slay	smoke	snow	shrove	sumac†

* These /sj/ words are more commonly heard without the glide /j/ following the /s/, as in [sɪut] or [sut].
† More commonly heard as [ʃumæk].

Less common consonant clusters with initial /s/ and /ʃ/ appear in borrowed words.

Schlegel	svelte	Schmidt	schnapps	schwa
Schleswig	svarabhakti	schmaltz	schnauzer	Schwab

CONSONANT CLUSTERS WITH /f/ AND /θ/

The voiceless fricatives /f, θ/ cluster with final /s/ when /s/ indicates the plural or possessive of a noun or the third person singular of a verb. They also cluster with each other, as in *fifth*. The /s/ clusters initially with /f/.

/fs/	/θs/	/ft/	/sf/
laughs	laths	laughed	sphere
giraffes	cloths	coughed	spherical

The /f/ and /θ/ also cluster with frictionless sounds.

/fr/	/fl/	/θr/	/θw/	/fj/
fry	fly	thrice	thwart	feud
freeze	flees	three	thwack	few

SOME SPECIAL /s/ CLUSTERS

/spl/	/skl/	/skr/	/kst/	/spr/	/str/
spleen	sclerotic	scrabble	text	spree	straight
splatter	sclaff	scrag	next	spruce	strong

/skw/	/ksθ/	/spt/	/pts/	/kts/	/n(t)s/
square	sixth	lisped	corrupts	acts	once
squirt		cusped	erupts	effects	dunce

/pst/	/sps/	/sts/	/sks/	/nst/
lapsed	lisps	boosts	desks	against
collapsed	grasps	fists	asks	bounced

Others

/ksθ/	sixth	/ksθs/	sixths
/pθs/	depths	/dθs/	widths
/fθs/	fifths	/lfθs/	twelfths
/tθs/	eighths	/ŋ(k)θs/	lengths

CLUSTERS WITH ADJACENT SYLLABLES

When the voiceless fricatives are in positions adjacent to other consonant sounds in separate syllables, the resulting combinations necessitate considerable agility of the parts of the articulatory mechanism as they move from one to the other position.

/skr/	/kstr/	/spr/	/kskr/	/stl/
ice cream	extra	express	smokescreen	ghastly
discredit	backstroke	expropriate	Max crept	mostly

/ftl/	/kstʃ/	/ms/	/ns/	/n(m)ʃ/
softly	mixture	Samson	Nancy	unsure
swift lion	fixture	Sam saw	fancy	dumbshow

Practice : Here are several sentences with the voiceless fricative sounds in prevocalic as well as in clustered positions with other consonants. Transcribe each sentence.

He left the wharf as the tramp steamer approached. Mister Shaeffer found a few fellows too close to the bushes. Philip Kraft couldn't quite see the three smokestacks. The smiling but flustered nurse administered the anaesthetic to the patient.

8.4. The Voiced Fricatives

The fricatives /v, ð, z, ʒ/ are the voiced counterparts of /f, θ, s, ʃ/ and are formed in the same way. They are not so forcibly emitted as are the voiceless fricatives, because part of the energy of formation and emission is dissipated by the voicing action of the vocal cords. Voiced fricatives initiate and conclude phrases in voiceless or partially voiceless forms. And they assume similarly voiceless forms when they precede voiceless consonants in the same phrases. The frictional duration of the voiced fricative is normally shorter than that of the voiceless sound of each pair.

A. *Fricatives Compared in Prevocalic and Intervocalic Positions*

When the voiced and voiceless fricatives are compared in prevocalic and intervocalic positions, you may note that the voiceless sounds are emitted with greater force and tension, the voiced sounds with less force and tension.

feel—veal	seal—zeal	thin—then	pressure—measure
fine—vine	scion—Zion	thigh—thy	evolution—delusion

a fast pace—a vast place	my Sue—my zoo
nefarious—knew various	you see land—New Zealand
author—oh there	we fail—the veil
too thin—to them	afford—avoid
facing—fazing	ether—to them
epistle—a fizzle	Arthur—northern

B. *Fricatives Compared in Final Positions*

In final positions in words and phrases, note that the voiced fricative approximates the ensuing silence by devoicing: "She uses too much rouge" [—— ru̥ʒ̥]; "Look alive" [—— əlaɪ̯]. Similar devoicing of voiced fricative sounds is heard when these sounds immediately precede voiceless consonants.

tough—have	wrath—tithe	fuss—fuzz	rush—rouge
life—live	cloth—clothe	mace—maze	bush—beige

v 〉 v̥

I'm five today.
Polish the stove pipe.
See that the pieces
  dovetail.

ð 〉 ð̥

Each made a ti*the* payment.
Notice how smoo*th*-faced he was.
It was a loa*th*some task to
  perform.

z 〉 z̥

She blows soap bubbles softly.
Adjust his nose piece.
The Aztec temple search proves
  futile.

ʒ 〉 ʒ̥

Sweep the garage floor.
Put the beige carpet there.
The rouge cream appears
  flattering.

Practice: Pick out each fricative sound. Read aloud and transcribe each sentence.

He was an avid authority on bees, flowers, and animals. She wore her corsage with great pleasure. No camouflage could conceal her frightened face. The flies buzzed over the floor. Five times the thunder crashed and the lightning struck. Sixteen bathers met in the bathhouse. The aircraft rose into the azure, cloudless sky. He ate the veal with zeal. David and Lev carried bags of horsehair down the path. Shoemakers and dress-makers are artisans or artists when perceived from different vantage points.

c. *Voiced Fricatives in Clusters*

Note that /z/ is sounded in the third-person singular of the verb, the possessive form, and the plural morpheme when it clusters with any word ending in a voiced consonant. When the word ends in a sibilant or affricate, the plural morpheme or the third-person singular of the verb or the possessive of the noun is [ɪz], [əz], or [ɪz], as in *roses, bushes, seizes,* and *Wallace's* [rouzɪz, buʃəz, sizɪz, wɑlɪsɪz].

/bz/	/zd/	/dz/	/ðz/
cabs	fazed	bids	writhes
fibs	raised	seeds	seethes

/gz/	/mz/	/nz/	/ŋz/
hogs	hams	sins	brings
begs	hymns	fins	hangs

/vz/	/ʒd/	/vd/	/ðd/
thrives	rouged	saved	breathed
proves	camouflaged	shaved	seethed

Note that /ʒ/ does not cluster with any other consonant except /d/ to form the /ʒd/. The affricate /ʤ/, as in *gem*, is considered a single sound, rather than a cluster of two sounds. Affricates are discussed later in this chapter.

d. *Unusual Clusters*

The voiced fricatives do not cluster with sounds other than /d/ and /z/, as already noted, except in certain borrowed words and names. Some of these clusters for /v/ and /z/ are noted below.

/vj/	/vl/
Vyatka (Russian)	Vladimir (Russian)
Vyernnyi (Russian)	Vlissingen (Dutch)

/vr/ | /vw/
vraisemblance (French) | Vuelta Abajo (Spanish)
Vries (Dutch) | reservoir (French)

/zl/
zloty (Hungarian)

E. *Clusters with Adjacent Syllables*

Here are examples of voiced fricatives adjacent to other consonant sounds in separate syllables.

/z+b/	/v+b/	/n+v/	/m+z/	/z+d/
husband	lovebird	envy	clumsy	Thursday
rosebud	love Betty	convert	flimsy	nosedive
Thisbe	give back	inversion	whimsy	Desdemona

/z+w, r, l/	/v+w, r, l/	/ð+r, l/
beeswax	a live whale	brethren
Israel	drive right	smoothly
noiseless	lovely	

F. *Dropping Final Voiced Fricatives*

The final /v/ of the words *of* and *have* may be dropped when the words are unstressed and in casual speech. The /v/ is not dropped when the ensuing word begins with a vowel (for example, "one of a kind"), but "one of the boys" may be heard as [wʌn ə ðə bɔɪz].

Practice: Transcribe the following sentences as you say them.

Two of them came to the house. Five of the men were elected. Many of those buildings should be fixed. Tug-of-war is a hard game. It is not pleasant to be stung by a Portuguese man-of-war. Take a cup of tea and relax. Put the pot of water on top of the stove. I could have come had I known. We might have seen the three of them yesterday. The tail of the plane was cracked.

8.5. Voiced and Voiceless Morphemic Endings

The /s/ and /z/ are the plural, possessive, and third-person singular morphemic endings that follow voiceless and voiced sounds in the same syllable (see Sections 8.5 and 8.6). The /s/ follows voiceless /p, t, k, f, θ/ in the same syllable; the /z/ follows all the vowels and all the voiced consonants /b, d, g, v, ð, l, m, n, ŋ/. Words ending in any of the sibilant sounds /s, z, ʃ, ʒ/ and the affricates /ʧ, ʤ/ add /ɪz, əz or ɪz/ to the stems.

Added /s/		*Added* /z/		*Added vowel* + /z/	
hips	baths	rubs	writhes	paces	bushes
hats	steeps	lauds	Paul's	Rose's	garages
laughs	kicks	hogs	hymns	rushes	catches
Seth's	loafs	lives	sings	rouges	Madge's

Practice : Read aloud and transcribe the following sentences.

Lloyd's wife's friends couldn't understand him. The foxes hid in the bushes near Ned's barns. She bought two hats and four dresses in the Hawaiian islands. The bank's loans amounted to millions of dollars. They boarded their horses for two weeks in Mr. Pace's stables. Ruth's friends were pleased to hear that she had bought two presents for each.

8.6. The Affricates

The release of the breath stream following a plosive through the constricted position of an immediately following fricative results in an affricative sound. English possesses two such affricate sounds: /ʧ/ and /ʤ/, the initial sounds of *chess* and *gem*. Each of these affricates consists of two phonetically identifiable forms: [t+ʃ, d+ʒ]. Both are heard as single linguistic units, however; that is, both are phonemic entities, single sound segments of the English language. The stop-plus-fricative characteristic identifies the affricative quality of these sounds.

Other plosives and fricatives do combine in speech, but there are valid reasons for maintaining that these others are merely combinations of two adjacent sounds, each retaining separate identities. The /ts/ of *cats*, *Pittsburgh*, and *Betsy*; the /tθ/ of *eighth*; the /dθ/ of *width* and *breadth*; the /dz/ of *fades* and *adds* or *adz* are thus considered combinations of separate and separable sound entities in English, whereas the /ʧ/ and /ʤ/ of *butcher*, *chew*, *catch*, *Jim*, *region*, and *ridge* are single sound entities not separable into distinctive parts.

Certain words borrowed from other languages do contain affricate forms common to the language of origin. A few such initial affricates are found in *tsar* (Russian), *tsetse* (Bantu) *zuccheto* (Italian), *zwieback* (German), *Tsitsihar* (Chinese), *Tsushima* (Japanese), *tsadik* (Hebrew). Those of us who use these borrowed forms do not consider them separable initial forms. Affricates are, then, single phonemic entities consisting of two acoustic features—an initiating stop and a fricative release. These sounds /tʃ/ and /dʒ/ are formed toward the palatal area, close to the area of articulation of /ʃ/ and /ʒ/. They are therefore prepalatal or palatal sounds.

The affricates are found in all positions in words—before, between, and after vowels and diphthongs. They cluster with /n/ and /l/ after vowels.

cheese—catcher—rich   gem—major—bulge
chew—pitcher—catch   Jew—ledger—surge
chip—poacher—beach   gyrate—mangy—plunge

Practice: The fricatives and affricates in the following selection are italicized. Read the selection aloud, and transcribe as you read. Describe each italicized sound.

Dr. *J*ohn*s*on *h*ad *f*or many year*s* *g*iven me *h*opes *th*at we *sh*ould go to*g*e*th*er and *v*isit *th*e *H*ebride*s*. We reckoned *th*ere would be *s*ome incon*v*enience*s* and *h*ard*sh*ip*s*, and per*h*aps a little danger; but *th*e*s*e we were per*s*uaded were magni*f*ied in *th*e ima*g*ina*t*ion o*f* e*v*erybody. *Wh*en I wa*s* at *F*erney in 1764, I men*t*ioned our de*s*i*g*n to *V*oltaire. He looked at me a*s* i*f* I had talked o*f* going to *th*e *N*or*th* Pole, and *s*aid, "You do not in*s*i*s*t on my accompanying you?" "No, *S*ir." "*Th*en I am *v*ery willing you *sh*ould go." I wa*s* not a*f*raid *th*at our curiou*s* e*x*pedi*t*ion would be pre*v*ented by *s*uch appre*h*en-*s*ion*s*, but I doubted *th*at it would not be po*ss*ible to pre*v*ail on Dr. *J*ohn*s*on to relinqui*sh f*or *s*ome time *th*e *f*elici*t*y o*f* a London li*f*e, *wh*ich to a man who can en*j*oy it wi*th f*ull intellec*t*ual reli*sh*, i*s* apt to make e*x*isten*c*e in any narrower *sph*ere seem in*s*ipid or irk*s*ome.

> *The Journal of a Tour to the Hebrides with Samuel Johnson, LL.D.*
> —James Boswell

chapter 9 *The Frictionless Consonants*

THE FRICTIONLESS SOUNDS are emitted through the mouth and nose with relative freedom from constriction of the articulators. Like the fricatives and vowels, they are all continuant sounds. Unlike the fricative sounds, they are all voiced sounds with no voiceless-voiced oppositions like those between /f and v/, /θ and ð/, and /s and z/). The frictionless sounds are either nasal or oral. The oral consonants are formed as glides or lateral sounds. All frictionless sounds are perceived by the listener as vowel-like sounds, for they do not possess the noise components so characteristic of the other consonant sounds, the plosives and the fricatives. They are also commonly known as "sonorant" or "semivowel" sounds. There are seven such sounds in American English: three nasals /m, n, ŋ/, one lateral /l/, and three semivowels /w, j, r/.

9.1. Special Characteristics

These unobstructed sounds possess very special characteristics, as an examination of their behavior in certain contexts of the stream of speech shows. The words *battle* and *kitten* contain final frictionless sounds that function as syllabics (vowels that carry the stress burden of syllables). Although /w/, /j/, and /r/ appear as glides in the prevocal positions, as in *wet*, *yet*, and *red*, in which they initiate the syllables and glide to the next sounds, they do not appear as glides at the ends of syllables. Intervocalically, as in *away*, *beyond*, and *arrow*, they do not check the initial syllables as do other consonants in these positions—

128

that is, they do not close the syllables. Instead, only the initial part of each of these sounds is heard at the end of the syllable. The full gliding motion of the articulators that normally results in the full acoustic qualities of these sounds does not take place at the close of the first syllable. As a result, the words *how* and *my* end in nonsyllabic vowels, rather than in glide-consonant sounds. *Fear* ends either in a post-vocalic /r/ [fɪr] or in a nonsyllabic vowel with no constriction or "*r*-coloring" at all [fɪə].[1]

9.2. The Nasal Sounds

The formations of the nasal sounds correspond to the positions assumed by the articulatory mechanism when forming the three sets of stops: The /m/ is formed by the lips, as are /p/ and /b/; the /n/ by contact between the tongue tip and the hard palate, as are /t/ and /d/; the /ŋ/ by contact of the back tongue with the soft palate, as are /g/ and /k/. The nasals differ from their plosive counterparts in that they are emitted when the breath stream is directed behind and over the soft palate, through the nasopharynx, and out through the nose. They are all continuant, vowel-like sounds, emitted with no constriction of the breath stream. They function as vowels in certain words like *mitten* and *schism*. Although they do not have voiceless opposites as do the plosive and fricative sounds, partially voiceless allophones of /m/ and /n/ do appear when they follow voiceless sounds, as in *smile* and *snow*.

A. *The Nasals and Plosives Compared*

When one is saying the nasal sounds, the velar valve is open, and the emission of air through the mouth is blocked by the lips for /m/, by the tongue at the alveolar ridge for /n/, and by the tongue at the soft palate for /ŋ/. There is also a noticeable difference in the breath pressure and the tension of the articulators between the plosive and nasal sounds.

---

[1] This text uses the [ɚ] vowel for the syllabic sounds only, as in *mother* [mʌðɚ] and *error* [ɛrɚ]. Nonsyllabic /r/ sounds, when pronounced as in *fear, far,* and *for,* are transcribed as [fɪr, far, fɔr]. Some other texts use [ɚ] for both syllabic and nonsyllabic sounds, transcribing *mother* and *fear* as [mʌðɚ, fɪɚ]. Still others transcribe "*r*-colored" vowels with an added /r/ symbol at all times, creating an impression of five sounds in the word *mother* [mʌðɚr] rather than the four we normally hear.

The offglide sound /ə/ for those speakers who drop r sounds in postvocalic positions is a nonsyllabic sound: [fɪə, faə, fɔə].

Prevocalically	*Intervocalically*
pen—Ben—men	upon—about—among
pie—buy—my	apiece—abut—amenable
pore—bore—more	apple—Abbot—almond
pop—bop—mop	supper—fable—famous
tie—die—nigh	attend—ado—deny
tear—dare—nary	retire—redye—renege
toe—doe—no	lotus—lady—linen
tip—dip—nip	fitting—fading—finish
(/ŋ/ does not appear in initial positions of words.)	seeking—nugget—singing
	sicker—pagan—singer
	shaker—sugar—gingham
	lucky—lager—tangy

In final position

cape—cab—come	fate—fade—fain
cop—cub—comb	cat—cad—can
rip—rib—rim	meat—mead—mean
mop—mob—mom	hurt—herd—horn
brick—brig—bring	hock—agog—gong
tuck—dug—dung	tuck—tug—tongue
caulk—cog—king	pack—egg—among
buck—bug—bung	pick—pig—ping

B. *The Nasals as Syllabics*

The /m/, /n/, and /ŋ/ may function as syllable sounds. Although more commonly heard with adjacent homorganic sounds, nasal syllabics are heard in other contexts too. They may appear in words and in phrases. Although speakers may avoid syllabic /ŋ/ in careful speech, there is sufficient evidence of its use in colloquial and informal speech among educated speakers to preclude an "uneducated" label. Syllabic /n/ [n̩] is the most common of the three.[2]

Syllabic /m/ [m̩, -pm̩, -zm̩, -bm̩]

I am (going)   happen   chasm   open   ribbon

(*Note*: *open* and *ribbon* are perhaps more commonly pronounced [-ən].)

---

[2] An interesting discussion of the incidence of this sound appears in James Abel, "Syllabic /n/?" *The Quarterly Journal of Speech*, LI (October 1965), 294–300.

Syllabic /n/ [-tn̩, -dn̩, -ʃn̩]

button	oven	sudden	laden	glistening
hidden	vision	cotton	mitten	brazen
written	fission	listen	creation	mountain

(*Note*: *vision, fission,* and *creation* are perhaps more commonly [ən].)

Syllabic /ŋ/ [-kŋ̩, -gŋ̩]

bacon	beckon	dragon	blacken	chicken

(*Note*: These forms occur only occasionally; [ən] is more common.)

Practice: In these sentences for comparing syllabic nasal forms with vowels + nasals, note that in careful, more formal speech, the tendency is to avoid these syllabic forms, whereas in more casual, colloquial, and intimate styles of speech they are more common.

Op*en* the door carefully before you get *in* the car. Buy three doz*en* yards of red ribb*on*, please. He happ*en*ed by very sudd*en*ly. A schis*m* was bound to occur once the doz*en* nations disagreed without list*en*ing to one another. The truck was lad*en* with rott*en* fruits. We list*en*ed as he related the vis*ion* he had had. He could*n't* find the butt*on* of his coat and madd*en*ingly shouted, "What rott*en* luck!" Have you checked the pronunciation of *chasm* and *schism* recently? The drag*on* came out of the wag*on*, eating all the bac*on*. Don't black*en* the bac*on* at the campfire. It may sick*en* many of the girls.

c. *Nasals in Unexpected Positions*

THE DENTALIZED NASAL

Whenever /n/ appears immediately preceding either /θ/ or /ð/, it assumes the tongue-teeth position of the following sound. Note your pronunciation of /n/ in each of the following phrases and sentences. (The symbol for dental /n/ is [n̪].)

Don't take *on* so.	Don't take *on* that burden.
We walked *in.*	He walked *in* through the door.
Was he see*n*?	Look at the sce*ne* through this lens.
Be sure to pla*n.*	Pla*n* the work carefully.
Whe*n* will he come?	Whe*n* the storm comes, take care.

THE LABIODENTAL /m/

The /m/ is similarly affected by a following /f/ or /v/ sound, so that it is formed in a labiodental position. Note the difference in the articulatory position of the /m/ sounds in the following sentences when there is no pause or break following the /m/. The symbol for labiodental /m/ is [ɱ].

He ca*m*e for his hat. It was a triu*m*phant tour. The temperature was a co*m*fortable 70°. He saw the sa*m*e view each morning. "Co*m*e forth," she shouted. The doctor checked the ly*m*ph nodes.

D. *Variations*

The /n/ and /ŋ/ vary with each other in certain words. In the lists below, the two pronunciations of each word vary freely with each other in informal, educated speech. Check your own pronunciation for your preferences.

Common /n-ŋ/ variations

pa*n*cake	sy*n*copate	i*n*cubus
co*n*crete	idiosy*n*crasy	i*n*quiry
sy*n*chronize	Co*n*greve	i*n*clination
co*n*quest	i*n*come	pa*n*creas

Common /ŋ-ŋk/ variations

length—lengthen   strength—strengthen

The last group of words may be heard with [n̪θ] forms too. Most educated speakers of American English seem to avoid these dental forms, although the incidence of such pronunciations seems to be on the increase.

E. *Special Nasal Forms*

All orthographic "n+g" or "n+k" forms result in either /ŋ/, /ŋ+g/, or /ŋ+k/ forms when they appear in the same syllables. The dropping of the final /g/ in early modern English has created two forms for words spelled with "n+g": /ŋ/ and /ŋg/. No English words today end in /ŋg/. *Sing, bring, thong, hung, tongue*, all end in /ŋ/. The /ŋ/ therefore appears in all derivative words from these forms: *singer, thongs, songster, hanging*, and so forth. A few exceptional forms in our language retain the /ŋg/ forms where we would expect /ŋ/. These words are noted later in this section. Other words containing medial "ng" spellings normally take /ŋ+g/ because they were not affected by the earlier dropping of final /g/. *Singer* thus appears as /sɪŋɚ/, whereas *finger* appears as /fɪŋgɚ/, *mingle* as /mɪŋgəl/, *Rangoon* as /ræŋgun/. The /ŋ+k/ applies in words like *anxious* and *sink*.

Here are examples of the /ŋ/ in final positions in words and in affixed forms and compounds.

long	longing, longshoreman
sing	sings, singer, singing, singable
bring	brings, bringer, bringing
hang	hangs, hanger, hanging, hangnail, hangman
gang	gangs, gangster, gangway
harangue	harangues, haranguing, harangued

Practice: These words and phrases contain /ŋ/ in medial positions in words. Note that these words all contain the /ŋ/ sound in the final positions of the stems, except for *gingham* [gɪŋəm], which was borrowed from the French *guingan*, and *anxiety*, which is not normally followed by /g/ [æŋzaɪəti]. For example, *singer* is pronounced [sɪŋə]; *gongs* [gɑŋz]; and *haranguing* [həræŋɪŋ]. Place names with these medial "ng" spellings are actually final "ng" words plus suffixes. *Farmingdale* means "dale of farming," *Washington* means "town of washing," *Nottinghamshire* means the "shire of the hamlet of Notting." All these place names, therefore, retain the "final /ŋ/." Pronounce and transcribe:

singer	Springfield	wronged
bringing	Bingham	hanged
hanger	Binghamton	twangy
longing	Nottingham	songster

A few words, through the history of use, have developed two variant forms, both of which are common to the educated pattern of English. One is no more preferable than the other today, although one may have a longer history of use. These words are heard with both medial /ŋ/ and /ŋg/ forms. In each of these the /ŋg/ is the older form and is perhaps preferred by most speakers.

English	clangor	hangar (/ŋ/ is the more common
England	language	pronunciation today)

Medial /ŋ+g/ clusters appear in words without the final orthographic "ng," which retain the older /ŋg/ of earlier modern English. A few words that retain the final /g/ when affixed forms are added are also included in the following list. They are shown in the final column.

finger	mingle	angler	longer
monger	single	angry	stronger
anger	singular	hungry	younger

ingot	mangle	isinglass	diphthongal
linger	inglenook	anguish	prolongation
Angola	tangle	languid	elongation

Here are examples of /ŋk/ clusters

ink	monkey	uncle	distinct
think	thanked	relinquish	blank
ankle	brink	shrink	linkage
	winked	shrank	

F. *The Nasals in Consonant Clusters*

The only sounds with which /ŋ/ clusters in the same syllable are /g/ and /k/. The other nasals (/n/, /m/) cluster with plosives, fricatives, and glides. Here are examples of nasals in consonant clusters or adjacent to other consonants in neighboring syllables.

Sibilants and nasals

smile	sneeze	dismal
smoke	sneer	asthma
smite	snore	Christmas
smear	snood	cashmere

Syllabic /m/ and /n/

lissome	cotton
prism	sudden
rhythm	often
oven	earthen

Nasals and plosives

paint	symbol	timber
empty	plump	glimpse
thimble	wonder	Camden
kingpin	find	infant

Plosives and nasals

topmost	Cockney
chutney	Hickman
madness	tiredness
signal	madman

Nasals and fricatives

comfort	worms	films
circumvent	homesick	rinse
pronounce	Ramsey	clumsy
Tom's	answer	nymphs

Fricatives and nasals

halfmoon	pavement
roughness	smoothness
rhythmical	arithmetic
deafness	evening

Nasals and glides or /l/

teamwork	downwind	gangway
manly	inlaid	wingless
ringlet	calmly	ramrod
farmyard	banyan	onion

/l/ and nasals

almost	elm
overwhelm	helm
Elmer	almanac
cheerfulness	walnut

Nasals and nasals

amnesty	enmity	hangnail	homemade
inmate	nothingness	penknife	immaterial
chimney	meanness	solemnity	unmannerly

Practice: Read the following selection aloud. Note each italicized sound. Indicate which nasals are syllabic sounds and which are syllable initials or syllable finals. Are there any [n̪] or [ɱ] pronunciations here? Transcribe each word with /m, n, ŋ/ sounds.

*M*erry days were these at Thor*n*field Hall; a*n*d busy days too: how differe*n*t fro*m* the first three *m*o*n*ths of still*n*ess, *m*o*n*oto*n*y, a*n*d solitude I had passed be*n*eath its roof! All sad feeli*n*gs see*m*ed *n*ow drive*n* fro*m* the house, all gloo*m*y associatio*n*s forgotte*n*: there was life everywhere, *m*ove*m*e*n*t all day lo*n*g. You could *n*ot *n*ow traverse the gallery, o*n*ce so hushed, *n*or e*n*ter the fro*n*t cha*m*bers, o*n*ce so te*n*a*n*tless, without e*n*cou*n*teri*n*g a s*m*art lady's-*m*aid or a da*n*dy valet.
The kitche*n*, the butler's pa*n*try, the serva*n*ts' hall, the e*n*tra*n*ce hall, were equally alive; a*n*d the saloo*n*s were o*n*ly left void a*n*d still whe*n* the blue sky a*n*d halcyo*n* su*n*shi*n*e of the ge*n*ial spri*n*g weather called their occupa*n*ts out i*n*to the grou*n*ds.

Jane Eyre
—Charlotte Brontë

9.3. The Glides and Lateral Sounds

The three glide sounds /r, w, j/ are acoustically similar to the vowel sounds /ɝ—ɚ, u, i/. The glides, which appear in prevocalic and inter-vocalic positions, move from positions approximating the respective vowels to those of other vowels. As these glides are initiated in some-what more constricted positions than are the vowels mentioned, they can move to these vowel positions too, as in "woo," "yeast," and "stirrer." The lateral is made in the alveolar position with the sides of the tongue free from contact. The /l/ can appear in any position in the syllable.

These four sounds are similar to sounds which are treated as consonants because they function as such in the language. The /l/ may function as a syllabic sound in certain words, such as *beetle* and *funnel*.

The glides and lateral are initiated in devoiced forms when they follow voiceless plosive and fricative sounds, so that *true, cue, plume, quick, slew, few, fry,* and *thwart* are heard as [tr̥u, kju, pl̥um, kw̥ɪk, sl̥u, fju, fr̥aɪ, θw̥ɔ(r)t]. The voiceless variants of these sounds approximate fricative, rather than frictionless, sounds when they occur.

Practice : Transcribe the glides and the laterals in the following words.

In prevocalic and intervocalic positions

weed	read	lead	yield	away
win	rim	Lynn	yen	around
wore	roar	lore	yore	bewitched
wide	ride	lied	belied	deride
wood	root	loot	use	beyond

In voiceless positions, compared with voiced allophones

dry—try	grow—throw	blow—plow
grew—crew	bright—price	brew—prove
Dwight—twice	view—few	gouache—quash

Contrasted with similar sounds in similar positions

weal—veal	wear—where	win—bin
wore—four	wide—why	wound—boom
wonder—money	watt—what	west—vest
yeast—least	weep—peep	read—feed
yore—tore	roar—lore	won—son

In clusters or when adjacent to other consonants

Gwen	twin	dwell	quote
Guam	twice	dwarf	queen
guava	tweed	Dwight	quite
Guatemala	twist	dwindle	Quebec
guano	twig	dwelling	question
greed	crest	drain	treed
grow	crow	drive	try
greet	Crete	dread	tread
grunt	crunch	drunk	trunk
grew	crew	drew	true
glove	club	blood	plunder
glean	clean	bleat	please
glaze	claim	blame	plain
gland	climb	blind	plum
glow	clue	blunder	plaid

subway—upward   black wig—cogway
sidewalk—network   tight waist—tightwad
ragweed—wigwam   acquire—acquit
goblet—poplar   public—stop Leon
beauty—pure   cab yard—shipyard
midyear—light year   abroad—unpressed

Nasals plus glide and /l/ sounds

teamwork	timeless	farmyard	foamlike
downwards	unless	companion	inlaws
ringworm	ringlet	ramrod	bring lots
gangway	wingless	inroads	kingly

Fricatives plus glides or /l/

thwart—toothless   birthright—Faith Young
northwest—with Len   stiff rod—fuse
halfwit—safely   Africa—views
fishworm—flashlight mushroom—push you

The /l/ and plosives

whelp—kelp
bulb—pulp
belt—felt
sold—cold

The /l/ and nasals

overwhelm—film
realm—almost
Pullman—walnut
shrill noise—will not

The /l/ and fricatives or affricates

alfalfa	else	wealth	pails	compulsion	gulch
alphabet	false	health	falls	convulsion	filch
sylph	wholesale	filthy	kneels	emulsion	mulch

The /l/ plus glides in adjacent syllables

/lw/	/lr/	/lj/
always	all right	all year
whirlwind	already	coal yard
ill wind	school room	school yard

Syllabic /l/ and /n/

kitten	lesson	reason	cattle	pedal	sizzle
fatten	person	season	turtle	needle	thistle
button	arson	chosen	beetle	cradle	muzzle
frighten	fasten	dozen	chortle	tunnel	funnel

A. *Variant /l/ Sounds*

Prevocalic /l/ tends to be "lighter" than postvocalic /l/. The /l/ sounds in *light* and *fill* differ in their formation and acoustic values. The former /l/, called "light /l/," is made with the tongue blade and middle higher in the mouth, whereas for the /l/ of *pill*, the tongue is somewhat retracted, and the middle and back of the tongue are raised toward the velum. "Dark /l/" is transcribed [ɫ].

The /l/ sounds preceding front vowels are "lighter" than those adjacent to back vowels. Thus a "lighter" /l/ precedes /i/ or /j/, whereas a "darker" /l/ precedes /u/. Compare your pronunciations of the /l/ sounds in each of the following words. Note that preconsonantal /l/ is also "darker" than prevocalic /l/.

leave	lift	left	laugh	lock
leaf	linen	lend	land	lot
seal	Jill	jell	pal	Sol
sealed	filled	jelled	Hal's	Sol's

law	lose
lawn	loop
Saul	pool
halls	ruled

DENTAL /l/

A dental /l/ sound is made whenever /l/ precedes either /θ/ or /ð/ in the same word, as in *wealth*, or in a phrase with no pause, as in *file the tax, call the man*. The word-final clusters /lt/ and /ld/ are also commonly dentalized when they precede the dental *th* sounds, as in *Walt thinks, killed the goose, called the company*. Compare the following:

call	called	call the man	called the man
fill	filled	fill the glass	filled the glass
sell	sold	sell the goods	sold the goods

PALATALIZED /l/

A front variety of /l/ with the tongue closely approximating the /j/ position appears whenever /l/ precedes the /j/ glide. Compare the positions of the tongue and the acoustic values of the /l/ sounds in the following sets.

will—will you	will—William
mill—million	bill—billion
fail—failure	He was ill.—He was ill yesterday.

B. *Added /r/ Forms*

An added, unhistorical /r/ appears in the informal speech of many people. This added /r/ seems to be more common to those who lose final /r/ sounds. It is fairly common among New Yorkers and Bostonians, and among others in the Northeast. Southern coastal speakers who lose final /r/s do not commonly add an unhistorical /r/. It is uncommon to speakers in the rest of the country, who typically do not lose final /r/. Attitudes toward the use of this /r/ range from considering it a mark of illiteracy or almost complete lack of education (a notion hardly warranted by the facts of usage), through indifference to acceptance because of its common existence in casual, educated speech. Most speakers consciously avoid it if they notice it, but there is little doubt that it is heard in the speech of many well-educated people. Social pressures may force some of us to avoid its use. Its continued existence over half a century (it was not uncommon in educated speech of the late nineteenth century) seems to indicate that, despite school pressures, it will probably remain. The following words and phrases, if you read them without self-consciousness, will soon show whether or not you add this /r/.

idea	What's the idea?	Whose idea is that?
law	Obey the law.	Law and order are essential.
saw	Careful with that saw.	I saw a star.
Utah	He lived in Utah.	Utah and Nevada are western states.
Shah	She married the Shah.	He looks like the Shah of Persia.
Ida	Her name is Ida.	Ida and Mary are girls' names.
fellow	He's an unhappy fellow.	He's the fellow I saw.
potato	Buy more than one potato.	Place the potato under the spoon.
tomato	What a tomato!	Put some tomato on the bread.
sofa	Lie on the sofa.	Carry the sofa over there.
follow	Don't follow.	Don't follow it.

C. *Linking /r/*

Speakers who drop the postvocalic /r/ in such expressions as "I came at four" [——fɔ]; "Close the door" [——dɔ]; and "They were"

[——wɜ] reinsert the /r/ when it becomes intervocalic. This change occurs when these sentences are changed to "I came at four o'clock"]——fɔrəklɑk], "Close the door in the hall" [——dɔrɪn——], and "They were over there" [wɜrouvɚ——]. The reinserted /r/ is known as a "linking r."

Linking r is not commonly used by many speakers of the south Atlantic regions of the United States. These "r-less speakers" do not reinsert the /r/ in intervocalic positions.

D. *Added /w/ and /j/ Glides*

These two sounds intrude in intervocalic positions in casual speech but hardly ever in careful, educated speech. Careful speakers do not find it difficult to avoid them when they desire. These glides intrude after /ʊ, u/ or /ɪ, i/ before other vowels. They intrude because of the motion of the articulators from the relatively close quality of the /i/ or /u/ sounds as the articulators glide to the positions of following vowels of more open quality.

do it	Sue is	see if	why are
go on	going	see any	enjoy it
know any	growing	they are	seeing

The /hw/ and /hj/ clusters are discussed in Chapter 8.

Practice: Pronounce the following words and phrases aloud and transcribe your pronunciations.

far	far over	They were far enough away.
fear	fear of	They had no fear of animals.
four	four of them	We had four other chairs.
more	more of it	They were more honest than most.
care	care about it	He had not a care in the world.

Read the following selection aloud. Note whether or not you use any added /r/ or other glide sounds and whether or not you use a syllabic /l/ at any time. Comment on any of the special allophones of these sounds. Transcribe all words with italicized sounds.

It had not been much after noon when Frank Greystock reached Portray Cast*l*e, and it *w*as ve*r*y nea*rl*y five when he *l*eft it. Of course, he had lunched *w*ith the two *l*adies, and as the conversation before *l*unch had been *l*ong and interesting, they did not sit down unti*l* near th*r*ee. Then *L*izzie had taken him out to show him the grounds and garden, and they had c*l*ambered together down to the sea beach. "*L*eave me here," she had said, when he insisted on going because of his friend at the cottage. When he suggested that she would want help to climb back up the rocks to the castle, she shook her head as though her heart was too full to admit of a consideration so trifling.

The Eustace Diamonds
—Anthony Trollope

chapter 10 *The Front Checked Vowels*

THE VOWEL SOUNDS are the freely emitted unobstructed sounds of the language that carry the stress, duration, pitch, and vocal quality of each syllable. As noted earlier, each syllable contains a vowel or vowel-like sound as its nucleus. Before attempting to apply any of the practice material in this chapter, it is wise to review the classification and description of vowels that appear in Chapter 6.

All the vowels we use are either "free" or "checked," that is, they either complete syllables or are checked in their formation by following consonants that end the syllables. Monophthongal or diphthongal variants may appear in the different dialects of the country. We do not find it useful to classify these sounds in the traditional manner of vowels versus vowel glides or diphthongs, since vowels are common variants of diphthongs and diphthongs are common variants of vowels in our language. This fact is true not only among the different dialects of American English but also of the internal patterns of a single dialect.[1]

There are six checked vowels in English.[2] They appear in such words as *big, beg, bag, book, bog,* and *bug.* These vowels normally appear in simple or monophthongal forms, although there are diphthongal

---

[1] See Hans Kurath and Raven I. McDavid, Jr., *The Pronunciation of English in the Atlantic States* (Ann Arbor: The University of Michigan Press, 1961), pp. 4 ff.

[2] These vowels are known as "checked vowels" because they do not normally appear as syllable finals in English. They are followed (checked) by consonant sounds that close the syllables. Other vowels like /i, o, u/ do exist as syllable finals in English. They can appear in both open and closed syllables, as in *no* and *note, see* and *seed.* Vowels that can appear as syllable finals are known as "free vowels."

A seventh checked vowel appears in eastern New England in such words as *whole, road, stone.* See the special section on this sound in Chapter 12.

variant forms that are heard as vowel glides culminating in [ə, ɪ, ɛ] sounds. (All these variant forms are illustrated later in this and the following chapter.)

The diphthongal variants of these checked vowels are heard more readily when syllables are prolonged. Such prolongation occurs as the stress on the vowel increases. These variant vowel glides are also perceived more readily when they are checked by voiced consonants in stressed syllables than when they precede voiceless consonants. The variant forms are also demonstrated in the practice material in this chapter.

10.1. A General Description of the Front Checked Vowels

The three vowels in *big*, *beg*, and *bag* are formed with high, mid, and low positions of the blade of the tongue, as noted in Figure 10.1.

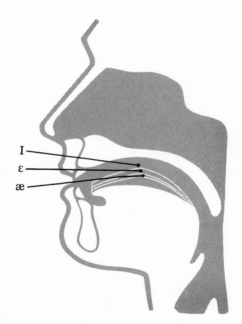

I

ɛ

æ

Figure 10.1. The Tongue Curves of the Front Checked Vowels /ɪ, ɛ, æ/.

SOURCES: Adapted from Arthur J. Bronstein, *The Pronunciation of American English* (New York: Appleton-Century-Crofts, 1960), p. 139; and Jon Eisenson, *Basic Speech* (New York: The Macmillan Company, 1950), pp. 83–85. By permission of the publishers.

The resonance chambers of the vocal tract are affected by the different positions assumed by the articulators during the formation and emission of these vowels. The differences may be noted in the schematic drawings that appear in Figure 10.2. The changes in the resonance cavities of the entire vocal tract, with resulting changes in the formants, allow for our perception of these vowels.

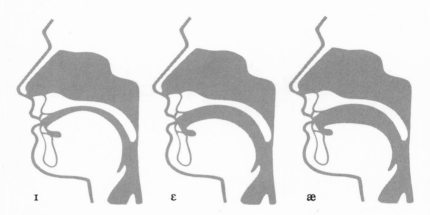

Figure 10.2. Schematic Drawings Showing the Shapes of the Resonance Chambers of the Vocal Tract during the Formation of /ɪ, ɛ, æ/.

sources: Adapted from Bertil Malmberg, *Phonetics* (New York: Dover Publications, Inc., 1963), Fig. 27, p. 33; and Peter Ladefoged, *Elements of Acoustic Phonetics* (Chicago: The University of Chicago Press, 1962), Fig. 75, p. 96. © 1962 by The University of Chicago, and published by The University of Chicago Press. By permission of the publishers.

A. *Checked by Voiced and Voiceless Consonants*

Note that, when checked by voiceless consonants, the front checked vowels are spoken with shorter durations than when they are checked by voiced consonants.

BEFORE PLOSIVES

bit	bid	bet	bed	bat	bad
slit	slid	set	said	sat	sad
nip	nib	rep	Reb	nap	nab
rip	rib	Shep	Deb	tap	tab

| Dick | dig | deck | leg | wrack | rag |
| brick | brig | peck | peg | track | drag |

| fitting | bidding | getting | heading | latter | ladder |
| bitter | bidder | betting | bedding | matter | madder |

| vicar | vigor | wrecking | legging | backing | bagging |
| snicker | snigger | Becker | begging | tracking | ragged |

| tippy | Tibbie | leopard | pebble | tapping | nabbing |
| nippy | Libby | stepping | treble | slapping | cabby |

| bits | bids | slept | ebbed | slapped | crabbed |
| tipped | cribbed | hex | pegs | ax | hags |

Practice: Transcribe the following sentences. Arrange words with /ɪ, ɛ, æ/ according to longer and shorter forms.

His dad took the cats to the hospital. Mac hired a cab near Dan's house. They wrapped the ax in a loose bag. Heading south, they made tracks quickly. The wicked fitter said he was neither a beggar nor a vicar. The new styles were shaggy, baggy trousers or snappy wraparounds.

BEFORE FRICATIVES AND AFFRICATES

/ɪ/	/ɛ/	/æ/
pithy—slither	death—feather	path—lather
myth—with	Seth—leather	lath—gather
gift—gives	heifer—ever	traffic—lavish
miff—lives	zephyr—heavy	laugh—salve [sæv]
if—sieve	effort—lever	Taffy—maverick
shift—sieved	deathly—Evelyn	staff—have
hiss—his	less—fez	mass—has
prissy—Lizzie	precedent—president	gas—chasm
mission—vision	special—pleasure	cash—casual
dishes—collision	pressure—treasure	Asher—azure
witches—frigid	wretched—pledging	matching—magic
bitch—bridge	ketch—ledge	batch—badge

Practice: Pick out all words in the following sentences with /ɪ, ɛ, æ/ before stops, fricatives, and affricates.

"Live and let live" is an old motto. The general staff had a meeting about traffic problems. It was a pity they had no cash. When Madge crossed the bridge, she had a special vision of Lester's calf in her path. Ethel hated to kiss in traffic. Philip started the myth by splashing the red ketchup over Seth's legs.

B. *Before Nasal and Lateral Consonants*

/ɪ/	/ɛ/	/æ/
Tim	phlegm	tamper
slim	temple	ham
crimp	Emma	stamp
pimple	empty	bramble
image	feminine	sample
tin	ten	tan
winsome	send	sand
inquire	unquenchable	candles
dwindle	endless	branches
inner	slender	anvil
wink	strength	vanquish
wing	lengthen	language
distinguish	Stengel	angles
relinquish	Engels	thank
England	Englewood	frankfurter
fill	fell	pal
silly	jelly	fallow
filched	welcome	Sally
sylph	belched	malleable
William	realm	infallible

Practice: Select and transcribe all the words with /ɪ, ɛ, æ/ before nasal and lateral sounds in the following sentences.

Manny rang the bell and pounded on the door. When they emptied the seventh box, a slender snake fell to the floor. William called his friends to help with the lemonade stand. Ample space permitted them to move the singers about. They found three handles on the temple box and thanked the vendor for his help.

C. *Stress*

These checked vowels (like the free vowels) are shorter when unstressed or less stressed than when fully stressed.

UNSTRESSED OR WITH INTERMEDIATE STRESS		FULLY STRESSED	
/ɪ/		/ɪ/	
forage	mirage	ridge	rib
private	historic	hit	hippodrome
witches	ingrain	ingot	inner
Senate	inhuman	inkstand	stingy
Philip	quintessence	stigmatize	Libby
/ɛ/		/ɛ/	
mentality	enrobe	penny	penniless
Mendoza	enroll	many	enter
engineer	democratic	energy	mentor
energetic	mendacious	Denmark	demonstrate
resolution	regimental	question	ready
/æ/		/æ/	
Massachusetts	affectation	massive	amnesty
Massenet	accelerate	mascot	algae
matinée	accolade	anchor	actress
algebraic	actuarial	access	actual
aquamarine	afternoon	aquaplane	activate

Practice: Transcribe those words containing /ɪ, ɛ, æ/ syllables in each of the following sentences.

They spent too many pennies in the market. It doesn't pay to be stingy in Paris. If he went to his friend's house, he'll be back by dark. Dan never finished his project on American inventions. Sally would rather sit and study than spend too many hours in bed.

D. *Compared with Free Vowels*

When compared with the free vowels in the same environments, the checked vowels are of shorter duration.

/ɪ-i/

slip—sleep	sin—seen	chip—cheap
dip—deep	fill—feel	pitcher—peaches
hit—heat	lip—leap	still—steal

/ɛ-e/

tent—taint	send—sane	special—spatial
let—late	fester—faced	edging—aging
Seth—faith	Lester—laced	wedges—wages

$$/æ-a/^3$$

cat—cart (ENE)   lackey—lark (ENE)   man—mine (South)
pack—park   nasty—nice (South)   hat—heart (ENE)

Practice : Pick out the three front-checked vowels in the following sentences. Transcribe the words in which they appear.

When Wendy sat on the steps, she saw a strange mark. He singed his pants. They were seen near the west gate. He planned his tasks well. While bringing the book to the maid, he fell. He hated to heat the food so quickly. He tried to save the wheeling toy but missed it as it sped past him. They greeted each other in very plain language. He sailed the seven seas while still a young man.

10.2. The /ɪ/ and Its Common Variants

The /ɪ/ is the high front checked vowel of *bit* and *thin*. It is a lax vowel pronounced with the tongue forward in the mouth and with the blade of the tongue slightly lower than for the vowel /i/. If you repeat the pair of words *it-eat* for a while, you will note that the tongue muscle is more relaxed for *it* than it is for *eat*; that the blade of the tongue, although high and close to the palatal arch for both sounds, is slightly lower for *it* than for *eat*.

The /ɪ/ is an uncommon sound to speakers of many other languages. Speakers of French, Italian, and Spanish have a tendency to substitute a tenser, closer sound /i/ for the stressed /ɪ/ of English. Speakers of the Slavic languages, Russian or Polish, tend to centralize the sound, giving it the approximate quality of /ɨ/. German speakers use a much tenser variety of /ɪ/ than do English speakers. Speakers of the conservative dialect of Japanese vary /ɪ/ with /i/ depending on the neighboring consonant.

The [ɨ] variant, a high central vowel, is used by many speakers in certain words like *sister*, *dinner*, and *milk*, whereas other speakers retain [ɪ] in these words. This variant is found in the speech of educated people and is not a form of careless or uneducated speech. For many, [ɪ] and [ɨ] are in free variation; for others, the use of [ɨ] is of such consistency that some linguists believe the sound should be accorded phonemic status as a separate vowel. Although its phonemic status may be questioned by some to whom it appears only an allophone of

---

³ This contrast, as in *hat-heart*, appears in the eastern New England dialect, in which free /a/ exists. Some /æ-a/ contrasts, as in *fan-fine*, appear in the South.

/ɪ/, there can be no question about its use by many educated speakers.[4]

The centering glide [ɪ°], as in whip [hwɪ°p] and fill [fɪ°l], is widely heard in the southeastern part of the country; the monophthongal form is common throughout the rest of the country.

Practice : Read aloud the following pairs, demonstrating stressed /ɪ/ and /i/ in initial, medial, and final syllables of words.

In initial syllables

it—eat	dip—deep
ill—eel	sit—seat
Italy—Eton	pick—peak
Icarus—easy	dim—deem
Isadore—eke	hit—heat
in—e'en	rich—reach
ignorance—eager	sick—seek
illustrate—Eli	lid—lead
Istanbul—eastern	ship—sheep
iterate—eater	kill—keel

In medial syllables

peninsula—immediate	funicular—unheated
Virginia—policeman	emission—agreement
vehicular—achievement	edition—inbreeding
meticulous—immediacy	elicit—northeastern
novitiate—repeated	felicitous—bereavement
Corinthian—careening	fertility—Amelia
eviscerate—impeachment	particular—parcheesi

In final syllables

within—settee	remit—machine
relive—employee	remiss—police
desist—grantee	dismiss—achieve
until—decease	submit—sixteen
abyss—belief	relist—agree
resist—repeat	assist—intrigue
instill—relieve	atheist—parakeet

Transcribe these sentences. They demonstrate stressed /ɪ/ and /i/ in different contexts, for comparison.

[4] See reports by Raven I. McDavid, Jr., in W. N. Francis, *The Structure of American English* (New York: The Ronald Press Co., 1958), p. 525; A. Bronstein, *The Pronunciation of American English* (New York: Appleton-Century-Crofts, Inc., 1960), pp. 148–50, 183–84; and H. A. Gleason, Jr., *An Introduction to Descriptive Linguistics*, rev. ed. (New York: Holt, Rinehart & Winston, 1961), pp. 36, 322–23.

When did she see the city policeman? The peninsula of Italy is a favorite tourist sight for English and American visitors. The village achieved a big industrial boost when fishing and agriculture were augmented by big-city investments in tin mining and ship building. The teachers were relieved when the city officials defeated the bill to increase class limits. It isn't easy to see over the tops of the hills. Phil was lifting the big bales of hay when his shoelace ripped. Amelia repeated her warning until the discipline in the classroom was restored. They had dinner at an inexpensive drive-in.

The variation of the vowels before /r/ is extensive, and generalizations can be made only with the greatest care. Considerable variation exists throughout the country, and educated speakers do use both forms. The generalizations noted here are based on the most recent evidence available.

Practice: With initially stressed orthographic *ir*, words tend to retain /ɪ/ in educated speech in all regional dialects. Note your pronunciation of each of the following words. Compare it with that of a friend from another region of the country.

Iroquois	irradiate
iridescent	Irrawaddy
iridescence	irreclaimable
irrigate	irredeemable
irritate	irreplaceable

Medial stressed /ɪ/ and /i/ vary dialectally before postvocalic /r/ at all social levels of the language.

When checked by /r/ (that is, in most of the country where the dialects of American English preserve the postvocalic /r/), as in *cheer, fearful, nearby*, the stressed vowel tends to be pronounced with either /i/ or /ɪ/, which is normally spoken with a slightly higher tongue position than the stressed /ɪ/ of *fit* and *bid*. It is perhaps closer to phonemic /ɪ/ than to /i/. In those eastern and south Atlantic areas where the postvowel /r/ is replaced by a vowel offglide [ə], as in [tʃɪə, fɪəfəl], four vowels may be heard in these words: the most recently published *Atlas* studies suggest that /i, ɪ/ are the predominant forms, but that mid-front /e/ and central /ɜ/ also appear in the South.

Practice: Check your pronunciation of the following words, and again compare it with that of friends from other regions of the country.

cheer—cheerful—cheered
fear—fearful—fierce
steer—steering—steerage
clear—clearing—Clearview

pierce—piercing—pierced
near—nearly—nearby
hear—hearing—hearsay
rear—rearing—yearly
beard—bearded—merely
appear—appearing—appearance

Here are sentences with words containing /ɪ/ and /i/ before /r/ for ear training and transcription practice.

They steered clear of the Clearview Expressway for fear of the speeding cars. Each year they appeared before the same street lamp and sang cheerful songs. The hearing aid seemed to help him identify the sounds more clearly. The new beard seemed to enhance his appearance.

Polysyllabic words with intervocalic or intersyllabic /r/ sounds have forms that seem to vary greatly from dialect to dialect, and there is evidence that these forms can appear in the same dialect region in free variation. These words are not derived from monosyllabic words ending in an historical /r/ (as in *cheer–cheering, near–nearer, fair–fairest*). Those that are so derived do retain the same forms in the polysyllable as in the base words [tʃɪr–tʃɪrɪŋ] and [tʃɪə–tʃɪərɪŋ].

The incidence of vowels plus /r/ in these polysyllables varies from /i/ to /ɪ/ to /ɪ/ in educated speech. In at least two of the words in the following list, *stirrup* and *syrup*, the predominant /ɪ/ forms vary with /ɛ/ and /ɜ ~ ʌ/ (~ = "varying with") forms too, according to recently collected evidence. The exact extent of this variation is unknown yet, but the indications seem to be that most educated speakers of the country use the /ɪ/ rather than the /i/ form in these words, tending to pull the intervocalic /r/ into the preceding vowel syllables, which lowers the /i/ toward /ɪ/.

Practice : Check your pronunciation of these words below, and again compare it with that of your friends.

mirror	lyric	Miriam
spirit	lyrical	(sometimes /ɛ/)
diphtheria	cirrhosis	myriad
syrup	dirigible	pirouette
serious	Hirohito	spiritual
miracle	lyricist	Syracuse
stirrup	pyridine	(sometimes /ɛ/)
pyramid	pyrrhic	Syria

Here are phrases and sentences with words containing intervocalic /r/ for ear training and transcription practice.

They were very seriously drawing pyramids and circles on their papers. Miriam placed his biretta on his head, deftly. The tyrannical Syrian loved to look at the syringas. The Syr Darya river is nowhere near the Syrian desert. The young boy grew into a virile man who specialized in virology. The glazier made superior mirrors for the expensive stores.

10.3. The /ε/ and Its Common Variants

The /ε/ is the mid-front checked vowel of *bet* and *lend*. It is a lax vowel made with unrounded lips. The height of the tongue blade is approximately halfway between that for /ɪ/, as in *bit*, and that of /æ/, as in *bat*. The mouth is, similarly, opened approximately halfway between the /ɪ/ and /æ/ sounds. When compared with the nearest free vowel, /e/, /ε/ is normally shorter, less tense; the lips are more open, the muscles of the tongue and cheeks more relaxed, and the blade of the tongue slightly lower and retracted from the hard palate.

Although the most common form is the monophthongal sound described, numerous variants of /ε/ are heard in educated speech. The [εᵊ] glide variants are generally heard in fully stressed syllables from eastern New England south and west in *bed* and *tell*, whereas upward glide forms [εᶦ] seem to be more common in folk speech, which is avoided by educated speakers (see Chapter 1). Variations ranging from /ɪ/ to /e/ are heard in words like *again, egg, beg, kettle,* and *yesterday*, whereas a retracted or centralized /ε/ form [ε˞] is influenced by adjacent consonants with labial motion like /b, v, w/, as in *very, fence, well, welcome, bury*. These variants seem to predominate in the folk speech; educated speakers, in general, seem to avoid them.

Practice : Read these words, which show the stressed /ε/ compared with /e (eɪ)/ in initial, medial, and final syllables of words, aloud in pairs. Transcribe your pronunciations.

In initial syllables

egg—ache	ebb—Abe
any—aim	Emma—aiming
ever—aviary	anything—amiable
eddy—aiding	element—ailing
edge—age	bet—bait
get—gate	let—late
send—sane	fence—faints
wedding—wading	well—wail
west—waist	wreck—rake
spread—sprayed	fled—flayed

In medial syllables

severity—abatement	temerity—restated
extensive—amazement	especially—Israeli
November—persuasion	September—invasion
December—relation	America—modulation
amendment—continuation	already—accumulation
develop—population	ineffable—investigation
effervescent—mutation	expression—expropriation
secondarily—extraneous	primarily—explanation
intention—attainment	suspension—discriminating
eleven—elation	deceptive—complainant

In final syllables of polysyllabic words

themselves—nosegay	unless—birthday
present (v.)—dovetail	express—phosphate
intent—wholesale	resent—fumigate
expects—investigate	respects—reiterate
directs—accumulate	elects—populate
dispensed—speculate	condensed—modulate
commenced—investigate	intense—graduate (v.)
relent—humane	depends—mutate
unbend—display	inspects—discriminate
pretend—retained	condemn—contain

Here are sentences with stressed /ɛ/ and /e (eɪ)/ in different contexts, for comparison.

Ethel's back was ailing yesterday when she went home. The mention of the excellent book brought pleasant memories to David. Gail could not gainsay Evelyn's examination achievement scores when the registrar posted them in Sage Hall. Temperamental babies require special, painstaking care.

In words like *fair, spare, chair, dairy,* and *Mary,* three different vowels are heard: /e, ɛ, æ/. The /e/ is found sporadically in New England but more commonly in the lower South, where it competes with /ɛ/ and /æ/. The /æ/ is more common in the upper South and in northeastern New England. The /ɛ/ is the common form in most of the country, /e/ being the least common of the three variant sounds. Less educated forms, generally avoided by educated speakers, contain either /ɪ/ forms or lowered /æ, a/ or the back /ɑ/ forms. Scattered instances of /ɜ/, as in [kjɜ] and [tʃɜ] for *care* and *chair,* may be heard in folk speech.

In polysyllables before intersyllabic /r/, derivative words like *sharing* and *caring* retain the same sound as the monosyllable /kɛr–

kɛrɪŋ/ or /kær–kærɪŋ/. In words not derived from monosyllables ending in /r/, considerable variation exists. *Mary, dairy, area,* and *various* are heard with the same vowels as *merry, error,* and *very* in those sections that retain postvocalic /r/. For example, speakers in upstate New York, the mid-Atlantic coastal regions, and in most of the north central, midwestern and western states hear *merry* and *Mary* as homophones /mɛri/. The South and coastal New England retain the /e/ of *gate* in the *Mary–dairy* words and the /ɛ/ of *get* in the *merry–cherry* words. (Diphthongal variants [eɪ, eɪ, eᵊ] and lengthened monophthongal /e/ [eˑ, eː] may be heard south of the Potomac and north of Connecticut as the normal, cultivated forms for the *Mary–various* words.) Speakers in metropolitan New York distinguish *merry* from *Mary* by pronouncing them /mɛri/ and /mɛəri/, respectively. The /ɛ/ is the normal educated form for the *very, merry, cherry* words throughout the country. Forms with /ɪ, ɜ, ʌ,* and *e/ may be heard in folk or uneducated speech for the *merry–cherry* words instead of the checked /ɛ/ of *get* common to educated speakers.

Practice : Check your pronunciation of the following words. Which forms do you use? Transcribe your pronunciations.

eremite—air
Eric—area
errand—airing
errant—aerial
error—aeriform
erudite—aerobic

Are the *er, ar, air, are* syllables the same or different in your speech? Which variant forms do you use? Compare and transcribe your pronunciations.

error—area	variation—verify	glare—Merrimac
Eric—airing	wary—wherry	mare—Maryland
berry—bare	Fairfax—feretory	pair—Perry
merry—Mary	fairy—ferret	Mary—perigee
very—varied	hair—Gerald	stairs—periphrastic
cherry—chairing	hairbreath—gerund	staring—serendipity
derelict—dairy	harebrained—meretricious	Sarah—serif
derogate—daring	harem—merit	sharing—sheriff
derrick—daredevil	flair—Merrill	tare—terror

Here are sentences for ear training and transcription practice.

Sarah was a fine dairy maid until she met the fair-haired man. Mary made the air in the entire area sweet smelling. They moved from Darien to Bethesda, Maryland. Geraldine married a merry man from Marietta, Ohio. When they could not share the chair, Perry got up and allowed Harry to remain seated. He read about the fair-haired women in the harem and wondered if he should read further.

10.4. The /æ/and Its Common Variants

The /æ/ is the lowest front vowel for most of us, as monophthongal /a/ is uncommon to most American speakers, except eastern New Englanders, for whom /pak/ and /kat/ are common for *park* and *cart*, and Southern speakers, for whom /a:v/ [a^{ə}v] and /na:n/ [na^{ə}n] are common for *I've* and *nine*. This vowel is generally lax, as in *bat* and *had*, although a tense variety quite often appears for the long variety heard in *bag* and *ask*. The mouth is open fairly wide, about halfway between the positions for /ɛ/ and /ɑ/ in *get* and *got*. The lips are unrounded and the tongue blade is lower than for /ɛ/ (see Figures 10.1 and 10.2).

Because this sound is perhaps the most complex of the checked stressed vowels, you are advised to read special studies and texts that treat it in greater detail than can be done here.[5] It is important, however, to keep some general points in mind and to note them in the practice sections given in this chapter.

A. *Short and Long Varieties*

The longer variety is the common form before final voiced stops (*snag, bad, cab*); the voiced affricate (*badge*); both voiced and voiceless fricatives in certain words (*ask, cash, bath, laugh, jazz, salve*); and nasals /m, n/ and /n/ plus consonants (*ham, tan, sand, branch*).

This longer variety, when used, is of equal duration with any of the stressed free vowels like /i, u, ɑ/, and it is regularly longer than any of the higher checked vowels /ɪ, ɛ, ʌ, ʊ/. It is commonly a glide or diphthongal form: Upgliding forms [æ^{ɪ}] and [æ^{ɨ}], as well as ingliding or centering forms [æ^{ə}], appear regularly in the speech of educated people in different sections of the country. The use of a raised (or

[5] See, for example, Kurath and McDavid, *op. cit.*, pp. 8–9, 135–41; Bronstein, *op. cit.*, pp. 154–60; R—M. S. Heffner, *General Phonetics* (Madison, Wis.: University of Wisconsin Press, 1949), pp. 102–03; Charles K. Thomas, *Phonetics of American English*, 2nd ed. (New York: The Ronald Press Co., 1958), pp. 90–91; Allan F. Hubbell, *Pronunciation of English in New York City* (New York: King's Crown Press, 1950), pp. 75–79; George L. Trager, "The Pronunciation of 'Short A' in American Standard English," *American Speech*, 5 (1929–1930), 396–400; Trager, "What Conditions Limit Variants of a Phoneme?" *American Speech*, 9 (1934), 313–15; Trager, "One Phonemic Entity Becomes Two: The Case of 'Short A,'" *American Speech*, 15 (1940), 255–58.

advanced) and lengthened variety [æˑ:, æˑᵒ, æˑ', æˑˣ] for the syllabics of such words as *crack, cash, bag,* and *fancy* is found perhaps more commonly in the speech of the middle and lower social levels than in educated speech, although there is mounting evidence of widespread use, even approximating [ɛˑ:ᵒ], in the speech of well-educated people in many sections of the country. A variety of this raised sound, spoken with a tensed, lowered palate that permits accompanying nasality, is associated with nonstandard American English speech. It may be heard in each of the categories described.

B. *Before Stops and Affricates*

A shorter /æ/ sound is normally heard before voiceless stops, non-final voiced stops, and the voiceless affricate. A longer variety is heard before final voiced stops and the voiced affricate. Certain sections of the country (for example, the low country of South Carolina and much of Georgia) retain long /æ/ [æ:] and centering or upward glides [æᵒ, æ', æˣ] before the voiceless stops and the affricate too.

Practice: Compare the following pairs of words. Transcribe your pronunciations.

nap—nab	lap—lab	elapse—scab
tap—tab	hatch—tags	collapse—scrag
slap—slab	catch—wagging	fact—flagged
bat—bad	latch—fag	haggard—drab
crap—crab	scratch—stagline	faggot—drag
fat—fad	patch—sad	factory—maddening
flat—plaid	slat—glad	factual—fagged
pat—pad	batch—badge	magic—nagging
sack—sag	flagellate—flags	magistrate—fad
crack—crag	paginate—padded	mackerel—madhouse

Here are sentences with /æ/ before stops and affricates. Transcribe each sentence.

Matty called his cat "Patches." They brought home bags of badges and flags. They placed padlocks on the doors of the blackguards' cells. The sagging sacks of crabs were dragged by the young lads to the backs of the stores. Sad lads rarely brag of their mad magic.

C. *Before Voiced and Voiceless Fricatives*

The /æ/ is long or is an ingliding or upgliding diphthong before voiced and voiceless fricatives. Certain words of the type of *ask, half, path* (known hereafter as the "ask words"), in which the vowel appears before the fricatives /s/, /f/ (occasionally /v/) and /θ/ (occasionally /ð/), have /a/ in educated eastern New England speech. Many educated speakers in that area use /æ/ for these same words; still others freely shift from /æ/ to /a/ in the same words or retain /æ/ for some of these words and /a/ for others. Similarly, /a/ is used by many speakers along the Georgia and South Carolina coast, although educated speakers in those areas normally use /æ/. Occasional prestigious pronunciations of lowered and retracted /æ/, as in [æˑ, æˠ, æˠᵊ] or even [æˣ, æᵊ, aᵊ], are heard in the speech of New York City (Manhattan), Philadelphia, and northern Virginia. In the rest of the country, non-lowered /æ/ is the normal, expected form.

Here are words with long /æ/ before voiced and voiceless fricatives ("ask words"). The lowered allophones of /æ/, as well as the use of /a ~ ɑ/, may be heard for these sounds in certain regions of the country.

/s/	/sp, st, sk/	/f, ft, v/	/θ, ð/
pass	ask	laugh	bath
glass	pasture	halve	wrath
lass	elastic	half	path
alas	basket	salve	lath
brass	clasp	craft	lather
castle	gasp	after	paths

Here are other words with long /æ/ before voiceless and voiced fricatives. These words are not of the "ask word" group and do not normally possess /a/ variant forms.

Before /s/	Before /f, v/	Before /z/	Before /ʃ, ʒ/	Before /ð, θ/
passage	affable	jazz	cash	lather*
ass	Daphne	spasm	cashier	blatherskite
gas	saffron	spasmodic	fashion	gather
gasoline	safflower	chasm	passion	fathom
blaspheme	Sappho	chasmic	crash	Bathsheba
blastoderm	sapphire	Tasman	mash	empathic
acid	scaffold	plasma	casuist	spathic
acetate	taffy	Erasmus	casuistry	Bathhurst
bastard	lava	hasn't	casual	Catherine

* One who works with a lath.

Practice: Read the following sentences aloud, and transcribe as you speak. Note whether or not the /æ/ before the fricatives and affricates retains the same quality in all the italicized words. How many different forms do you use?

He *asked* me for a *basket* of apples for the *gymnast*. He tried to *catch* the *elastic* of the gown, then *casually* turned down the *path*. *After* his *bath*, *Erasmus* drank a *draught* of beer. The *aircraft* pilot could not *master* the complicated *passage* through the *pass*. He *grasped* the *mastiff* with both hands, trying to *pacify* him. *Daphne* gave her friend a *sapphire* and a *safflower* seed to see.

D. *Before Medial and Final Nasals*

The /æ/ tends to be long before medial and final /m/ and /n/, /n/ plus consonants, and final /m/ and /n/ plus suffix forms; it is shorter before medial and final /ŋ/. These words are not of the "ask–glance" word group and do not normally possess /a/ variants in educated speech.

		Before medial and final /ŋ/		*Before medial and final* /m/	
slang	sang	bespangle	Sam	stamp	clamshell
tangle	sank	hanky-panky	ham	Tammy	clammy
mangle	hang	crankshaft	spam	sample	sham
crank	handkerchief	stank	ram	hamster	Stamford

	Before /n/		*Before* /n/ *plus consonant*		
tan	clannish	Hannibal	sand	rant	finance
channel	bran	panacea	cant	hands	romance
ban	banana	Panama	hand	clans	clansman
ran	gannet	planetarium	expand	brand	grand

Practice: The /æ/ can be either short or long in the same phonetic environment, in an apparently inconsistent pattern. In the lists below, longer (and sometimes raised) varieties are heard for the words in the two left-hand columns and shorter, not normally raised, varieties can be heard for the words in the two right-hand columns. Compare them with your own pronunciations, transcribing as you say them.

laugh	Cathy	Africa	laboratory
laughter	jazz	Afghanistan	Labrador
after	cashier	sapphire	fabulous
rafter	snagged	saffron	banish
craft	lab	Havemeyer	braggart
salve	banjo	travesty	cant
bask	bragging	mathematics	classic
basket	can't	Catherine	amateur
plaster	classes	hazard	banana
math	classify	haggard	amino

E. *Before Nasals Plus Consonants*

Certain words in which the vowels appear before nasals plus consonants (as in *dance, glance*) possess the same variant /a/ forms as those noted in the previous section for the "ask" words.

Blanche	demand	sample	can't
branch	command	example	chant
chance	Flanders	sampler	grant
dance	Alexander	sampling	plant

Practice: Say these sentences aloud, and transcribe them as you say them.

Mr. Crandall was a fine banjo player for the canteen in Panama. His handkerchief was hanging in the clam bar. Blanche poured the wine from the decanter on the sand while she and Sam were dancing. The frangipani odors were sweet enough to cancel the uncomfortable odors of the factory. He demanded that she hand him the price of the brandy sample.

F. *Further Comparisons*

The /æ/ is an uncommon sound in many languages, and speakers of these languages find it difficult to distinguish a sound between higher, more front [e, ɛ] and lower and further back [a, ɑ]. Speakers of those languages that possess only mid front vowels and no low front vowel like the English /æ/ do tend to substitute /ɛ/, if their own languages possess it, or /a/ or /ɑ/. German, Norwegian, French, Spanish, Russian, Thai, Japanese, and Italian speakers, among others, have difficulty distinguishing the /æ/ sound from the [e, ɛ] and /a, ɑ/ sounds around it. The comparisons below will help establish the appropriate differences.

/e-eɪ/	/ɛ/	/æ/	/ɑ/
Hague	leg	lag	lock
trade	tread	fat	hot
bacon	beckon	batten	gotten
straight	dread	drab	drop
late	let	lack	lock
raid	red	radish	rotten
pain	pen	pan	pod
sale	sell	Sally	Solly
rake	wreck	rack	rock

Practice : Here are sentences for ear-training practice. Note especially each word with /e, ɛ, æ, ɑ/ sounds. Transcribe these sentences.

Kate put the cat on the cot after locking the door. The battle scenes were drab entertainment. Betty put the pot back on the stove so Madeline would have some hot tea later. Whenever Pat and Ned stopped Sally on the street, the three sang folk songs. Cathy got fat after eating too much candy and too little salad. Sadie traded her camera for Lester's record collection.

G. *Before Intersyllabic* /r/

Most speakers in the eastern and southern parts of the country use /æ/ in words like *marry* and *parrot*, although the /ɛ/ of *merry* may be heard commonly in southwestern New England, northern West Virginia, western New York State, and northeastern Pennsylvania. The /ɛ/ is characteristic of the central part of the country and of the area west of the Mississippi and north of Oklahoma (see Section 10.3).

Some /a ∼ ɑ/ variants for /æ/ occur sporadically in words like *married, narrow, harrow, wheelbarrow, barrel*; these forms are not infrequent in western Pennsylvania and the South.

Practice : Here is a list of words with /æ ∼ ɛ/ before intersyllabic /r/ arranged in two columns by the orthographic vowels of the first stressed syllable. Check your pronunciation of these words. Some people who pronounce *Harriet* or *character* with /æ/ commonly say *Maryland, ferry*, and *herald* with /ɛ/. Some say *Mary, dairy, fairy* with [e, eᶦ, eᵊ], others with /ɛ/, as in [mːɛri], or [mɛəri], [dɛəri].

Compare your pronunciations of the following words with those of your friends from elsewhere. Transcribe your pronunciations.

arrant—Eric	Karen—Merrick
Aragon—keratin	Laramie—Merrimac
aerial—cerebrate	larynx—merry
airy—ceremony	Marion—Perry
barren—kerosene	Mary—pericarditis
barricade—cherub	marigold—Pericles
Carol—cherry	marrow—peril
carry—derelict	narrow—peripatetic
character—ferry	narrate—periscope
charily—ferrous	pairing—perish
clarify—Gerry	Paris—serendipity
dairy—herald	paradise—serenade
Darien—heir	parallel—scherzo
embarrass—Heracles	parrot—sherry
fairy—heritage	Saracen—Sheridan
Farragut—herod	scarab—stereotype

pharynx—heroin	sharing—sterile
garret—Jeremy	Sharon—terrapin
garrison—Geraldine	tarantella—terrible
Gary—gerund	tarragon—territory
Harold—Jericho	tarry—Terry
hairy—Jerrold	vary—Vera Cruz
Harriet—meretricious	variable—verify
harem—merit	wary—very
Jarrow—Merivale	Zarathustra—whereabouts

Two selections for further review of front checked vowels are presented here. Read them aloud. Identify each front checked vowel. Note whether or not any of these vowels are pronounced differently in the speech of your friends. Transcribe the selections for practice in ear training and transcription.

Having shown that no one of the powers transferred to the Federal government is unnecessary or improper, the next question to be considered is, whether the whole mass of them will be dangerous to the portion of authority left in the several States.

The adversaries to the plan of the convention, instead of considering in the first place what degree of power was absolutely necessary for the purposes of the Federal government, have exhausted themselves in a secondary inquiry into the possible consequences of the proposed degree of power to the governments of the particular States.

The Federalist, No. 45
—attributed to James Madison

It is not a new observation that the people of any country (if, like the Americans, intelligent and well informed) seldom adopt and steadily persevere for many years in an erroneous opinion respecting their interests. That consideration naturally tends to create great respect for the high opinion which the people of America have so long and uniformly entertained of the importance of their continuing firmly united under one federal government, vested with sufficient powers for all general and national purposes.

The Federalist, No. 3
—attributed to John Jay

chapter **11** *The Central and Back Checked Vowels*

THE CENTRAL, stressed, checked vowel, as in *bug*, and the two back checked vowels, as in *bog* and *book*, complete the system of checked vowels in English. Of these three, only the high back vowel /ʊ/ can be paired with a phonically similar free vowel /u/ in all regional dialects of American English. Every dialect possesses a phonically paired free vowel for each of three checked vowels: The two front vowels /ɪ/ and /ɛ/ of *bit* and *bet* are phonically paired with the two free vowels /i/ and /e/ of *beet* and *bait*, and the back vowel /ʊ/ of *book* is paired with the /u/ of *boot*. The three checked vowels, /æ/, /ɑ/, /ʌ/ are not commonly paired with stressed free vowels in all the regional dialects of English.

11.1. Description

The typical positions assumed by the tongue during the emission of the checked vowels of *book*, *bog*, and *bug* may be seen in Figure 11.1. The lips are somewhat rounded for /ʊ/, unrounded for /ɑ/ and /ʌ/. The different cavity volumes of the vocal tract for each of these vowels, with resulting changes in the formants for each vowel, permit our perception of each vowel sound. The relationships of these cavities to one another during the emission of these three vowels are noted in the schematic drawings of Figure 11.1. The teeth are slightly

162

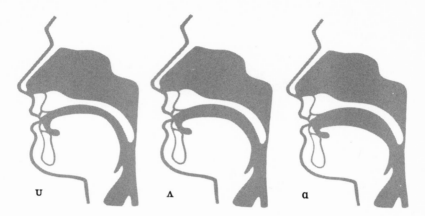

Figure 11.1. Schematic Drawings Showing the Shapes of the Resonance Chambers of the Vocal Tract during the Formation of /ʊ, ʌ, ɑ/.

SOURCES: Adapted from Arthur J. Bronstein, *The Pronunciation of American English* (New York: Appleton-Century-Crofts, 1960), pp. 138–40; and Jon Eisenson, *Basic Speech* (New York: The Macmillan Company, 1950), pp. 83–85. By permission of the publishers.

apart for the high, back /ʊ/, partially so for the mid-central /ʌ/, fully open for the low, back /ɑ/.

11.2. Compared in Prevoiceless and Prevocal Positions

These checked vowels, like other syllabics in the language, are somewhat longer when they precede voiced consonants than when they precede voiceless ones. Compare these sets of words.

BEFORE PLOSIVES

but—bud	rot—rod	put—should
nut—dud	hot—hod	foot—could
butter—budding	trotting—trodden	putting—pudding
shutter—shudder	sotted—sodden	footing—wooden
sup—rub	mop—mob	coop (also /u/)[1]

---

[1] Comparatively few examples of stressed /ʊ/ remain in our language. A good portion of these sounds that developed from Middle English long /o/ words has shifted to /u/ in many regional dialects, so that *root* may be heard as /rʊt, rut/, *hoop* as /hʊp, hup/, and *roof* as /rʊf, ruf/. See, for example, Raven I. McDavid, Jr., "Derivatives of Middle

cup—cub
puppy—double
twopence—Tubby
tuck—tug
chuck—chug
pucker—bubble
suckling—ugly

sop—sob
topper—robin
proper—probably
lock—log
hock—hog
socket—soggy
flocking—logging

hoop (also /u/)
whooping cough
(also /u/)
Cooper (also /u/)
hook
book
cookie—sugar
bookish—
boogie-woogie
(also /u/)

BEFORE FRICATIVES AND AFFRICATES[2]

/ʌ/		/ɑ/		/ʊ/	
fuss	fuzz	gossip	project (n.)	push	pussy
roughing	loving	crotch	hodge-podge	bush	hoof
buff	other	posh	collage		(also /u/)
rush	southern	hospital	grovel	bushel	hooves
crutch	fudge	possible	lozenges		(also /u/)
				Pushkin	roof
					(also /u/)
				ambush	woof
					(also /u/)

BEFORE NASAL AND LATERAL SOUNDS

/ʌ/		/ɑ/	
sum	cull	psalm	collar
bumble	skull	bombing	trollop
come	lulling	Congo	lollipop
thunder	cruller	Thompson	hollow
tongues	dullard	thongs	dollar

The /ʊ/ before nasals and lateral sounds is uncommon in English. Many speakers substitute vowels other than /ɑ/ in the preceding words. These variants are discussed later in this chapter.

English [o:] in the South Atlantic Areas," *Quarterly Journal of Speech*, 35 (December 1949), 496–504; and Arthur J. Bronstein and Esther K. Sheldon, "Derivatives of Middle English ō in 18th- and 19th-Century Dictionaries," *American Speech*, 26 (May 1951), 81–89. There are no common final /-ʊb, -ʊg/ forms.

[2] Since few pairings are possible, most of these sounds are not arranged in similar environments.

11.3. Stress

These checked vowels are shorter in less stressed syllables than in fully stressed syllables.

IN LESS STRESSED SYLLABLES	IN FULLY STRESSED SYLLABLES
/ʌ/	/ʌ/
uncomfortable	uncle
unless	underwear
unfit	pumpkin
subordinate	tungsten
umbrella	subway
/ɑ/	/ɑ/
obbligato	operate
obsolescence	oblong
occupation	occupancy
omnipotent	omnibus
colonization	colonize
/ʊ/	/ʊ/
(The /ʊ/ in less	umlaut
stressed	pussy
syllables is	footsore
not common	bookstore
in English.)	hoodwink

When compared with phonically similar free vowels in similar phonetic environments, these checked vowels are of shorter duration. Because all dialects do not possess phonically similar sounds that can be easily paired with checked /ɑ/ and /ʌ/, the following lists will be meaningful, perhaps, only to speakers of the dialects that demonstrate such pairings. All dialects do possess the pairing of /ʊ/ with phonically similar free /u/.

/ʊ-u/[3]

Cooper	pull—pool
roof	look—Luke
room	could—cooed
soot	bullet—Boola-Boola
hooves	hood—who'd

[3] Some speakers use /ʊ/ for all words in the left-hand column, whereas others always use /u/.

Practice : Checked /ɑ/ and /ʌ/ are compared here with phonically similar free vowels in similar phonetic environments, as they appear in certain regional dialects. Transcribe your pronunciations.

cop—carp	topper—tarpaulin	shock—shark
cot—cart	hopping—harpist	other—artist
hot—heart	crock—hark	hod—hard
pod—pardon	lock—lark	hockey—harken
clock—Clark	pocket—parked	shop—sharp

suck—sock—soak	rub—rob—robe
shun—John—shone	won—wan—won't
fund—fond—phoned	cup—cop—cope
hull—holly—whole	cluck—clock—cloak
sup—sop—soap	stuck—stock—stoke

Transcribe these sentences containing central and back checked vowels, as you say them aloud.

She put her stockings in her pocketbook. John drank a cup of hot milk when he caught cold while fishing for cod. They locked their stocks in the vault. The opera star fell unconscious. The children sucked their lollipops in the hot sun while their collars wilted. The gossiping mothers forgot to cook supper until the sun had set. The southern sunshine was very hot. Bookish students were munching too much fudge in the stuffy room. They put the bushels of good food in the back room. The lucky boys found their funds at the edge of the pond. Thunderous clouds couldn't still the gossiping tongues.

11.4. The /ʌ/ and Its Common Variants

The /ʌ/ is the low central or mid-central unrounded vowel in *hug* and *bundle*. It is the only central checked vowel in the language. It is made with relatively relaxed articulators. The middle of the tongue is slightly raised toward the palate. It is phonically close to the vowel of *crop* in certain dialects, to the vowel of *road* in other dialects, and to the vowel of *carp* in still other dialects. When compared with each of these dialect sounds, it is always more advanced or central in tongue position. The lips are always neutral, unrounded; the mouth opening is partial rather than full.

The /ʌ/ is an uncommon vowel in many languages. For example, speakers of French, German, Spanish, Yiddish, Russian, and Japanese have difficulty in pronouncing it, tending to substitute sounds that vary from the low, back /ɑ/ to a mid, or high, back unrounded or rounded vowel. Speakers of such languages can approximate /ʌ/

fairly easily if articulatory precision is constant, and ear training helps to establish the acoustic differences between /ʌ/ and what seem to be similar sounds in the low and back parts of the vowel system.

Stressed /ʌ/ also possesses an ingliding, diphthongal variant [ʌᵊ]. This variant is most common in the South, but it may also be heard sporadically in other sections.

A. *Compared with Low Back Vowels*

As speakers in different regional areas of the country may use different vowels in the compared words, check your pronunciations with those of your friends. Note differences in articulatory positions that result in different acoustic values for the sounds, as well as in differences in duration between /ʌ/ and other sounds.

IN INITIAL SYLLABLES

/ʌ/	/ɑ/	/o/	/ɑ(r)/	/ɔ/
ugly	Og	Oklahoma	Arctic	augur
ulcer	olfactory	oldster	Carlsbad	awls
ultra	Oliver	oleander	Arlington	paltry
lux	locks	soaks	larks	hawks
under	onto	owned	Arno	awning
husband	posse	pose	parse	pause

IN MEDIAL AND FINAL SYLLABLES

/ʌ/	/ɑ/	/o/	/ɑ(r)/	/ɔ/
inundate	inoculate	ignoble	anarchic	inauspicious
alumni	allopathy	Aloha	alarming	unlawful
conundrum	incongruous	connoting	imparting	inaudible
illustrious	illogical	eloping	enlarging	appalling
entrusting	impossible	imposing	restart	resort
insult (v.)	restock	resold	embark	inaugurate

B. *The /ʌ/ Variants in Special Words*

A number of words normally containing /ʌ/ in educated speech also possess variant forms ranging from /ɑ/ to /ɔ/, with no apparent regional pattern. These pronunciations exist in educated speech, but no complete consistency is present, either for person or for region.

Practice : Check your pronunciation of the following words. (Note that all possess orthographic *o* in the syllable concerned.)

Bromley	compass	donkey
Bromwich	conjure	frontier
Bronson	(to practice magic)	frontispiece
constable	clough	hovel
combat	([klʌf, klaʊ])	mongoose
combatant	Coventry	Pomeroy

Before the fricative /ʃ/ and the affricates /ʧ, ʤ/, upgliding allophones of /ʌ/ ([ʌ', ʌˠ]) and the mid-central /ɜ/ ([ɜˠ, ɜˀ]) sounds are sporadically substituted for monophthongal /ʌ/. This variation is heard in the southern mountain region, especially in western Virginia and northeastern North Carolina, with scattered occurrences elsewhere. These variant forms seem to be more prominent in folk or common speech than in the speech of the well-educated.

Practice: Some words containing these variants appear below. Transcribe your pronunciations.

mush	much	budge
muskmelon	touch	budget
crush	touchy	fudge
rush	crutch	sludge
usher	clutch	nudge
hushabye	such	trudge

The use of /ɛ/ for /ʌ/ in these and other words, for example, [ʃɛt] for [ʃʌt] or [sɛtʃ] for [sʌtʃ] is uncommon in educated speech.

c. *Variants before Intersyllabic* /r/

Three common variants exist for the stressed vowels in disyllabic words like *worry* and *courage*. These three pronunciations for the two words mentioned are

1	2	3
[wʌri]	[wɜri]	[wɝi]
[kʌrɪdʒ]	[kɜrɪdʒ]	[kɝɪdʒ]

Type 3 with the constricted syllabic [ɝ], may be heard in the Middle Atlantic area, upstate New York, western New England, and the middle and western sections of the country. Speakers in the Middle Atlantic area use Type 1 too.

Type 2, with the syllabic /ɜ/ and unsyllabic /r/, may be heard in eastern New England and in the South along with Type 1. It exists alongside Type 3 in the remainder of the country. Type 1 is regularly heard in metropolitan New York, where Type 2 is also heard occasionally.[4]

Practice: Transcribe your pronunciations of these words.

furrow	borough	curry	nourish
worry	currency	curried	flurry
courage	squirrel	stirring	scurry
furry	hurry	turret	scurried
thorough	hurrying	surrogate	Murray
burrow	surrey	flourish	murrain

Some /ʌ/ variants also exist in the derivatives of words with *-ir*, *-er*, *-ur* in their final syllables, along with [ɜr], [ɝ] forms:

slurring	spurring	stirring
purring	inferring	erring
occurring	furrier	preferring

Practice: Transcribe the following sentences containing words with the /ʌ/ sound. Listen to your friends say these sentences aloud. Do you note any differences in their pronunciations of these sounds?

The ugly husband decided to eat his supper alone. Her brother was found under the car. The upper tooth had to be cut from the gum. Among the sundry items of equipment, he located three sun helmets, one old musket, and one painting of a mongoose walking near a donkey. They rushed the muskmelon to market on Sunday evening. We trudged through the slush with much comfort in our new shoes. Except for the two brothers, no illustrious men were among the captured. Her mother worried when she saw the hovel they would be forced to live in. They sent Bromley and Pomerance forward, as these men showed great courage under fire.

11.5. The /ɑ/ and Its Common Variants

The /ɑ/ is the lowest vowel in the English phonemic system. The mouth is open wider for this vowel than for any other, and the lips remain unrounded. The upper surface of the tongue is almost completely flat in the mouth, although the entire tongue muscle is retracted

[4] The complex nature of the evidence on these variants is discussed in detail in the following sources: Charles K. Thomas, *Phonetics in American English*, 2nd ed. (New York: The Ronald Press Company, 1958), pp. 200–01, 127; Hans Kurath and Raven I. McDavid, Jr., *The Pronunciation of English in the Atlantic States* (Ann Arbor, Mich.: The University of Michigan Press, 1961), pp. 116–127; C. K. Thomas, "Notes on the Pronunciation of Hurry," *American Speech*, XXI (1946), 112–15; A. J. Bronstein, *The Pronunciation of American English* (New York: Appleton-Century-Crofts, Inc., 1960), pp. 175, 178, 50.

toward the pharynx, with the back of the tongue slightly raised. Compared with the /a/ of eastern New England *ask* (see Chapter 10) or *car* (see Chapter 12), the dorsum of the tongue is lower under the velum, as the tongue is drawn back and down; and a narrow channel results between the pharyngeal wall and the tongue base. The checked, stressed /ɑ/ of *hot, bog,* and *crop* is a low, back, unrounded lax vowel (see Figure 11.1).

The /ɑ/ is the regular vowel for "short *o*" before the stops /p, b, t, d, k/, intersyllabic /l/, and for orthographic *a* plus *r* in words like *far, harm,* and *chart* when postvowel /r/ is preserved. The /ɑ/ varies regionally preceding the voiced /g/ of *log*; when orthographic *a* follows /w/, as in *watch*; and when it precedes intersyllabic /r/, as in *forest* and *moral.* It does not appear in at least two regions of the country (eastern New England and western Pennsylvania) and it contrasts with a more retracted variety in certain regions where postvowel /r/ is lost. These variants are illustrated in the following pages. Free /ɑ/ of *pa* and *calm* is discussed in the next chapter.

The /ɑ/ in the "ask words," as an occasional variant of regular /æ/, has been discussed in Chapter 10. It appears occasionally in educated metropolitan New York, eastern New England, and northern Virginia speech alongside the more commonly used /æ/ form in these words. Samples of these words appear in Chapter 10 and need not be repeated here.

A. *Before Stops*

This vowel is the regular form except for speakers in eastern New England and western Pennsylvania, who use a higher, further back, slightly rounded sound /ɒ/ for the vowels of these words. Speakers in these regions (and in the Ohio Valley) tend to use the same free vowel in the words *crop, top, lock* that they use in *saw* and *law*, whereas all others in the country use the free vowel /ɔ/ in the latter words only, retaining /ɑ/ for the syllabics of the former words. Although /ɒ/ is the regular educated form for these short *o* words in eastern New England, /ɑ/ is not infrequent. In metropolitan New York, although /ɑ/ is regular, /ɒ/ is not infrequent. The South shows predominantly /ɑ/, with occasional retracted [ɑ˕] approaching rounded or unrounded /ɒ/ frequent in all sections. Throughout the remainder of the country, /ɑ/ is regular.

Lengthened varieties of this sound [ɑ·, ɑ:], as well as ingliding diphthongal forms [ɑˤ, ɑə], also appear.

BEFORE LABIAL, ALVEOLAR, AND VOICELESS VELAR STOPS

Practice: Compare your pronunciations with those of friends from other regions of the country.

/p/	/b/	/t/	/d/	/k/
top	job	not	nod	hock
crop	hobnob	dot	clod	pockmark
foppish	rob	got	God	rock
flop	probably	motto	modern	lock
opera	problem	otter	shod	clock
opposite	snob	shot	product	jockey
popular	hobnail	cotton	toddle	docket
proper	robber	knotted	dodder	stockade
popper	globule	flotsam	model	Bangkok
copy	globular	glottis	moderate	clockwork

BEFORE VOICED VELAR SOUNDS

The incidence of this sound before velar /g/, as in *hog* and *log* (before /k/ in certain exceptional words like *mock* and *mockingbird*), and before velar /ŋ/, as in *prong* and *honk*, is regular in the East. In certain parts of the South, /ɔ/ is regular and /ɑ/ not infrequent, whereas in other parts /ɑ/ is normally used in educated speech. The /ɒ/ occurs regularly in these words in eastern New England. The free vowel /ɔ/ is the regular form in the remainder of the country and /ɒ/ a frequent variant. The word *dog* retains /ɔ ~ ɒ/ forms in all areas, as do words like *song*, *wrong*, *long*, and *strong* and their derivatives.

bog	toggle	logger	logroll	bronco
cog	hogwash	dogeared	noggin	bronchi
dog	soggy	dogmatize	Ogden	prong
fog	hogshead	dogmatic	Og	honk
log	joggle	dogma	prognosis	gong

B. *Before Affricates, Fricatives, and Nasals*

The /ɑ/ is also found in "short *o*" words before the affricates /ʧ/ and /ʤ/, as in *Scotch* and *lodge*; before the fricatives, as in *possible* and *ophthalmic*; and before the nasal /n/ of *sonnet* and *on* and the nasal /m/ of *bomb* and *Tom*. Before the nasals and affricates, /ɒ/ is the common variant in eastern New England and western Pennsylvania, where /ɑ/ is less frequent. Elsewhere /ɑ ~ ɒ/ variants follow the pattern for "short *o*" words noted before plosives. For *on* and *gone*, however, the free vowel /ɔ/ is the more regular throughout most of the southern and southwestern parts of the country, while the /ɑ/ is common in the northeast, central, and western parts of the country. The /ɒ/ is a variant throughout.[5]

/n/	/ʧ/	/dʒ/	/m/
on	Scotch	lodge	bomb
gone	crotch	logic	pomp
onslaught	botch	cogitate	Pompeian
sonnet	cochineal	hodgepodge	comet
conduit	splotch	ontogeny	Bombay
blond	notch	Roger	comic

/s/	/z/	/ʃ/	/v/
osculate	osmosis	Ossian	Ovid
oscillate	Osgood	posh	novel
possible	Rosalind	bosh	novelette
hospital	positive	gosh	novice
Moscow	Moslem	mackintosh	novelty
nostril	Bosnia	galoshes	poverty

c. *Variants before Intersyllabic* /r/

The /ɑ/ before intersyllabic /r/, as in *orange* and *tomorrow*, varies from /ɑ/ to /ɔ/, the vowels of *far* and *for*. The unrounded vowel is regular in the eastern coastal region of the country, the rounded vowel in the remainder of the states. Eastern New England regularly retains /ɒ/ for this sound, although an /ɑ/ variant is not uncommon.

Before /l/, as in *doll* and *golf*, /ɑ/ is the regular sound of the mid-Atlantic section, the northern part of the country west from New England, and the South. /ɒ/ is regular in eastern New England. The rest of the country uses /ɒ ~ ɔ/ forms. The vowels before inter-syllabic /l/, as in *college* and *folly*, follow the /ɑ ~ ɒ/ pattern of "short o" before the stops. Lengthened and ingliding diphthongal forms /ɑ·, ɑ:, ɑ², ɒ²/ appear as variants for all the vowels before /l/ and /r/.

Practice: Transcribe your pronunciation of the following words.

orange	borrow	doll	oligarchy	hollyhock	hollow
forest	corollary	Dolly	solve	holiday	jolly
tomorrow	coronary	golf	loll	lollipop	mollify
coronation	Doric	involve	solvable	mollusk	olive

[5] This cross-country isoglossal line is charted in C. K. Thomas, "The Linguistic Mason and Dixon Line," in D. C. Bryant, ed., *The Rhetorical Idiom* (Ithaca, N.Y.: Cornell University Press, 1958), p. 254.

corrugate	foray	solvent	dissolve	oratory	orator
Doris	horoscope	college	Bolívar	politics	polish
forage	horrid	collar	collate	polyp	pollinate
horrible	morrow	colloquy	colony	Solomon	polyglot
moral	sorry	colonize	dolomite	solitary	solitaire
warrant	florist	follicle	follow	solenoid	solemn

D. *After* /w/

In words like *wash* and *qualify*, this sound varies regionally from /ɑ/ to /ɔ/. /ɑ/ is regular throughout most of the country, although the rounded forms /ɒ, ɔ/ are not infrequent throughout the central and western parts of the country. /ɒ/ is regular in eastern New England, /ɔ/ in the southern mountain section.

wash	wander	qualify	squab
wasp	want	quality	squander
waddle	wanton	qualitative	squabble

Practice: Transcribe the following sentences containing words with /ɑ/ forms. Check your pronunciations against those used by others.

The squadron feasted on a fair quantity of squab. He lost his wallet in Holland. They washed their feet after wandering in the forest. Lollipops, oranges, and olives do not go too well together. The golfers quarreled incessantly following each play. The horrible fact was that the colic had already spread throughout Hollywood. The volunteers for the squad stepped out. It was pleasant watching Doris solve the problem. The Bosnian osteopath was the best in the city. They read somber sonnets after returning from the concert. The Brontë sisters are dominant literary figures. They quarantined the quadruplets in the lodge.

11.6. The /ʊ/ and Its Common Variants

The /ʊ/ is a high, back, lax, checked vowel, as in *good* and *book*. It occurs only in the middle of words. The tongue is pulled back and up towards the velum, and the lips are slightly rounded. If you repeat "*boat–book–boot*," conscious of the muscle tensions and lip and tongue motions, you will note that the lips are more rounded for /o/ and /u/; less rounded for /ʊ/; the tongue backs steadily as we move from /o/ to /ʊ/ to /u/; the tension of the muscles is greater for the free vowels /o/ and /u/ than for /ʊ/.

Like its counterpart /ɪ/ in the front-vowel group, /ʊ/ is an uncommon sound in the phonemic systems of many other languages. Romance language speakers have difficulty avoiding the use of a tenser vowel like /u/ in its place. German speakers use a tenser variety of /ʊ/ than is common in English. Native speakers of Korean tend to substitute their higher, much rounder /u/ for the English /ʊ/ form, whereas speakers of the conservative dialect of Japanese vary /u/ with /ʊ/, depending on the adjacent sound.

Three common allophonic variants exist. The two diphthongal forms culminate in /ɪ/ and /ə/. The [ʊ°] is common in the South and the southern mountain regions, although the ingliding diphthong is not uncommon elsewhere in lengthened syllables. Upgliding variants with /ɪ/, sounding as [ʊᴵ], are heard in the upper South, especially before the /ʃ/ of such words as *push* and *bushel*. The monophthongal form is common throughout the country. Finally, a fronted or centralized variety of /ʊ/, [ʊ˖], may be heard in New England, the South, and the central and western parts of the country.

Occasional substitutions of /u/ and /ʌ/ for /ʊ/ may be heard in scattered instances: *butcher* and *bushel* with stressed /u/, *took* and *put* with /ʌ/. Such pronunciations are uncommon in educated speech.

STRESSED /ʊ, ʌ, AND u/ COMPARED

Stressed /ʊ, u, ʌ/ are compared below. Similar environments for /ʊ/ and /u/ are not too common.

> took—tuck—too
> look—luck—fluke
> hood—huddle—who'd
> book—buck—boot
> bushel—buskin—boost
> put—putt—putrid
> butcher—crutches—booth
> full—cruller—fool
> pulley—pulchritude—pool
> stood—stud—stewed

The variation noted for /ɪ ~ i/ before postvocalic /r/, as in *fear* and *nearly*, is mirrored with /ʊ ~ u/ variants in *poor* and *surely*. But to these two variants, a third, /o/, must be added. The use of /o/ in these same words is found only in the northeastern tip of New England, throughout the South at all social levels, and in the folk speech of the West. The /ʊ ~ u/ is regular in most of the country.

Normally /u/ before postvocalic and intersyllabic /r/, as in *tour–touring*, moves toward the lower and more relaxed and open /ʊ/. Variants of lowered /u/, raised /ʊ/ and ingliding diphthongal sounds with [ə] ([ʊə ~ uə]) or with constricted nonsyllabic [ɚ], [ʊɚ ~ uɚ], are also heard.

/ʊ ~ u/ BEFORE POSTVOCALIC AND INTERSYLLABIC /r/

boor	boorish
sure	tourist
surely	injurious
moor	Moorish
poor	purist
demure	durable
poorly	curious
inure	inuring

Practice : Transcribe the following sentences containing words with the /ʊ/ forms. Again, check your own pronunciations against those of friends, especially if they are natives of other regions of the country.

The good cook prepared a sugary dessert. They took the butcher home, pushing him in his wheelchair. We should bring all the wood into the shed before the downpour. She was sure she had seen the curio on the last tour of Europe. Her hood looked warm. Pure water was unavailable during their stay in the Moorish inn. No tourist should behave boorishly. The good and poor people remained demurely outside.

This selection is for review of stressed central and back checked vowels. Read it aloud, and identify each such vowel. Transcribe the sounds, and compare them with those transcribed by friends, noting any differences. Make a second list of the stressed, front checked vowels from the same selection.

> Once a poor widow, well along the road
> To old age, in a little house abode
> Beside a forest, standing in a dale.
> This widow, of whom I tell you now my tale,
> Even since the day when she was last a wife
> All patiently had led a simple life;
> Small were her earnings and her property,
> But what God sent she used with husbandry,
> And kept two daughters and herself. Of sows
> Three and no more she had about the house,
> Also a sheep called Molly, and three kine.
> Her sooty hall and bower were nothing fine,
> And there full many a slender meal she ate.
> No poignant sauce was needed for her plate;
> No dainty morsel passed her throat; her fare
> Accorded with the clothes she had to wear.

With surfeit she was never sick, but in
A temperate diet was her medicine,
And busy labor, and a heart's content.
Gout never kept her from a dance; nor bent
With stroke of apoplexy was her head.
Of wine none drank she, neither white nor red;
Her board was mostly served with white and black;
Milk and brown bread, of these she found no lack;
And bacon, or an egg, was not uncommon,
For in her way she was a dairywoman.

"The Nuns' Priest's Tale" from *The Canterbury Tales*
—Geoffrey Chaucer

chapter 12 *The Free Vowels*

THERE IS some discussion of the free vowels in previous chapters. But let us take them up specifically here, even though some of the data are repetitious.

The free vowels and their variant forms are those that can exist as syllable finals in our language. They differ in this way from the checked vowels, which cannot stand alone. All the free vowels occur in all parts of words—in initial, medial, and final syllables.

Most of the free vowels are commonly diphthongal in form, with monophthongal variants not uncommon. The free vowels in fully stressed syllables are normally diphthongs (as in *see, say, so* and *Sue*), and three of them are always diphthongal, even in less stressed and shorter syllables (as in *sigh, sow* [female hog], and *soy*), except for certain regional restrictions and certain occasional expressions. But for those three /aɪ, aʊ, ɔɪ/ sounds, all the other vowels normally have monophthongal forms in less stressed syllables and complex glides in fully stressed syllables. As stressing decreases, the monophthongal form shortens.

The stressed free complex sounds are falling diphthongs—that is, the major stress of the syllabic proceeds from strong to weak /áɪ,óŭ,éɪ, áŭ/. All these complex vowels are upgliding, diphthongal, or centralizing diphthongal forms. The latter are heard in words with orthographic /r/ like *four, bore, spurred, prayer*.

Free vowels are normally longer than checked vowels in the same environments. In addition, because they can occur as syllable finals, they are more prominently identified as carriers of the voice and voice qualifiers.

177

12.1. The Free Vowels Identified

There are ten free vowels in American English plus one variant and one regionally restricted sound. Let us identify the free vowels common to almost all speakers of American English first.

Seven vowels with common complex forms appear in such words as *see, create; Sue, cashew; say, vacate; sir, certain; so, Mohican; Shah, father; saw, Choctaw.* They are classified as two front vowels (*see, say*), four back vowels (*Sue, so, saw, Shah*), and one central vowel (*sir*). Two are high (*see, sue*); three are mid (*say, so, sir*); two are low (*saw, Shah*).

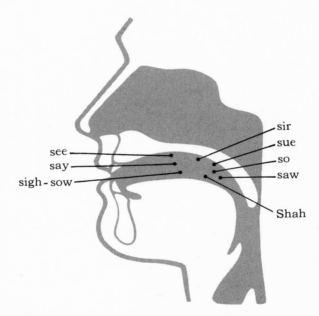

Figure 12.1. The Relative Tongue Curves of the Free Vowels.

SOURCES: Adapted from Arthur J. Bronstein, *The Pronunciation of American English* (New York: Appleton-Century-Crofts, 1960), pp. 138–140; and Jon Eisenson, *Basic Speech* (New York: The Macmillan Company, 1950), pp. 83–85. By permission of the publishers.

Three additional free vowels are normally complex, as in *sigh, sow,* and *soy.* They are initiated with low forms. The first two (*sigh* and *sow*) are normally initiated with low central or low back vowels. *Soy* is normally spoken with an initiating low back vowel. These three complex sounds are discussed in the next section.

The common relative articulatory positions of the tongue in forming these stressed free vowels (or the stressed elements when these vowels are complex) are shown in Figure 12.1. Figure 12.2

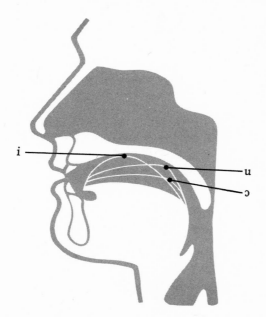

Figure 12.2. Schematic Drawings Showing Approximate Relationships among Resonance Chambers during Formation and Emission of /i, ɔ, u/.

SOURCES: Adapted from Arthur J. Bronstein, *The Pronunciation of American English* (New York: Appleton-Century-Crofts, 1960), pp. 138–140; and Jon Eisenson, *Basic Speech* (New York: The Macmillan Company, 1950), pp. 83–85. By permission of the publishers.

shows the vocal-tract configurations typical of three of the vowels /i, ɔ, u/.

To recapitulate, let us note the predominant articulatory areas of these vowels or of their stressed aspects in complex forms: Two are articulated as high vowels /i, u/; three are articulated as mid vowels /e, ɜ, o/; five are articulated or initiated as lower vowels /ɔ, ɔɪ, aɪ, au, ɑ/.

In addition to these ten vowels, American English possesses a regionally restricted free vowel in areas where postvocalic /r/ is lost. This additional vowel ranges from /a-ɑ/ in New England's *car* or *garden* to a more retracted /ɑ-ɒ/ in the same words in metropolitan New York and the South. And, to complicate matters further, the variant /ɪʊ ~ ju/ for /u/ appears as a complex sound in such words as *new* and *duty*. Variants of these free vowels may appear with an added centering form, as in [ɔə] for /ɔ/ in *for*, as [ɜə] for /ɜ/ in *sir*; with an initial glide [ɪ] or [ɪ], as in *see* and *seem*; with an initial glide [ʊ] or [ʊ], as in *sue* and *fool*; or with an offglide [ɪ] or [ʉ], as in *third* or *tune*. The additional vowels and their variants are described throughout this chapter.

12.2. The Free Vowels Compared

Typically, these vowels, like the checked vowels described earlier, are longer before voiced consonants than before voiceless ones. And free vowels are typically longer when they are stressed syllable finals than when they are checked by voiceless consonants. These two situations can be perceived in the words and phrases that follow. No listings appear here for /ɑ/ in closed syllables, as they were given under checked /ɑ/ in the previous chapter.

IN CLOSED SYLLABLES

/i/	/u/	/e/
seat—seed	soot—sued	mate—made
leak—league	hoop—boob	lake—plague
beet—Bede	ruse—whose	mace—maize
greet—greed	stoop—tube	lace—lays

/ɜ/	/o/	/ɔ/
Bert—bird	boat—bode	sought—sawed
spurt—spurred	moat—snowed	sauce—pause
Burke—berg	dope—lobe	ought—awed
irk—erg	soak—rogue	caught—cawed

/aɪ/	/aʊ/	/ɔɪ/
sight—side	kraut—crowd	Royce—Roy's
height—hide	mouse—rouse	oyster—boys
white—wide	shout—shroud	quoit—destroyed
vice—wise	a lout—aloud	choice—toys

IN OPEN AND CLOSED SYLLABLES

/i/	/e/	/u/
see—seat	may—mate	sue—forsooth
she—sheet	shay—shake	shoe—shoot
plea—pleat	bay—base	ensue—suit
lea—leaf	slay—slake	bamboo—boot

/ɑ/

pa—pot
Shah—shot
rah-rah—rotten
ma—mock

/ɜ/	/o/	/ɔ/
err—earth	go—goat	saw—sauce
sir—surf	so—soap	saw—sought
fir—first	show—shoat	awe—ought
spur—spurt	toe—toast	gnaw—nought

/aɪ/	/aʊ/	/ɔɪ/
I—ice	how—house	boy—boisterous
my—mice	now—mouse	joy—Joyce
try—thrice	sow—souse	Roy—Royce
high—kite	row—route	annoy—oyster

Free vowels are relatively long in at least three other situations too. When they appear as finals before pauses, they are longer than when they do not; when they appear as finals or before the final consonants of a closed syllable, they are longer than when they precede unstressed syllables; and like the checked sounds, they are longer when they precede the nasals and the lateral /m, n, ŋ, l/ plus voiced consonants than when they precede the same sounds and a voiceless consonant. These situations are illustrated below.

AS FINALS BEFORE PAUSES AND IN NONFINAL POSITIONS

I see.	I see the house.
Listen to his plea.	His plea is worthy.
We can't go.	Go if you can.
Come now.	Now is the time.

Bring the toy.	The toy is broken.
Don't try.	Don't try too hard.
If you can't go, tell him.	If you can go home, tell him.
Watch the show, quietly.	Watch the show quietly.
Stack the hay, then come.	Stack the hay bales, and then come.

AS FINALS OR BEFORE FINAL CONSONANTS IN CLOSED SYLLABLES AND
BEFORE UNSTRESSED SYLLABLES

see—seeing	now—nowadays
seed—seeded	Please stay—Please stay awhile
pleat—pleated	Do you see?—Do you see it?
go—going	Go slow—Go slowly

BEFORE NASALS AND THE LATERAL PLUS VOICED AND VOICELESS
CONSONANTS

owned—won't	hounds—ounce	joins—joints
honed—don't	bounds—bounce	joined—joint
fawned—flaunt	walls—waltz	cold—colt
songs—songstress	falls—false	hauled—halt

She feigned illness—She was faint, ill
The ball bounds away—The balls bounce away
Please don't—Lee groaned

12.3. The High Free Vowels and Their Variants

As you have already been introduced to most of the free vowels in the drill material on the checked vowels, this section considers these vowels in small groups and thus provides additional comparative material for analysis and perception.

The /i/ is the highest front vowel in the phonemic system of the English language. It is normally made with the blade of the tongue high toward the hard palate. The lips are spread, the articulatory muscles are tense, and the mouth opening is very slight. The /u/ is the highest back vowel of our system, made with the back of the tongue near the soft palate. The lips are rounded, the articulatory muscles are tense, and the mouth opening is slight. If you say /i-u/, /i-u/ quickly, you will note the quick motion of the lips from a spread to a rounded position, with the muscles remaining tense. If you say /i-ɪ/, /i-ɪ/ for a while or /u-ʊ/, /u-ʊ/, placing your hand along the lower jaw so that your fingers can feel the muscles of the face and under the chin, you will note why /i, u/ are considered tense vowels, and /ɪ, ʊ/ lax ones. Both /i, u/ are commonly diphthongal in syllables of any duration and tend toward the monophthongal in shorter, less stressed syllables.

Both possess at least three common forms: monophthongal or slightly lengthened [i, i·, u, u·]; upgliding diphthongal [ɪi, ʊu]; and ingliding or centralized [iᵊ, uᵊ]. Such complex variant forms do not commonly appear in certain other languages that have /i/ and /u/, for these sounds normally remain tense and long but monophthongal. Compare, for example, German *Sie* and *Schuh* with English *see* and *shoe* or French *oui* and *rue* with English *we* and *rue*.

A. *Compared with Similar Checked Vowels*

Note that the free vowels /i, u/ are regularly longer and tenser than the corresponding checked vowels in similar phonetic environments.

Final /i/	*Medial* /i/	*Medial* /ɪ/
see	seep	sip
he	heat	hit
he	heed	hid
we	weep	whip
she	sheep	ship
agree	greet	grit
plea	pleat	lit
we	weak	wick
pea	peak	pick
lea	leaking	liquor

Final /u/	*Medial* /u/	*Medial* /ʊ/
too	tool	full
pooh	pool	pull
shoe	shooed	should
woo	wooed	would
who	who'd	hood
blew	lewd	stood
boo	"pooch"	bush
chew	chute	shook
Pooh-bah	pooh-poohed	pudding

B. *In Stressed Syllables*

Initial syllable	*Final syllable*	*Medial syllable*
ease	surcease	increasing
aegis	appellee	appreciate
easy	appointee	Assisi
neater	increase	Polyphemus
pleasing	believe	kinaesthesia
ether	entreat	Geneseo
mealy	pongee	Eritrea
gleeful	guaranteed	idea
leonine	redeem	Medea
Cheops	achieve	achievement

Let him *be*. Try to in*crease* your production. She bought a *knee*hole desk. Pl*ease* be s*eat*ed quietly. *Clean* products are more *eas*ily *seen*. *Free*zing the *meat* will preserve it.

Initial syllable	*Final syllable*	*Medial syllable*
sue	ensue	ensuing
shooting	tatoo	leguminous
losing	canoe	inhuman
foolish	papoose	constitution
coupon	balloon	restitution
whooping	diffused	confusion
sumac	assume	unsuited
spooky	destitute	accrual
Julius	attuned	Medusa
ducal	reduce	enthusiasm

The lawyer *sued*. The oppor*tu*nity came. He did not ap*prove*. Place the *crou*tons in the *soup*. The *news*paper story as*sumed too* much. *Su*san *Crews* was con*fused* by the *nu*merous *cou*pons that ac*crued*.

The /i/ and /u/ before postvocalic and intersyllabic /r/ with variants /ɪr/ and /ur/ have been covered in Chapters 10 and 11. Refer back to them for review.

C. *Stressed /i/ and Variant Forms*

Commonly, stressed free /i/ is diphthongal; most noticeable in stressed final positions, as in *see* or *settee*; somewhat noticeable in checked syllables before voiced consonants, as in *cream* or *fleas*; less noticeable in checked syllables before voiceless consonants, as in *fleece* or *leaf*; least noticeable when receiving less stress, as in *create* or *Neapolitan*, in which /i/ may vary with /ɪ/. As the syllables lose stress in the phrase, the regular complex forms become shorter and more noticeably monophthongal, as in "Brìng me some téa, pleâse" versus "Pleâse bring the tèa nów."

At least three sets of variants of the free vowel /i/ can be heard in these circumstances, ranging from monophthongal [i, i·, i:] through upgliding [ɪi, ij] (the former with a lower beginning) to a centralizing diphthong [iᵊ, iᵊ].

Before /l/, a centralizing offglide /ə/ is not uncommon: [iᵊ] or [ɪiᵊ], as in *ceiling* or *feel*, [sɪiᵊlɪŋ, fiᵊl]. The breaking of the diphthong into a disyllable in such words [si-əlɪŋ, fiʲ-əl] is not common to educated speech.

Practice: Check the pronunciation of these words, arranged in special phonetic environments.

In open stressed syllables	With nasals	With /l/	With voiced consonants	With voiceless consonants	In less stressed open syllables
see	seem	seal	seize	cease	create
aegis	cream	feel	bead	beet	Neapolitan
aeon	steam	peel	breathe	beat	Aegean
appellee	wean	anneal	breeze	eke	Aeolia
beetle	clean	reeled	Louise	beach	beatific
appointee	preen	heals	breve	geese	Atlee
Edith	supreme	she'll	seethe	screeching	Aegeus
eagle	green	we'll	liege	Easter	Fujiyama
decent	nectarine	wheel	sleeve	crease	neology
Fuji	tangerine	appeal	Ganymede	fleeting	reorder

D. *The /u/ and Common Variants*

The /u/, like the /i/, possesses numerous variants: a monophthongal form [u, u·], centralized forms [ʉ, ʉ·, ɪʊ, ʉ], an upgliding form [ʊu], a centralized rising form [ʉʉ], and a centering or ingliding [uᵊ]. The high back /u/ is not uncommon in the northern part of the country. The centralized forms are very common in the South and not uncommon elsewhere, especially after palatals /j/ and /l/, as in *chew, shoe, blue, music*. The offglide /ə/ is common before velarized /l/, as in *fuel* and *school*, although the disyllabic forms, as in [skʊuʷ–əl] or [fjʊu–əl], are not common to educated speech.

The diphthongal variants are most common in this order: as stressed finals, as in *blew*; when checked by voiced consonants, as in *food*; when checked by voiceless consonants, as in *lute*; when less stressed, as in *Louella*, in which /u/ may vary with /ʊ/. As the syllable loses stress, the sound becomes less noticeable as a diphthongal form. For example, "He compòsed a melôdious túne" versus "The tùneful mêlody was most compléx." The following words are arranged in special phonetic environments so that you can check these various forms.

In open syllables	*With nasals*	*With /l/*	*With voiced consonants*
too	tune	fuel	prove
flew	croon	school	soothe
lucid	broom	schoolroom	fuse
Pluto	room	rule	news
Lou	prune	fool	fusion
usurp	fume	ghoul	improved
mutiny	flume	mule	unmoved
humid	tuneful	stool	stoothed
canoeing	spumes	poolroom	huge
neuter	noonday	tools	rouge

With voiceless consonants	*In less stressed syllables*
proof	Lucinda
sooth	Louella
tooth	cashew
roof	issue
scoops	duality
scoot	Fujiyama
loosely	Judaea
stoop	unto
useful	into
sloop	ubiquitous

After /l/ and /r/	*After /t, d, n/*[1]	*After /j/ and palatals*
lucid	tune	music
lute	duty	feud
absolutely	newspaper	beauty
resolution	contumely	mule
blue	renew	putrid
crude	tubular	shoe
rule	numerous	choosy
ruminate	intuitive	Schubert
proof	induce	amuse
broom	reducing	mutation

Practice: Here are sentences with the high free vowels in different contexts for comparison. Transcribe them, noting the variant forms of /i/ and /u/ you use in these words.

He gathered the peas in the fields, while kneeling. She pleaded with him not to take his shoes with him into the pool. We all agreed it was a most pleasing achievement for Susan. Judy served the tea to Edith with too much condescension for comfort. The shoemaker was an expert in the Hebrew language. Her niece arrived in Shreveport and then called Lucinda. The mutiny took place on a humid day on the high seas. The sloop caught up with the canoes in three minutes. The breeze felt clean whenever they approached the beach. They found that the music put him into a stupor.

12.4. The Mid Free Vowels and Their Variants

The /e/ and /o/ are the mid front and mid back vowels, both made with the tongue lower in the mouth than for the respective front and back /i/ and /u/ sounds. For /e/, the blade of the tongue lies approximately halfway between the high point for /i/, which is close to the palate, and the low front point for /æ/, in which the upward tongue curve is very slight. Similarly for /o/, the back of the tongue, which is high toward the soft palate, is lowered about halfway between that position and the position for /ɑ/, for which it rests almost flat in the mouth. The mouth is half open, approximately midway between the positions for higher /i/ or /u/ and lower /ɑ/. A recheck of Figure 12.1 will help to clarify these statements.

[1] These words are also heard with variant /ju/.

The lips and tongue muscles are tense for both vowels. The lips are spread for /e/; they are rounded for /o/. The difference in tension can be felt if you will repeat quickly /e-ɛ/, /e-ɛ/, /e-ɛ/ or /o-ʊ/, /o-ʊ/, /o-ʊ/. Both vowels /e, o/ are commonly diphthongal in syllables of any duration, tending toward the monophthongal forms in shorter, less stressed syllables.

The /ɜ/ is a central vowel, formed with the central portion of the tongue raised toward the back of the hard palate. The position of the tongue for /ɜ/ is not so high as it is for the centralized /ɨ/ and /ʉ/, as used by some speakers in words like *fish* and *fool*, and it is higher than the position for the low vowels /a ∼ ɑ/ of *part* or *pot*. The tongue is

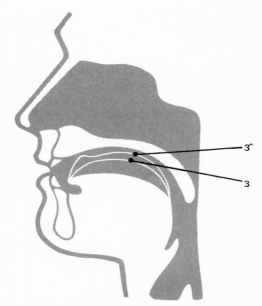

Figure 12.3. The Tongue Positions for [ɝ] and [ɜ] in American English.

SOURCE: Adapted from Arthur J. Bronstein, *The Pronunciation of American English* (New York: Appleton-Century-Crofts, 1960), pp. 138–40; and Jon Eisenson, *Basic Speech* (New York: The Macmillan Company, 1950), pp. 83–85. By permission of the publishers.

moderately retracted toward the middle of the mouth. Two major variants exist. One is a noticeably constricted form in which the tongue bulge is fairly high and the sides of the tongue are away from the teeth and gums. For this constricted form, the tongue tip turns slightly upward toward the ridges of the hard palate. The sound [ɝ] may be either fully or slightly constricted.

The sound may also be unconstricted when the tongue bulge is not quite so high and the tongue tip remains low behind the incisors. The positions of the two forms [ɜ-ɝ] may be compared in Figure 12.3. The mouth is open, and the articulators are tense. The [ɜ] may have an unrounded, neutral lip position or be made with rounded lips. The constricted form normally possesses forward and rounded lips.

Both constricted [ɝ] and unconstricted [ɜ] have diphthongal variant forms that culminate either in higher /ɪ, ɨ/ or in central /ə/ forms. And, of course, all varieties may be lengthened. Certain other languages that possess /e/ and /o/ tend to retain them in monophthongal forms, rather than in complex forms. Compare, for example, French *les* and *l'eau* with English *lay* and *low*, or German *geht* and *Ton* with English *gate* and *tone*.

A. *Compared with Checked Vowels in Similar Environments*

Note that the free vowels are regularly longer and tenser than the checked vowels are.

Final /e/	*Initial and medial /e/*	*Initial and medial /ɛ/*
may	ailing	Elsa
repay	shale	Nelson
spray	gate	get
fray	freight	fret

Final /o/	*Initial and medial /o/*	*Initial and medial /ɑ/*
show	ocean	shot
row	oatmeal	rotten
crow	rode	ostracize
forgo	goads	gods

Final /ɜ/	*Initial and medial /ɜ/*	*Initial and medial /ʌ/*
sir	certain	Sutton
refer	earn	fun
inter	turncoat	upper
purr	early	uncle

B. *In Initial, Medial, and Final Stressed Syllables*

/e/

ache	mistaken	mistake
nature	instantaneous	intake
patronage	oasis	rephrase
placate	tomato	promenade
nation	implacable	dilate
satiate	apparatus	exclaimed
stationery	appreciation	repay
phrasing	pronunciation	engaging

/o/

only	enclosure	encode
posing	unbroken	repose
soapy	unwholesome	enclose
soaking	encomium	extol
boat	exploded	unclothed
owner	immobile	morose
growth	melodious	hello

/ɜ/

urge	uncertain	invert
first	subversion	return
thirsty	superbly	superb
birthright	insertion	absurd
spurning	interminable	chauffeur
shirtwaist	commercial	prefer
cursory	interpret	inter

Practice : Transcribe the following sentences, and note the variants of the mid vowels you use.

No thirsty travelers came to the oasis. They urged Joseph to show his true nature. Don't go! Stay! Will she play? Take that turn, after the first crossroad. They stayed until Nona had her turn. No person should play the piano with his toes. He spoke slowly, weighing his words. He exerted his paternal privilege and paid for all the guests.

c. *Stressed /e/ and Variants*

Commonly stressed free vowel /e/ is diphthongal. The complex nature of the vowel is most noticeable in the fully stressed final position as in *repay*. In stressed syllables before voiced and voiceless consonants, it is quite noticeable in descending order, as in *grade* and *great*. When less stressed, as in the first syllable of *vacation* and the last syllable of *reiterate*, the complex sound tends to give way to the monophthongal form /e/. Similarly, as the syllable or word loses stress in the phrase, the regularly complex form becomes shorter and monophthongal. ("Did he páy?" versus "Did he pay his wáy?" "Listen to the horse néigh" versus "Gôôd nèighbors are better than bád neighbors.")

An upgliding [eɪ] is the common form in most of the country, along with variant [eɪ]. A more open [ɛɪ, ɛɪ] is heard in upper New England, Philadelphia, Pittsburgh, and northeastern North Carolina. An open, lowered [ɛɪ, ɛɪ, ɛə] is not uncommon before /l/, as in *pail* and *failure*, although the higher /eɪ/ is perhaps more common.

Monophthongal [e, e·] and a centralized [eə] are distinctive to the South.

In open syllables	With nasals	With /l/
say	same	sail
maybe	sanely	railroad
patience	fame	failing
pray	crane	shale

With other voiced consonants	With voiceless consonants	In less stressed syllables
grade	great	vacation
rage	raked	vacate
babe	pace	reiterate
craved	implicate	chaotic

The /e/ before postvocalic and intersyllabic /r/, with variants [ɛr] and [ɛər], as in *dare* and *Mary*, are covered in Chapter 10. Refer back to that section for review.

Practice: Transcribe these sentences illustrating the free mid vowel /e/ in different contexts. Note the variant forms used.

Play the game. Say the sentence with great care. They noticed both plain and stained-glass windows. The mayor met the train just as it entered the railroad station. Eight hundred females braved the throngs attending the retail sales. The crane operator was actually a famous tenor. "Stay the day," she suggested, "and we'll bathe in the brook, catch some game fish, and let our cares sail away." The runner quickened his pace, winning the great race by eighteen seconds.

D. *Stressed /o/ and Variants*

Stressed /o/ is regularly diphthongal. Like /i/, /u/, and /e/, /o/ is most noticeably diphthongal in fully stressed final positions, as in *go* and *slow*. It is also noticeably diphthongal in checked syllables before voiced consonants, as in *rode* and *rogue*, and almost fully diphthongal before voiceless consonants, as in *wrote* and *broke*. When the syllable is less stressed, as in *obey* and *window*, the diphthongal form tends to be shortened to monophthongal [o]. And, as the syllable or word loses stress in the phrase, the regularly complex form shortens and becomes less noticeably diphthongal: "He nóted the error" versus "He made a notátion of each êrror." "Did he gó?" versus "Did he go upstáirs?"

At least four common variants of /o/ should be noted. The first is the upgliding [oʊ ~ oᵘ] forms, which are predominant throughout the country. A raised [o⁺ʊ] is common in the South. The second is a monophthongal variant heard in the northern and central parts of the country. It is also found as the predominant form in the South, where centralized [oᵊ] can also be heard. The New England short *o* is a fronted and lowered [o⁒], fairly close to the /ʌ/ of *run* and *won*. This third variant is heard most commonly before alveolar /t, d, n/ (*coat, road, stone*) but less commonly elsewhere (*whole, home, post*). It is commonly short and monophthongal. When prolonged, as in "Let's go home" or "Give him his coat," it may be heard as [oᵗᵊ]. *Rode* and *rowed*, *shone* and *own* contrast in this area: [oᵗᵊ] versus [oᵘ]. Fourth, a more centralized form of /o/, almost approaching /ɜ/ (that is, with an almost mid-central open vowel [o₊]), is heard with growing frequency in the United States. It can be transcribed as [ɵ] or [ö]. It is common in the Middle Atlantic region, the upper Ohio Valley, and northeastern North Carolina. It is also heard sporadically as far west as Colorado and as far south as New Mexico and Oklahoma.

In open syllables	*With alveolar* /t, d, n/	*With /l/ and* /m/	*With other voiced sounds*
oh	rode	whole	stove
slow	rowed	home	rose
grow	stone	souls	clothes
rowing	coat	foam	rogue
showcase	moan	told	robe
chauffeur	phoning	molten	cloves

With other voiceless consonants	*In less stressed syllables*
broke	tomato
most	fellow
postman	obey
broach	notorious
approach	domain
slope	rotation

Before postvocalic and intersyllabic /r/, as in *hoarse* and *oral*, /o/ varies with /ɔ/ throughout the country, with some fairly noticeable regional restrictions. The historical distinction between *hoarse* with /o/ and *horse* with /ɔ/ is retained in much of the country. It is perhaps most noticeable in the South, where words like *hoarse* are almost universally heard with [o·ᵊ], [ouᵊ], or [ouə] in educated speech. The loss of the offglide [ᵊ] in [fo:] and [do:] for *four* and *door* is rare in educated southern speech and occasional in the middle social group.

In eastern New England speakers usually retain the distinction between *four* and *forty*: [foə, for] versus [fɒə, fɔə, fɒr, fɔr], but in western New England, some speakers use almost similar vowels [oˇ versus ɔˆ] for the different words, whereas others use only one. In New York City, all social levels use /ɔ/ in both *hoarse* and *horse, oral* and *aural*, while most speakers in the Southwest and in the north central areas make no distinction between these words, using /ɔ/ for both. The direction of change seems to be clearly toward dropping the distinction, except in the South.

Practice : The following drill material includes words in distinctive lists. Check your pronunciation against those of your friends. Transcribe.

/o ~ ɔ/	/ɔ/	/o ~ ɔ/	/ɔ/
oral	aural	excoriate	accordion
glory	lorgnette	export	extort
four	forty	explore	escort
story	torpedo	floor	for
boarder	border	force	forbear
mourn	morning	ford	forceps
Borah	born	fore	formality
Borneo	Borgia	forearm	formaldehyde
chlorate	chord	forthright	formative
chloroform	corkscrew	forum	Formosa

/o ~ ɔ/	/ɔ/	/o ~ ɔ/	/ɔ/
choral	corduroy	foreword	forswear
chore	chortle	forewarn	fortitude
core	corn	glory	forfeit
courtier	corporal	gore	Gorgon
courtyard	incorporate	hoard	gorge
dory	dorsal	hoary	horn
door	dormer	porch	horseplay
doorman	endorse	porosity	porcupine
Korea	Korzybski	port	porpoise
lore	Lorelei	portable	pornographic
Moore	morbid	portend	Sorbonne
morass	morning	portulaca	sordid
more	Norse	quorum	thorn
Nora	Norwalk	roar	torque
orate	northern	sore	tort
ore	orb	thorax	New York
Orestes	orchestra	tore	snort
orient	organize	torn	scorch
oriole	orgy	soar	scorn
Orono	ornament	spore	scorpion

Here are sentences with free, mid vowel /o/ for transcription and listening practice.

Orestes traveled to Portugal for the glory of his country. The doorman opened the courtroom door so Nora could enter. The dentist conducted the oral examination with dispatch and forwarded his report to the otologist for an aural examination. The postman approached the new home with caution. She swallowed the tomato juice quickly before trying the oatmeal. The chauffeur told her the weather was cold and snowy. The doting parents did not know how Joseph managed to close his door so quietly. Rose bought a new cloak to go with her new suit. He phoned the groaning man's son as soon as he could. The boys threw stones through the windows of the old home. Tom was known as a notorious criminal before he became a repentant window-washer.

E. *The /ɜ/ and Its Variants*

This mid central vowel possesses at least three monophthongal forms, each of which may also be heard with offglide vowels. The monophthongal form may be pronounced as a fully constricted, slightly constricted, or unconstricted sound. The unconstricted sound is transcribed [ɜ]; the slightly constricted one, [ɝ]; and the fully constricted one (with tongue-tip inversion toward the hard palate), [ɝ]. Each of these forms is spoken with the lips in neutral or rounded position.

The unconstricted /ɜ/ is found where postvocalic /r/ has been lost—in much of eastern New England, in the metropolitan New York area, and in the South. The [ɜ:, ɜə] are the common variants in these areas. A [ɜɪ] is also heard for nonfinal /ɜ/ in the South at all social levels, most noticeably before alveolar /t, d/, as in *word* and *hurting*. Educated speech in metropolitan New York has an occasional [ɜɪ] in a nonfinal position, especially among older native inhabitants, but it is more commonly associated with less educated speakers there.

Constricted [ɝ, ɝ] is the regular form throughout the country. It is heard in western New England and in the entire Middle Atlantic area, as well as throughout the middle and western sections of the country. Fully constricted varieties are more occasional in the North and Southwest.

The lengthened and diphthongal forms (excluding the special form [ɜɪ] already mentioned) occur in the same phonetic distribution as do other free vowels—ranging from most obvious lengthening and diphthongization in fully stressed final syllables and before voiced consonants, as in *spur, heard*; through less obvious lengthening and diphthongization before voiceless consonants, as in *hurt* and *purse*; to least lengthening in less stressed syllables, in which they are regularly monophthongal, as in *surreptitious* and *purchasability*.

The /ɜ/ variants before intersyllabic /r/, as in *worry* and *squirrel*, are noted in Chapter 11 and should be reviewed there.

In open syllables	Checked by alveolar stops	Checked by other consonants	Before intersyllabic /r/
sir	bird	turn	furry
her	hurt	thirst	surrey
burr	absurd	purse	thorough
were	divert	irked	furrow
certain	dessert	burst	courage
myrrh	referred	search	purring
myrtle	occurred	worm	borough
Percy	curds	spurn	recurring

Practice: Here are sentences with free, mid vowel /ɜ/ for transcription and listening practice.

Gertrude turned to her older sister, whom she preferred. The worthy nourishment helped turn the tide of the disease. The roads diverged, and

Burt felt absurd. The leg hurt when he turned. They lived in a hurried way, always worrying. If she stroked the cat's fur, she heard purring noises. They preferred to infer, rather than to analyze and search. When he caught the third perch, Kurt gave thirty other worms to Myrtle. They burst through the heavily furnished place, ripping curtains, disturbing the pet birds, and cursing in one-syllable words.

12.5. The Low Free Vowels and Their Variants

A. *The Low Vowel /ɔ/*

This sound, pronounced as in *awe*, is formed with the back of the tongue slightly elevated from the position of the lowest back vowel /ɑ/. The lips are slightly rounded, and the muscles of articulation are tense. The mouth opening is approximately halfway between that for the /ɑ/ of *Shah* and the /o/ of *show*, although the sound is more low than mid. Its relationship to these two neighboring sounds and to the

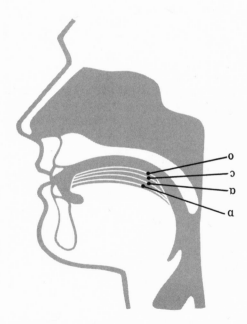

Figure 12.4. The Tongue Curves for the Four Back Vowels /o, ɔ, ɒ, ɑ/.

SOURCES: Adapted from Arthur J. Bronstein, *The Pronunciation of American English* (New York: Appleton-Century-Crofts, 1960), pp. 138–40; and Jon Eisenson, *Basic Speech* (New York: The Macmillan Company, 1950), pp. 83–85. By permission of the publishers.

/ɒ/ in *hot* and *cod* of eastern New England and western Pennsylvania can be seen in Figure 12.4.

The sound is normally long in stressed syllables with common variants [ɔ:] or [ɔə]. It is longest in final open syllables and before voiced consonants, shorter before voiceless consonants.

The most common variant is the /ɒ/ sound in *cross* and *dog*, in which the regular /ɔ/ does not appear in eastern New England and western Pennsylvania. The /ɒ/ in these words is not uncommon in metropolitan New York.

An upgliding [ɒᵊ] variant is heard in the educated speech of Georgia and South Carolina. The /ɔ/, with long and ingliding forms [ɔ:,ɔᵊ,ɔə], is regular, however, in most of the country in such words as *saw, talk, cross,* and *dog.* The word *water* seems to move from /ɔ/ through /ɒ/ to /ɑ/ as we go from east to west.

Variants for /ɔ/ before intersyllabic /r/, as in *horrible* and *warrant,* are discussed in Chapter 11; those for *four* and *forty,* in Section 12.4.

B. *The /ɔ/ in Different Phonetic Environments*

Initial syllable	*Medial syllable*	*Final syllable*
awe	unlawful	Montauk
awning	inaugurate	deformed
dawdle	absorbent	baseball
haunted	enforceable	because
raucous	defrauded	across

In final open syllables	*Before voiced consonants*	*Before voiceless consonants*	*In less stressed syllables*
saw	sawed	sought	authority
claw	Gaul	caught	Cornelius
Wainshaw	shorn (or /o/)	wrought	automobile
raw	prawn	gawk	inauspicious
gnaw	maudlin	forth (or /o/)	forswear

C. *The Free /ɑ/*

The /ɑ/ of *shah* and *father* is a low back or low back central sound. The description of the checked /ɑ/ can be repeated here, for the sounds do not contrast for most speakers of American English, except perhaps in length. Free /ɑ/ tends to be long or diphthongal; checked /ɑ/, short. This sound is made with the tongue muscle almost completely flat and slightly retracted. The tongue is farther back than for the eastern New England /a/ of *car*, and it is lower and more to the front than is the /ɒ/ of *hot* heard in the same region. The mouth is open.

The /ɑ/ is the final sound in words like *pa* and *shah* for all speakers throughout the country. It is the sound used in such pre-/r/ words as *car* and *garden*, as well as in such words as *calm* and *psalm*. There are comparatively few words in the language in which free /ɑ/ is common. The /ɑ/ is more commonly heard in checked syllables. Checked /ɑ/ was discussed in Chapter 10, and you should refer back to that section for a full review of this sound.

The /ɑ/, with lengthened and centralized forms [ɑ:,ɑ°, ɑə] is the normal checked sound for such words as *calm* and *psalm*. It appears as a free vowel in *pa* and *ma* and, in the "r-less" regions of the East, in *car* and *garden*. In the remainder of the country, it is followed by post-vocalic /r/ [kɑr, gɑrdn̩]. This sound varies from a lower front [a] through a low central [ɑ˕] heard in eastern New England in *car* and *heart* to a more retracted sound varying from /ɑ/ to /ɒ/ heard in metropolitan New York, Maryland, Virginia, South Carolina, and Georgia. Contrasts are made in "r-less" areas between *hard* and *hod*, both with /ɑ/, but with the first long or diphthongal, the second shorter and monophthongal.

The /ɑ/ as a checked sound in the "ask words" and in such words as *hot* and *horrible* has been discussed earlier (see Chapter 11). Note that many free /ɑ/ words are borrowed from other languages.

Open syllables	Before /r/	Checked /ɑ/	Free /ɑ/ in closed syllables
pa	part	pot	calm
sonata	market	mocking	Kant
hurrah	farther	clod	palmistry
father	martyr	mop	mirage
Shah	shark	bomb	camouflage

D. *The /ɔ, ɑ, and ʌ/ in Similar Environments*

Medial /ɔ/	Medial checked /ɑ/	Medial checked /ʌ/
taller	collar	cruller
lawn	Lonnie	lunch
bawdy	body	budding
sawed	sod	suds
wrought	tonsure	puddle

Practice : Here are sentences with free vowels /ɔ/ and /ɑ/ for transcription and listening practice.

Paul saw them talking across the street. The hockey players stored their hockey sticks in a cart in the barn. The horse-drawn cart stood athwart a puddle on the lawn. Palmetto bugs and palm trees are part of the Florida scene. The small boys played ball, calling to each other in raucous voices. The law sought fairness for all. Saul's car hit the wrought-iron fence at the edge of the garden, near the reservoir. It took the two partners to subdue the carp. It was nice to know he would be able to see Chagall's paintings, read Kant and Čapek, and listen to Brahms and Scarlatti when he visited that city. Carmen shopped in the market, while her father carried Arthur in his arms. The sharks held their party in Sanchez's house. They saw the hawk withdraw as the animal gnawed the bonds loose. It was a heartening sight when the travelers, in their scarlet tunics, docked at Le Havre.

Listen to a reading of the following selection, and note all the words with free vowels. Make a list of these words, and transcribe them as you say them. Note the special variations in these vowels compared with the pronunciations used by your friends. Make a second list of the words containing checked vowels. Transcribe them too.

Confucius said, "There are three friendships which are advantageous, and three which are injurious. Friendship with the upright; friendship with the sincere; and friendship with the man of much observation:—these are advantageous. Friendship with the man of specious airs; friendship with the insinuatingly soft; and friendship with the glib-tongues:—these are injurious.

"There are three things men find enjoyment in which are advantageous, and three things they find enjoyment in which are injurious. To find enjoyment in the discriminating study of ceremonies and music; to find enjoyment in speaking of the goodness of others; to find enjoyment in having many worthy friends:—these are advantageous. To find enjoyment in extravagant pleasures; to find enjoyment in idleness and sauntering; to find enjoyment in the pleasures of feasting:—these are injurious.

"There are three errors to which they who stand in the presence of a man of virtue and station are liable. They may speak when it does not come to them to speak;—this is called rashness. They may not speak when it comes to them to speak;—this is called concealment. They may speak without looking at the countenance of their superior;—this is called blindness.

"There are three things which the superior man guards against. In youth, when the physical powers are not yet settled, he guards against lust. When he is strong, and the physical powers are full of vigor, he guards against quarrelsomeness. When he is old, and the animal powers are decayed, he guards against covetousness.

"There are three things of which the superior man stands in awe. He stands in awe of the ordinances of heaven. He stands in awe of great men. He stands in awe of the words of sages. The inferior man does not know the ordinances of heaven, and consequently does not stand in awe of them. He is disrespectful to great men. He makes sport of the words of sages."

Book **XVI**, *Analects of Confucius*

chapter 13 *The Regularly Diphthongal Free Vowels*

13.1. The Diphthongs Compared

The three remaining free vowels have been identified in the preceding chapter. They appear in the words *buy, bough,* and *boy,* and they are, for almost all speakers of American English, regularly complex sounds. Like all such complex sounds, they are blends of sounds with different initiating and culminating articulatory positions.

All three sounds upglide, moving from low initiating positions of the tongue to higher positions of the tongue; all three shift from stressed to unstressed sounds, as is common with most such diphthongs (except [ɪi, ij, ʊu] for example). They are always long sounds and demonstrate greater duration in the following cases: in final positions before pauses than when not, before voiced consonants than before voiceless ones, before nasals plus voiced consonants than before nasals plus voiceless consonants, in final positions or before final consonants of closed syllables than before unstressed syllables.

Practice: In the following examples, these sounds are shown in the different contexts mentioned before. Say each word aloud, listen, and transcribe.

IN SIMILAR PHONETIC ENVIRONMENTS

sow—sigh—soy   owl—aisle—oil
bow—buy—boy   power—pies—poise
cow—kite—coy   trowel—thrice—destroys

gown—guy—goiter
tower—tie—toy
jowl—Giles—joy
prow—pry—Roy
lounge—lime—loin

Raoul—rile—broil
cowl—Keily—coil
count—kind—coin
jounce—gyrate—joist
louse—lice—cloister

BEFORE VOICELESS AND VOICED CONSONANTS

out—crowd
mouth (n.)—mouth (v.)
oust—browse
house (n.)—house (v.)
lout—loud
scout—cowed
route—shroud
quoit—destroyed
foist—toys
Joyce—joys

light—lied
ice—eyes
rice—rise
thrice—tries
life—live (adj.)
strife—strive
tripe—tribe
knifes (v.)—knives (n.)
white—wide
oyster—noise

BEFORE NASALS PLUS OTHER CONSONANTS

pint—find
bounce—bounds
ounce—lounge
pounce—pounds

fount—found
mount—mound
count—crowned
anoints—loins

WHEN FINAL OR BEFORE FINAL CONSONANTS

Here is a comparison between the sounds when final or before the final consonants of closed syllables and appearances before unstressed syllables.

[aɪ]	[aʊ]	[ɔɪ]
pry—prying	how—tower	soy—Sawyer
fright—frightened	bound—bounded	toy—foyer
side—sidling	round—roundabout	annoy—annoying
sprite—sprightly	plow—plowing	joy—lawyer
light—lightly	down—downy	cloy—cloying
sign—sighing	grouse—roustabout	joys—boisterous

13.2. The /aɪ/ and Common Variants

A number of common allophonic variants of this diphthong appear in American English. There are, however, two principal members of this phoneme: [aɪ] and [ɑɪ]. The variation appears in the first element of this complex sound, from the low front /a/ of the eastern New England *car* to the low central checked /ɑ/ of *stop* or the free /ɑ/ of *ah*.

To the four variants of the initial element of this diphthong that appear in American English must be added the nature of the unsyllabic offglide, which may in turn vary from upgliding /ɪ,i/ to upgliding and centralizing /ɪ,ə/. The relative prominence of the upglide (or inglide) also varies, as does the length of the initial element. These variations are only briefly noted here; for a detailed explanation, check the phonetic texts and dialect *Atlas* sources noted previously (Chapter 1, footnote 10; Chapter 10, footnote 5).

The diphthong with a low front initation is common throughout the country, with [aɪ], [aɪ], and [a·ɪ] the most common forms. The [ɑɪ] and [ɑɪ] are heard in metropolitan New York, in the East and South along the coast to Florida, and through much of the Midwest and West as common variants. The low central beginning [ɑɪ,ɑɪ,ɑ·ɪ] is in free variation with [aɪ,aɪ,a·ɪ]. Excessive backing of the beginning vowel to [ɒɪ,ɒ·ɪ] is uncommon in educated speech.

A centralizing diphthong ending in [ə] ([a·ə] or [ɑ·ə]) before voiced consonants is common to some southern areas. *Night* and *nine* thus differ there not only in the quality of the vowel but also in the duration. This same "slower" sound does appear throughout the country for the word *I* in such expressions as "I'll try" and "I'm coming," in which the pronoun is pronounced [a·ɪ,ɑ·ɪ,a·ɪ,ɑ·ɪ] or [a·ə,ɑ·ə].

Practice : Comparisons of this diphthong in different phonetic contexts are shown in the following lists. Repeat the sounds in these words, and transcribe your pronunciations.

IN INITIAL POSITIONS

I	idea	iota
eye	island	iodine
eyeful	iambic	Islip
isolate	iceboat	isle

I'm	ice cream	isinglass
I'll	idyl	Isaac
irate	iconoclast	ivy

IN FINAL POSITIONS OF SYLLABLES

sigh	my	primarily
try	cry	finally
comply	July	silent
reply	lie	prying
high	belie	lyceum
buy	sky	highest
imply	migraine	trying

BEFORE VOICELESS AND VOICED CONSONANTS

ice—eyes	snipe—tribe
nice—tries	rice—rise
lice—lies	fright—fried
Christ—cried	blight—blind
bite—bide	pint—pined
night—snide	spice—spies
like—slide	light—lied

IN INITIAL, MEDIAL, AND FINAL SYLLABLES

lying	presiding	allied
finer	environment	baptize
slyly	Oneida	suffice
writhing	politely	notified
whining	decisive	confide
mighty	concisely	deride

Two major variants of /aɪ/ before /r/ appear in American English: One is the diphthongal form with a lowered and retracted initial vowel [aɪ ~ ɑɪ]; the other is the reduction of the diphthongal vowel into a monophthong [a ~ ɑ]. A third variant, substituting [ɔ] for [aɪ], seems unique to one area of the East, southern New Jersey and the peninsula of Delaware, Maryland, and Virginia. In this variation, the words *far*, *fire*, and *for* are all pronounced as monosyllabic [fɔɚ]. Most speakers throughout the country use the [aɪ] form for this sound before /r/, with occasional [ɑɪr] for [aɪr].

When postvocalic /r/ is lost (as in eastern New England, metropolitan New York, and the South), two forms occur:

1. A disyllabic [aɪ-ə] appears for such words as *tire* and *fired* [taɪ-ə; faɪ-əd]. (These words remain monosyllabic where postvocalic /r/ is retained.)

2. In those sections of the South where /aɪ/ becomes a centralizing diphthong [aˑ°], these words are monosyllabic [taˑ°] and [faˑ°d].

In the following list, /aɪ/ before /r/ is compared with similar sounds in similar environments.

fire	four	far	forest
tire	tore	tar	torrid
spire	spore	spar	porridge
mire	more	marring	Morris
pliers	lore	larva	lorry

Practice: Here are phrases and sentences with /aɪ/ and /aɪr/ forms for listening and transcription.

My good friends tried to replace the tire for me. Five men reported they were hired yesterday, after the fire. His wife, attired in a tiger-skin coat, was an attractive sight. Next time he would remember to take both the iodine and the quinine. The white jet was a high-flying plane. He drove nine miles during the night. They wired the entire house, despite the riotous party next door. Four of the five were baptized. Lyle denied the need to pry any further.

13.3. The /aʊ/ and Common Variants

There are two principal forms of the diphthongal vowel in words like *how*, *out*, and *sound*. These two forms are the [aʊ ~ ɑʊ] variants, the former perhaps the more common. Other variants of this diphthong are not uncommon in educated speech, and there are, of course, social variants too.

Although [aʊ ~ ɑʊ] forms are the more common in the northern part of the country, a more fronted form is common in the South [aʊ ~ æʊ]. It is longer or "slower," [aˑʊ, æˑʊ], especially when final or when preceding a voiced consonant. Although [æʊ] and [aʊ] both exist in the speech of educated southerners, the [æʊ] elsewhere is associated with rustic or less-educated speech.

This diphthong, with a centralized beginning vowel variously transcribed as [əʊ, ʌʊ, ɜʊ], is regular before voiceless consonants in parts of Virginia and Maryland, as well as in South Carolina and Georgia. In these areas, *house* and *hound* have different diphthongs. The [əʊ ~ ɜʊ] form is a relic in certain other parts of the country. It is heard sporadically, for example, in coastal Maine, upstate New York, and upper Michigan.

The diphthong is normally longer in the South (except for those places using [əu ~ ɜu] forms) than elsewhere [æ·u, a·u, ɑ·u].

Practice : In the following sections, transcribe your pronunciations, and note the variants you use.

IN INITIAL AND FINAL POSITIONS

owl	now
ounce	cow
outcome	plow
hour	highbrow
outrage	allow

BEFORE VOICELESS AND VOICED CONSONANTS

devout	oust	noun	countenance
shout	without	crowd	account
house	outside	rouse	allowed
rout	outcome	down	aloud
doubt	snout	ounce	shroud
pout	holdout	bounce	cloud
drought	about	round	mountain
mouth	south	ground	counter
ouch	throughout	confound	soundly
grouse	shouting	espouse	pound

IN INITIAL, MEDIAL, AND FINAL SYLLABLES

owlish	encounter	around
sounding	allowance	allow
township	empower	surround
bounteous	redoubtable	impound
counsel	resounding	account
crouching	accounting	without
countenance	undoubtedly	espouse
cloudlike	announcer	renown
shouting	carousing	announce
powered	surrounded	carouse

BEFORE POSTVOCALIC /r/ AND /l/

When postvocalic /r/ is lost, disyllabic forms are common for such words as *flower* and *tower* [au-ə ~ ɑu-ə]. Elsewhere both monosyllabic and disyllabic forms exist side by side [flaʊ-ɚ ~ flaʊr]. Words like *sour* and *scour* remain monosyllabic.

Before final /l/, as in *towel* and *Powell*, an offglide [ᵊ] is not un-common. These words are either monosyllabic or disyllabic in ed-ucated speech [taʊ-əl ~ taʊᵊl ~ taʊl]. Words like *fowl* and *scowl* remain monosyllabic in educated speech [skaʊl ~ skaʊᵊl].

Here are some examples for listening and transcription practice:

sour	tower	scowl	towel
scour	flower	jowl	vowel
hour	empower	foul	scowled
flour	coward	fowl	afoul

In the following examples, /aʊ/ before /r/, /ɚ/ and /l/ is compared with similar sounds in similar environments.

tower—tire—tore   fowl—file—foal
shower—shire—shore   howl—aisle—whole
power—pyre—pore   hour—ire—oar
sour—sire—sore   flower—flyer—slower

Practice: Here are sentences with /aʊ/ forms for transcription and listening.

The powerful basketball team encountered little opposition. The guards impounded the money, their countenances glowering. No flowers were permitted on the bower. The announcer and accountant were fast friends. They allowed the foundling to sit on the ground for a full hour. The cows walked through the flowering fields, over the plowed ground and toward the mountain path.

13.4. The /ɔɪ/ and Common Variants

Three common variants of /ɔɪ/ appear: [ɔɪ, ɒɪ, oɪ]. 1. The most common form [ɔɪ] is regular throughout the country; its initial element is the rounded [ɔ] or [ɔ·]. 2. A less rounded and lowered initial sound [ɒɪ] is heard in western Pennsylvania and in the speech of those New Englanders and residents of metropolitan New York who use the [ɒ] sound for the "short *o*" in *hot* and *stop*. For these speakers [ɒɪ] is the regular form. 3. The [oɪ] or [o·ɪ], the third common variant, is heard in Maryland, Delaware, South Carolina, and adjacent areas and predominates in certain areas over the regular [ɔɪ]. [ɔɪ], with occasion-al variant [ɒɪ], is regular throughout the middle and far West.

A monophthongal [ɔ·] or centralizing [ɔ·ᵊ] is heard in the South, so that *boil* and *ball*, *oil* and *all*, *coil* and *call* are homophones there.

Diphthongal variants [ɔɪ, ɔɨ, oɪ, oɨ] are longer forms in the South [ɔ·ɪ, ɔ·ɨ] than in the rest of the country.

IN INITIAL, MEDIAL, AND FINAL SYLLABLES

oyster	annoyance	annoy
oil	rejoicing	enjoy
boiling	deploying	enjoin
toiler	recoiling	embroil
coilspring	embroider	rejoice
cloister	enjoyable	decoy
royalty	avoidance	avoid

COMPARED WITH OTHER VOWELS IN SIMILAR ENVIRONMENTS

boil	ball	bile	bowel
foils	falls	files	fouls
doily	dawdle	dilate	Dowling
choice	jaws	chime	joust
ploy	law	lie	plow
lawyer	claw	liar	glower
poison	paws	pies	spouse
Floyd	flows	flies	flower

Practice : Here are sentences for listening and transcription.

She saw Floyd fall. The lawyer recalled Saul's lawful behavior. The diners rejoiced at the oyster bar. All the oil was boiled while the royal pair watched. The annoying boys coined an expression known only to those loyal to the group.

Read the following stanzas aloud, and note the free vowels, including the regularly diphthongal forms. Transcribe both stanzas, and underline all words with free vowels. Note especially your pronunciation of any variant forms of these vowels.

> I weep for Adonais—he is dead
> O, weep for Adonais! though our tears
> Thaw not the frost which binds so dear a head!
> And thou, sad Hour, selected from all years
> To mourn our loss, rouse thy obscure compeers,
> And teach them thine own sorrow, say: 'With me
> Died Adonais; till the Future dares
> Forget the Past, his fate and fame shall be
> An echo and a light unto eternity!'

Where wert thou, mighty Mother, when he lay,
When thy Son lay, pierced by the shaft which flies
In darkness? where was lorn* Urania
When Adonais died? With veilèd eyes,
'Mid listening echoes, in her Paradise
She sate, while one with soft enamoured breath,
Rekindled all the fading melodies,
With which, like flowers that mock the corse† beneath,
He had adorned and hid the coming bulk of Death.

"Adonais"
—Percy Bysshe Shelley

* Archaic for *forlorn.*
† Archaic for *corpse.*

chapter 14 *The Unstressed Vowels*

ALL THE VOWELS covered so far appear in stressed syllables and in syllables of weaker stress. The stressed /i/ of *be* thus appears in the weak stressed initial syllable of *meander*; the primarily stressed /æ/ of *lack* in the phrase "Whàt do you láck?" appears with intermediate stress in "He làcks good sénse" or "The Làckawànna Ráilroàd. . . ." The first two syllables of *Montgomery* contain two differently stressed /ɑ/ sounds; the first syllable of *uninteresting* is a shorter and less stressed version of the strongly stressed /ʌ/ of *under* or *funny*; the /u/ of *Plúto* is spoken with intermediate stress in *plùtónium* or in one common pronunciation of *into* [íntù].

14.1. Stress

Changes in stress are generally noted in at least one of three ways and usually in combination. As greater stress is placed on a syllable, the syllabic is spoken with increased duration or with a change of pitch. As stress is decreased, the syllabic tends to be shorter in duration, lower in pitch. Usually fully stressed syllables are louder than are less stressed syllables, and weakly stressed syllables are spoken with less intensity. Perhaps decreased or increased intensity is less important than the other two factors of pitch and duration. And as we move to syllables with weakest stress, we normally tend to speak them with the least duration and the lowest pitch and loudness.

Finally, as syllables lose stress, the degree of muscle tension also decreases. Normally tense vowels /i/, /e/, /o/, and /u/ are quite lax in the last syllables of such words as *readied*, *Tuesday*, *tomorrow*, and *into*.

210

14.2. Comparisons

All the vowels discussed so far have their weak forms in the same contexts as the stressed forms. Thus free vowels, when weakly stressed, appear in weakly stressed free or checked syllables. The /i/, /u/, /e/, /o/, and /ɔ/ do appear in syllables of weak stress, and like their stressed counterparts, they appear in both free and checked syllables. These points may be noted in the following word lists, in which free fully stressed vowels are compared with free weakly stressed vowels and in which fully stressed checked vowels are compared with less stressed or weakly stressed checked vowels. Weakly stressed free /ɑ/ is uncommon in English.

Free vowels in open syllables	*Free vowels in closed syllables*	*Free vowels in weakly stressed open syllables*	*Free vowels in weakly stressed closed syllables*
see	sees	Rosie	Rosie's
be	deed	candy	candied
day	daze	Monday*	Mondays*
sue	sued	issue	issues
too	tooth	value	valued
fir	third	cover	covered
cur	curse	burner	burners
awe	awed	inaudibility	alternative†

* These words perhaps more commonly have unstressed final /i/.
† A weakly stressed /ɔ/ is uncommon in closed syllables.

Checked vowels in fully stressed syllables	*Checked vowels in syllables of intermediate or weak stress*
did	candid
ridges	sausage
sister	houses
thin	something
kingly	walking
resist	taxes
full	awful
nonsense	Montezuma
solve	solvability
concert	gondolier
cup	hiccough
under	unattached

When spoken with weak stress, the two high free vowels /i/ and /u/ resemble the lowered forms /ɪ/ and /ʊ/. The last syllables of *ready* and *into* do possess variants with /ɪ/ and /ʊ/, although for most speakers they are closer to /i/ and /u/. (Comparisons of *taxis* with *taxes*, *readied* with *candid*, *posies* with *poses*, *theses* with *thesis* demonstrate this distinction.)

14.3. The Unstressed /ə/

The unstressed syllables of *sofa*, *among*, and *felony* possess the same sound in all regional dialects of American English. The free vowel /ə/ is a mid central vowel, spoken with the lips in neutral position. It is always short, lax, and unstressed. It may vary with the tongue position, approaching /ɪ/, /ɨ/, or /ʊ/, and some speakers use these sounds in place of /ə/. The words *comical*, *children*, *suppose*, for example, may be spoken [kɑmɪkəl, tʃɪldrən, sʊpoʊz] by some and [kɑməkəl, tʃɪldrɪn, səpoʊz] by others.

The /ə/ is closest in tongue position to the central vowel /ʌ/ of *but*, but it is usually somewhat higher and more to the front. It is considered by some an unstressed /ʌ/, but /ʌ/ never appears in open syllables, whereas /ə/ does. It is commonly separated phonemically from /ʌ/ as a separate vowel though always unstressed.

The /ə/ appears only in syllables of weakest stress, in what may be called "unstressed syllables." It is never long, even partially so, and of course it has no diphthongal variants.

The /ə/ also appears as the final vowel of *cover* and *under* in those Atlantic coastal areas of the country where postvocalic /r/ is lost. Where /r/ is retained, an unstressed [ɚ] appears.

In the following lists, /ə/ is compared with other vowels in weakly and less stressed syllables.

Practice: Check your own pronunciations of the words in these comparison lists. Which sounds do you use? Transcribe.

In initial syllables		*Other sounds*	
among	magenta	create	eradicate
around	medallion	creation	extenuate
alone	monopoly	erupt	exhaust
away	annoy	detail	record (v.)
appoint	admire	research	prepare
adopt	achieve	deny	predominance

In initial syllables

address (v.)	acclaim
analysis	accomplish
macadam	potato

Other sounds

elastic	vicissitude
disabled	Sumerian
illusion	notation

In medial syllables

general	degradation
genesis	microphone
Medici	national
despotism	philosophic
alabaster	stenographer
limousine	attainable
passable	lamentation
nitrogen	metamorphosis
viaduct	abolition
salamander	cataract
legendary	parable
excellent	laudable

Other sounds

lubricant	Livia
Louisiana	silicate
merriment	simian
copybook	sociology
copycat	architectural
cultivator	animosity
absurdity	curiosity
charmingly	emigration
Tennyson	assimilation
oxygen	appreciate
predicate	pancreas
capillary	impious

In final syllables

Cuba	candor*
sofa	ardor*
Russia	wander*
comma	actor*
toga	record (n.)*
Eva	copper*
data	color*
Ithaca	baker*
geisha	Robert*
Lukas	liver*
mammoth	butcher*
Monmouth	lizard*

Other sounds

scented	candid
fishes	comedies
taxes	taxis
thesis	Rosie's
basis	monkey
comic	minute
wanted	gasket
relic	savage
bonded	walking
candied	laughing

*For "r=less" speakers.

14.4. The Unstressed /i, ɪ, ə/ in Contexts

Practice: Investigate your pronunciation of the unstressed syllables in the following lists, noticing which forms you use as you transcribe. Compare your pronunciations with those listed in a recent authoritative dictionary and with those used by your peers from different regional areas of the country.

Initial checked vowels

illuminate	ignoble		
imagine	illiberal		
impress	illogical		
important	indicative		
inconvenient	inferior		
Ignatius	inspire		

Initial free vowels

eliminate	behave
eject	believe
elation	detach
Elaine	regret
Elizabeth	remain
begonia	result

Final checked vowels

wanton	slogan
bucket	lengthen
careless	April
towel	monkeys
awful	candid
wicked	candies
mountain	roses
wicket	taxis
pocket	oases
mention	ration
causes	portion
lemon	savage
picket	tubful

Final free vowels

Tony	Anna
China	Emma
sofa	comma
candy	Nova Scotia
monkey	rusty
ferry	story
fairy	heavy
idea	Indonesia
Asia	opera
era	father
Russia	mother
drama	wonder
data	manner

A. *The /ɪ, ə/ Variants in Initial Syllables*

The /ɪ/ is the common colloquial form, with variant /ə/, whereas /ɛ/ is used in more formal discourse for the initial checked, unstressed syllables of the words containing the prefix *ex–*.

Practice: Transcribe your pronunciation. Do you use the same forms when these words are in context?

exact	except	existence	exert
exacting	exceptional	explain	exonerate
exacerbate	excessive	explicit	expand
exaggerate	excursion	extensive	expect
exalt	excuse	extrapolate	expensive
example	executive	extravagant	experience

B. *The /i, ɪ, ə/ Compared in Medial Syllables*

These sounds may all be heard in the medial, unstressed syllables of certain polysyllabic words.

Practice: Transcribe your own pronunciations.

deify	cilia	meteor
activity	policy	probable
evident	specify	article
comical	critical	opposite
happiness	stultify	examination
imitate	typical	mystical
evidence	magnify	animate
notification	represent	Lidice
bellicose	atrocity	impediment
beautiful	recognition	sincerity
hypocrisy	amicable	erroneous
supposition	antiquity	odious

c. *The /ə/ in Medial Closed Syllables*

The /ə/ is the common form for the unstressed vowels of medial closed syllables. The /ɪ/ is the common vowel, however, for medial orthographic *i*.

Normally medial /ə/		*Normally medial /ɪ/*	
balancing	gentlemanly	Washington	Englishman
commonly	niggardly	Farmingdale	punishment
womanly	open-handed	Nottingham	establishment
husbandry	Onondaga	limitless	offensively
loathsomely	piquancy	sophistry	harbinger
fealty	pigeon-toed	mimicry	Provincetown

Practice: Here are sentences with certain unstressed syllables italicized for identification of the vowels used. Practice reading them aloud. Compare your usages with those of your friends. Transcribe these sentences.

Whenev*er* the oth*er* wom*en* walked by, she hurr*ied* t*o* h*er* house. No comm*on* pe*o*ple *were* *per*mit*ted* t*o* ent*er* th*e* king's pres*ence*. Golf play*ers* contin*ually* prac*tice* put*ting*. *The* Congress re*ferred* th*e* bill t*o* one *of* its committees. *The* Prime Mini*ster* con*vened* th*e* Parli*ament* in ord*er* t*o* con*sider* his *suggestions for* levying new tax*es*. New bud*get* requests *were* *pre*pared *for the* President's *per*usal prior t*o* th*e* pre*paration* of his State *of the* Un*ion* mess*age*. A not*orious* crim*inal* man*aged* t*o* el*ude* th*e* *po*lice by chang*ing* his *ad*dress, face, *employ*ment, and habits *un*til his best friend *in*formed the authorities.

Read the following selection, and note all the unstressed forms. Do your friends use the same unstressed forms that you do? Transcribe all words containing unstressed forms.

Thou think'st 'tis much that this contentious storm
Invades us to the skin; so 'tis to thee,
But where the greater malady is fix'd,
The lesser is scarcely felt. Thou'dst shun a bear;
But if thy flight lay toward the roaring sea,
Thou'dst meet the bear i' th' mouth. When the
     mind's free
The body's delicate; the tempest in my mind
Doth from my senses take all feeling else
Save what beats there—Filial ingratitude!
Is it not as this mouth should tear this hand
For lifting foods to't? But I will punish home.
No, I will weep no more. In such a night
To shut me out! Pour on; I will endure.
In such a night as this! O Regan, Goneril!
Your old kind father, whose frank heart gave all,—
O, that way madness lies; let me shun that;
No more of that.

                    Act III, Scene IV, *King Lear*
                    —William Shakespeare

part five | **the voice**

chapter **15** *Pitch*

THERE ARE four dimensions of sound that we can perceive: pitch, loudness, quality, and duration. When we voluntarily modify any one of the factors that produce vocal sounds, we frequently make involuntary changes in the three remaining dimensions, and we always change the total configuration of the sound. In this chapter, we shall deal with pitch.

15.1. Pitch and Frequency

The pitch of a voice is our interpretation of the number of times the vocal folds rise and fall in a second. The actual rate of vibration of the vocal folds is its frequency. Physicists can analyze the fundamental frequency of a sound and give it a precise label. Furthermore, they can produce any frequency they wish in the laboratory with an instrument called an "audio-oscillator." The frequencies that we can interpret range from vibrations as slow as 16 cps (cycles per second) to those as fast as 20,000 cps. Sounds above or below these limits cannot be heard by the human ear and therefore do not have the dimension of pitch. The slow sounds are low pitched and the rapid sounds high pitched. And here is where the ambiguity begins.

A. *When Low Is High*

The terms "low" and "high" are meaningful only in relation to fixed referents. But as we usually use them without specifying our referents, we do not always convey what we mean. In Figure 15.1(a), you see a continuum of all the sound frequencies that can stimulate

219

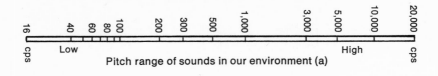

Pitch range of sounds in our environment (a)

Range of frequencies of speech sounds – voice, vowels and consonants (b)

65 — 312
Low — High

Pitch range of fundamental frequency of a Low Male Voice (c)

85 — 392
Low — High

Pitch range of fundamental frequency of a High Male Voice (d)

120 — 590
Low — High

Pitch range of fundamental frequency of a Low Female Voice (e)

160 — 792
Low — High

Pitch range of fundamental frequency of a High Female Voice (f)

220 — 520
Low — High

Pitch range of fundamental frequency of voices of 8-year-old Boys and Girls (g)

Figure 15.1. Diagram of Frequency of Vibration of Sound Source to Demonstrate Comparative Pitch Ranges.

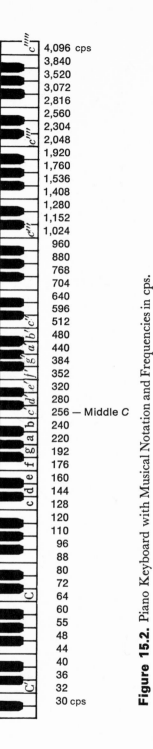

4,096 cps	
3,840	
3,520	
3,072	
2,816	
2,560	
2,304	
2,048	
1,920	
1,760	
1,536	
1,408	
1,280	
1,152	
1,024	
960	
880	
768	
704	
640	
596	
512	
480	
440	
384	
352	
320	
280	
256	— Middle C
240	
220	
192	
176	
160	
144	
128	
120	
110	
96	
88	
80	
72	
64	
60	
55	
48	
44	
40	
36	
32	
30 cps	

Figure 15.2. Piano Keyboard with Musical Notation and Frequencies in cps.

the human ear. In Figure 15.1(b), you see a portion, the low-frequency region, which represents the sounds that encompass speech. On this continuum 3,000 cps is in the category of high, and 300 cps is in the category of low. In Figure 15.1 (c, d, e, and f) the range of pitch of four speaking voices (exclusive of falsetto) that were used in a study on vocal-pitch levels is shown.[1] Note that the high male voice comprises a lower range of frequencies than does the low female voice. Note further that the 300-cycle sound, which is considered low in terms of the total range of audible sound, is close to the highest limit of the low male voice.

It is clear, then, that the terms "high" and "low" are meaningless except as comparatives; and, because we ordinarily use them grammatically as incomplete comparatives, the absence of precise information is obvious. If we had machines that could count the vibrations emanating from vibrating bodies, we could solve the problem by using numbers to identify pitch. We do not have access to such machines outside laboratories, so we must rely on a scale that is only approximate—one that is not absolutely accurate but is close enough for our purposes.

[1] Harry Hollien, "Vocal Fold Thickness and Fundamental Frequency of Phonation," *Journal of Speech and Hearing Research*, 5 (September 1962), 238.

B. *Musical Notation*

To illustrate these concepts, it is useful to conduct a simple demonstration. Use the musical notes of a piano, a pitch pipe, a cello, or whatever musical instrument you have. Assign a number to each note in the scale. Remember that the frequencies of any two identical notes struck on different pianos not similarly tuned will present different numbers of vibrations and will therefore sound different. Figure 15.2 shows the notes of the musical scale, their frequencies, and the intervals between them.

As the human voice does not usually go below 65 cps or higher than 1,300 cps, this chapter deals with pitch between these limits. Two factors are of concern: what the human voice produces and what the human ear perceives. We can voice a greater number of intervals between pitches than can be played on any piano or other musical instrument. Although the scale in Figure 15.2 shows the interval between adjacent *b* and *c'* as that between 240 cps and 256 cps, the human voice can actually be produced at quite a few pitches between these two limits. The human ear can perceive as many as four other pitches between *b* and *c'*. With fine auditory discrimination, people can actually recognize sounds that are only 3 cps apart (below 1,000 cps). (Auditory discrimination is the controlling factor in pitch variation.) These two instruments, the larynx and the ear, make available numerous possibilities for vocal expression.

15.2. Factors Affecting Pitch

Each of us has a maximum range of pitch that he produces as vocal tone. The potential range is limited by the dimensions of the larynx, the structure located in the upper part of the neck. It takes a certain amount of practice for each of us to reach the highest and lowest notes within his range. But, what is more significant, we cannot produce clear laryngeal sounds above or below our pitch limits. It is thus necessary to find out what these limits are. See p. 229 for instructions.

A. *Loudness Limits and Pitch*

Occasionally, we wish to produce pitches at either end of the vocal compass, and it is reasonable to do so. But if called on to project our voices for a considerable period of time, we cannot afford to use just any part of the vocal range. We shall have to stay mostly in that area in which we can achieve maximum loudness with minimum energy. Just as there are anatomical limitations to the pitch range for each of us, so are there anatomical limitations to the loudness range of each voice. There is a minimum level of loudness below which we cannot go without converting to a whispered form of speech. There is also a maximum loudness that we cannot surpass by increasing the energy output. We shall discuss this point in detail in Chapter 16.

B. *Breath Pressure and Vocal Folds*

If one used the voice at either end of his pitch range at the maximum limits of loudness (the actual maximum is much less at the lowest pitch than at the highest) for an extended period, the chances are that he would eventually injure the vocal fold tissue. Unfortunately, he might suffer no pain to apprise him of the injury. A speaker is unlikely to cause organic changes in the mechanism if he uses the minimum limits of loudness at the extremes of pitch. He will probably not be easily heard and will be advised to "speak up" or to talk more loudly.

C. *Optimum Pitch*

"Optimum pitch" is the term used to designate the series of pitches within the total range of a speaker's voice that permits most effective use of the voice. In theory it calls for the production of a voice with maximum power and minimum effort. In actual practice we translate "maximum power" into "adequate loudness" and "minimum effort" into "absence of excess tensions" and "use of reasonable amounts of breath." There are a number of discernible pitches that satisfy these conditions. They are likely to be pitches in the middle of the lower half of the total pitch range. When the proper balance has been established between laryngeal tension and breath pressure and between breath pressure and vocal-tract shape, a clear, moderately loud voice of appropriate harmonic structure at a particular pitch is heard.[1a] The

---

[1a] Dr. Friedrich Brodnitz, an eminent laryngologist, decries the focus of attention on pitch in many programs of vocal reeducation—this in spite of the fact that he and most speech therapists agree with the concept of optimum pitch. Brodnitz' criticism is justified. His comments are applicable to those who forget that optimum pitch is dependent upon pitch-pressure-resonator relationships. For further discussion, see Friedrich S. Brodnitz, "The Holistic Study of the Voice," *Quarterly Journal of Speech*, XLVIII (October 1962), 280–84; Mildred F. Berry and Jon Eisenson, *The Defective in Speech* (New York: Appleton-Century-Crofts, Inc., 1956), p. 193; Giles W. Gray and Claude M. Wise, *The Bases of Speech* (New York: Harper and Row, 3rd edition, 1959), p. 52; Margaret C. L. Greene, *The Voice and its Disorders* (London: Pitman Medical Publishing Co., Ltd., 1957), p. 97; and Charles Van Riper and John V. Irwin, *Voice and Articulation* (Englewood Cliffs, N. J.: Prentice-Hall, Inc., 1958), p. 298.

ear of the trained listener is the instrument for the recognition of optimum pitch. The ear of the speaker is its monitor.

D. *Tension, Pressure, and Flow*

It is not difficult to recognize the functional interplay of events in activities less complicated than phonation. Consider the flow of water from a faucet. If you turn the handle to a given position, you can observe and measure the amount of water that flows out during a given period. Indeed, you have probably timed the process on many occasions in the past. You run the water for your bath and know just how long it takes to fill the tub, assuming, that is, that you always turn the handle the same distance and that all other factors are equal or similar to what they have been in the past. If too many other people in your household turn on other faucets at the precise moment you begin to run your bath, you may find that it takes longer to fill the tub than usual. If so, you may decide that time is essential and be willing to take your bath with less than your usual quota of water, or you may turn the handle farther to allow for an increased flow. Your balance between the turn of the faucet and the time it takes to fill the tub is interfered with as soon as the pressure is diverted to serve additional outlets.

If you think now of your voice as a flow of air from your lungs and of your mouth and nose as two possible outlets for that air, you can make an analogy to the water flowing into the tub. With only one vocal outlet, most of the pressure that is exerted when the air is first forced out of the lungs will continue to move vigorously either through the mouth or the nose. When you allow the air to emerge through the mouth and nose simultaneously, however, you diminish the rate of flow because you add another outlet for the pressure and thereby diminish its power.

E. *Breath Pressure and Pitch*

There are languages—French, for example—for which this condition is customary. For the French vowels /ã/ and /ɔ̃/, the desired qualitative effect is nasal. English vowel sounds are not expected to be nasalized. But should they be produced in that manner and should you wish to utter them with as much intensity as you utter oral vowels, you will have to "turn on the tap" a bit more or call for more breath pressure. As soon as you increase the pressure, you affect the pitch of your voice unless you alter the degree of tension in the pitch-producing mechanism itself. Later, we shall explain this point in detail.

F. *Breath Pressure and Quality*

If you have a nasal voice, you have to use more breath than for an oral voice in order to achieve a certain degree of sound pressure level. Without a change of breath pressure, the nasal voice is exceedingly soft—the diversion of the breath stream is similar to what causes the trickle of water when all the faucets are turned on. Depending on what decisions you make about pressure, you will have either a very soft nasal voice—almost inaudible— or a nasal voice that is loud and shrill. The latter type of nasality is always higher pitched than is the soft nasal voice.

G. *Pitch Changes in Speaking*

Although we are concerned only with the speaking voice, it may be well to remind you that the identical mechanisms or body structures are also used in singing. The mechanisms function similarly for both types of utterance. The only real difference involves timing.[2] When you sing you try to maintain a given note or pitch for the duration of the syllable and to change your pitch discretely, rather than continuously, as you move on to the next syllable. When you speak, you do not maintain one precise pitch throughout the syllable, even on uninflected or unstressed syllables. The changes in the rate of vibration may not always be recognized as pitch changes because of their subtlety, but on terminal syllables you are always aware of pitch glide. The constant movement of pitch throughout an utterance increases the difficulty you may have in developing pitch discrimination. In this chapter, we shall start with discrete pitch practice, and when we have sharpened our listening, we can proceed with continuous pitch practice.

15.3. Analysis of Habitual Pitch

As you recall, pitch is only one of four dimensions of sound. To make certain that we are all listening to the same aspect of sound, we shall keep pressure, quality, and duration constant as we alter the pitch. Consequently, our demonstrations will be simple, unlike the difficult, complex production of sound in connected speech. At this beginning stage, we recommend that you divorce your practice from the communication of ideas, so that you can concentrate on *how* you sound rather than on *what* you say.

[2] See again Chapter 4, "The Melody of English."

A. *The Time Factor*

In connected speech, a particular sound lasts for a short period of time. A long vowel sound like /ɔ/ or /ɑ/ in a stressed position continues perhaps for 0.2 sec., and most vowels that you utter last only 0.1 sec. or less each. As it is difficult to make critical judgments about events that have such brief exposures to your ear, you will prolong sounds for periods of time sufficient to enable you to study them with care. This method will allow you to check each aspect of the sound, to compare or contrast it with other sounds, and then to accept or reject it. Begin your practice by maintaining a sound for approximately ten times as long as you would normally.

When you prolong a sound at a single pitch level, the result resembles singing more than speaking. We shall use the word "intone" to mean a prolongation of the sound for at least one second, preferably two, with no appreciable changes in pitch, loudness, or quality for that particular tonal event.

B. *The Quality Factor*

In order to keep the qualitative aspects of the sound constant, it is necessary to fix the movable structures of the passageway through which the air travels after it has been modified by the action of the laryngeal constrictors. The structures that have to be held in position by voluntary action are the jaw, the tongue, the soft palate, and the lips.

CONTROL OF THE JAW

We shall start with the easiest exercise, which can be censored most accurately by your own eyes—the movement of your jaw. Open your mouth wide enough so that the distance between the edges of your upper and lower front teeth is approximately 3/4 in. Actually measure the opening with a ruler, and try to get a visual impression of the distance between the teeth. Hold the jaw in that fixed position for two or three seconds. You should be aware of certain feelings or tensions in different parts of your face. If you measure with a ruler first and then use your eyes to make comparative judgments, becoming aware at the same time of the jaw position through the muscle sensations of kinesthesia, you will eventually be able to assume this jaw position and to maintain it without relying on your eyes or the ruler. The feel of the positioning will guide you.

CONTROL OF THE TONGUE

To produce this first practice sound, keep your tongue quiet. Let it remain close to the resting position it has when the jaw is closed. Keep the tongue on the floor of the mouth cavity—its edges in contact with the bottom teeth, its top surface arched gently with no humps. Be sure not to retract the tongue, because when you pull it back, the throat passage (pharynx) is narrowed, and the quality of the sound will be affected by the restriction of the pharynx. Use your eyes to check the position of the tongue and your muscle sense to recognize the feel of its resting position.

CONTROL OF THE SOFT PALATE

The third structure you are to control is the movable portion of the roof of the mouth. Some of you will find this difficult, but it is essential for the acquisition of normal English voice quality. The goal is to close off the nasal passage at its commencement in the throat or oropharynx. If you cannot achieve a complete cut-off voluntarily at this time, take note of the fact, and remember that, when you achieve the desired movement, your voice quality will change again, and for the better.

If you observe the top of your mouth cavity, you will note that its back part resembles the architecture of a mansard roof—a gentle oblique slope of tissue from the horizontal line back toward a final steeper slope toward the vertical (see Figure 5.8). The bottom edge of the slope is scalloped rather than straight-edged. The scallop or pendulous portion is the uvula, which is an obvious landmark for you but in itself not so important as the area immediately above it. You can change the architecture of the roof of your mouth by decreasing the steepness of the slope and causing an extension of the horizontal plane, which is what we mean by "raise your soft palate."

You raise your soft palate, involuntarily, every time you swallow in order to prevent food or drink from going up into your nose. One way to raise the soft palate voluntarily is to yawn, inhaling air through your mouth only when it is wide open. Yawn, and watch the roof of your mouth flatten and lengthen. Observe the sensation you have in your throat and the back of your mouth as you watch your palate move up. Now try to move the palate similarly without inhaling any air. Compare what you see and feel now with what you saw and felt when you were yawning. Work for an upward movement and extension of the palate guided only by the feel of the muscles.

CONTROL OF THE LIPS

The lips are the last structures that must be maintained in fixed position to sustain one quality of sound. The specific posture of the lips can be readily assumed under the guidance of your eyes and can be maintained by your own muscle sense. Move your lips to form a circle approximately as large as that of a quarter. A lip aperture with the radius of a dime is not adequate for this exercise.

c. *Visual and Kinesthetic Control*

Some of you may be surprised that so far we have made no reference to a specific sound or to the ear, which is the usual guide to the control of voice quality. We have omitted the reference deliberately and in spite of the fact that one of the basic procedures in all voice training involves improvement in auditory discrimination. The omission has not been made without reason. Our habitual reliance on the ear as the selector of the pitch-loudness-quality characteristics of the sound to be produced results in a censorship device that often prevents us from attempting to make sounds that differ from what we are accustomed to producing. Our hearing insists that the response fit into a remembered pattern. Only by using visual and kinesthetic sensory discrimination to control what we do can we produce a whole series of new sounds without being restricted by our previous auditory habits. In other words, we are trying to develop a new stimulus-response pattern. Ultimately the ear will again be put in charge. As we mentioned earlier, the techniques proposed for vocal change are based on the assumption that you have normal hearing and that you have "a third ear" or listener to help you at the beginning of your practice—a listener who will help you reinforce the correct discriminations made after each vocal performance.

PHONATION OF SOUND

Now that you have some idea of how to shape the resonators, put your jaw, tongue, palate, and lips into the positions described, holding them as stationary as you can, and utter a sound. Maintain it for at least two seconds. We will designate the sound with the symbol ⵦ in order not to evoke your habitual phonemic responses (see Figure 15.3). Repeat the sound, and listen to it. What label do you wish to apply? Does the quality resemble any speech sound?

PITCH IDENTIFICATION

As soon as you can produce the sound at will, find out what the fundamental tone or pitch is. For identification of this pitch you will need to refer to a musical instrument, preferably a piano or, if that is not available, a pitch pipe.[3] Male students can use a pitch pipe that can produce sounds from middle C (*c′*) to the octave below (*c′* to *c*).

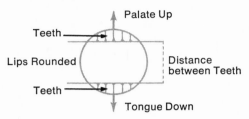

Figure 15.3. Symbol to Indicate Jaw, Tongue, Palate, and Lip Positions.

Women may need an additional pitch pipe that produces sounds in the octave above middle C (*c′* to *c″*). In other words, the frequencies produced should include rates of vibration from about 128 cps to 512 cps. To keep us from resorting to lengthy phrases each time we make an evaluation of frequency, we shall assign alphabetical and numerical labels to the pitches. The piano keyboard shown in Figure 15.2 gives you the necessary information.

To determine what pitch you are producing, intone ♀ and then strike the piano keys, one at a time, in an effort to match the pitch of the piano note to your voice. Keep in mind that the two sounds are qualitatively different. Starting with middle C (*c′*), keep changing the piano note until you find the best match. When you have located the pitch of the voice that you have been intoning, record its alphabetical and numerical designation.

Now reverse the process, striking the note you have recorded and intoning ♀ on that note.

15.4. Range of Pitch

Now that you are able to identify the pitch that you most frequently use (your habitual pitch), try to find out what your upper and lower pitch limits are. You will need the piano or a singer with a sense of "absolute" or "perfect" pitch to help you. Start to intone ♀ at the pitch you have recorded at a loudness level that will reach a listener no more than six feet away from you.

[3] Pitch pipes for the octave below *c′* and for the octave above are manufactured and distributed by Harold Lindner, 58 Warren Street, New York, N.Y. 10007.

A. *The Highest Pitch Limit*

Intone the next higher musical note and the next until you can go no higher. Keep the articulators fixed in the positions you start with. Check the lip and jaw openings by looking in a mirror or asking your listeners to tell you of any slackening of mouth posture. You may need to increase the amount of energy you use as you go up the scale. When you reach the topmost pitches, your voice will be falsetto. The mode of laryngeal production will then shift, and you will need an increased amount of breath pressure. Repeat the procedure several times until you and your listeners think that you have reached your highest pitch potential. Record this note.

B. *The Lowest Pitch Limit*

Then return to your habitual pitch, and repeat the exercise as you intone consecutively lower musical notes. Repeat this procedure until you reach your lowest pitch. You may have to diminish your breath pressure to reach the absolute bottom of your range. Do not expect the sound to be clear and richly resonant. It may sound gravelly or rasping. Repeat the intoning until you and your listeners are satisfied that you can go no lower. Record the note. In all likelihood your range will be at least 2 or 2 1/4 octaves. If it is less, you have probably not reached your upper or lower limit. Keep practicing until you have established your maximum range.

C. *The Optimum Pitch Range*

To find your optimum pitch range, which is not the same as your maximum range, intone ♯ on the lowest note you recorded, then intone successively higher notes. If you cannot follow the musical scale of the piano, do not be discouraged. Use the piano notes to judge the nearest pitch. When you are able to start at the very bottom of your pitch range, your optimum pitch will be at approximately the fourth, fifth, or sixth note above the one you start with. The decision as to which note is best should be made by your instructor with the help of others in the class who have good auditory discrimination. Record the note selected.

For example, if the lowest note that you can sound is G in the second octave below middle C, then the *c* below middle C may be your best pitch. This note should be the one you intone with the least amount of energy at a loud enough level to be heard easily. The ear of the expert listener is more significant than any formula for arriving at optimum pitch.

D. *Optimum Pitch and Pitch Contours*

When we refer to your optimum pitch, middle C (*c'*), for example, we do not mean that the fundamental tone exactly corresponds to the similar note on the piano, nor do we mean that you should always speak on this note. We do mean that much of your speech will be at a frequency near that of this note and that the frequency of this note will probably be the mode of your utterance. (The mode of the frequencies appearing in each syllable pronounced is the most often used frequency of the entire sequence of sounds). Obviously, if you are to speak with the intonation pattern of English, you will have to start many utterances above this note and finish them below it. In Chapter 4, the numbers 1, 2, and 3 were used to refer to different pitch levels. In the sentence "*What* are you doing?" with a 321 contour, you might say the first word at level 3, which could be *d'* or *d'♯* if the optimum pitch is *c'*. The next syllables would glide through *c'* on level 2. The last word would end on *b♭*, or might even go as low as *a* for level 1. The label "optimum" or "best" pitch, therefore, is not limited to a single tone but is an indication of the central tendency or midpoint, as well as of a number of pitch intervals above and below the midpoint.

The pitch intervals we use in speech are smaller than the intervals between the notes of our musical scale. We can produce as many as twenty different pitches in a pitch contour 321 within the range from *d'* to *a*. The piano can produce only six notes. In the same range an octave below, only eleven pitches can be spoken, although six notes are still available on the piano. With sufficient practice you will be able to recognize and discriminate fine differences in pitch.[4] At the very least you can improve your pitch discrimination, which is a learned function. Fine pitch discrimination is a prerequisite of skillful pitch production.

E. *Habitual Use of Optimum Pitch*

If your optimum pitch and your habitual pitch are the same, you will not need to make any changes in pitch level. In that event, we suggest that you omit the exercises that follow unless your voice lacks pitch flexibility.

---

[4] The pitch-discrimination test of the Seashore Measures of Musical Talents can be purchased from the Psychological Corporation, New York. It is a record of pairs of sounds that differ only in pitch. The listener is asked to judge whether one sound is higher or lower in pitch than is the other. Test scores have been standardized according to percentile ratings.

Practice : Use the piano or a pitch pipe to project the desired pitch sample. First produce the desired note. Then immediately try to match your vocal pitch to that note. Intone ⅄ . Your instructor and class will judge whether or not you have matched the note within a reasonable degree. The class is to respond by telling you to intone higher or lower or that you have succeeded in the match. Repeat the procedure until you can match correctly more than 50 per cent of the time.

When you can produce the match easily, you are ready to use your own judgment after each pair of sounds (sounds of pitch pipe and intoned voice) has been produced. When your judgments are fairly accurate, you are ready to practice on your own. It is worth mentioning here that, if you really wish to change your pitch level, you will have to spend time in daily practice. Half an hour twice a day would be ideal. Half an hour once a day would be the minimum practice time.

Now practice intoning sentences.

Practice : Sound your note (optimum pitch) on pipe. Then intone ⌗ on the pitch played. Next intone the sentence on a single pitch, each syllable for the same duration and at the same level of loudness. *Each* time you stop to replenish your breath, repeat the entire procedure: Play the note, intone ⌗ , then continue intoning the phrase. Within the breath group, there must be liason between all syllables. This practice gives us an opportunity to listen to one pitch with many different qualities. See Chapter 17 for a detailed explanation of qualitative changes in voice that are associated with vowel differences. Here is a sample sentence for optimum pitch c' :

"Now is the time for all good men to come to the aid of the party."

1. Inhale.
2. Play c'.
3. Intone ⌗ at c'.
4. Judge the pitch match between c' and intoned ⌗ .
5. When the pitch of voice is fairly close to c', intone ⌗

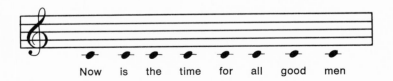

Inhale. Play c'. Intone ⌗ at c'. Judge the pitch match between c' and intoned ⌗ . When ⌗ is close to c', intone

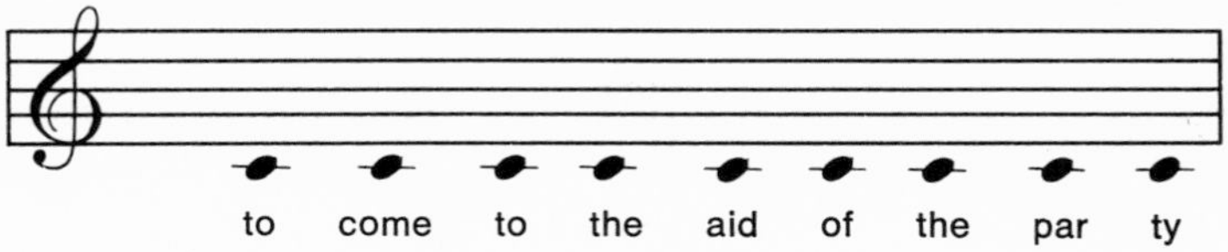
to come to the aid of the par ty

Judge the pitch match between each of the intoned syllables.

Practice Chart:

1. Inhale.
2. Play ———. (Insert your optimum pitch.)
3. Intone ϕ at ———. (Insert your optimum pitch.)
4. Judge the pitch match between 2 and 3.
5. When ϕ is close to the note played, intone a phrase. (Insert optimum pitch notes on clef.)

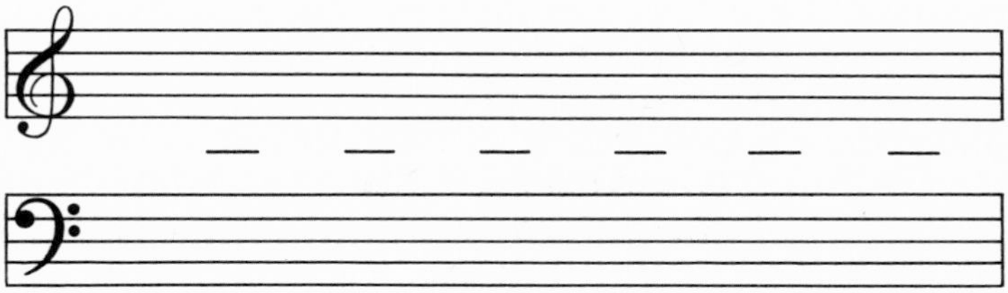

6. Judge the pitch match between ϕ and each syllable intoned after the phrase has been completed. Repeat these procedures until the sentence is completed.

If you cannot intone eight or more syllables in one breath group, stop whenever you need to, take another breath, and start the introductory procedures again. There is no need to say a particular number of syllables on one breath as we are not, in this exercise, concerned with the meaning. You can use any sentences you like for practice. When you try this exercise, you will discover that it takes practice to maintain a single pitch, an equal rate of duration for each syllable, and equal loudness. Repeat the same sentence until you are able to perform easily.

Where there is smoke you should look for ash. Time and tide wait for no woman. All is not fair in love and in war. A stitch in time may save embarrassment. Hitch your wagon to a satellite.

When you have practiced sufficiently, try to intone sentences in the same way, but intone a lower note for the last syllable.

Inhale. Play a note. Intone ♯. Intone all syllables except the last on the optimum pitch. Intone the last syllable on a pitch that is approximately one musical interval lower. Next, try to say each sentence with appropriate timing, stress, and pitch contours, following each exercise with final syllable lower than the optimum pitch guide.

Inhale. Play note. Intone ♯. Intone one phrase at the optimum note sounded. Intone the last syllable below the optimum note. Inhale. Say sentence.

Use the sample of the intoned speech as a reminder of pitch for initial utterance. Then say the sentence as you concentrate on meaning.

The final step is to read and speak at the optimum pitch level without the aid of the preliminary models. Let your listeners check your pitch level while you are reading and speaking.

Here are further sentences for practice.

Silence and tact may or may not be the same thing. . . .
All that is not pertinent in art is impertinent. . . .
I have seen thoughts and fancies playing upon people's faces like the wind upon young heather. . . .
A man should be just cultured enough to be able to look with suspicion upon culture at first, not second hand. . . .
Woe to the specialist who is not a pretty fair generalist and to the generalist who is not also a bit of a specialist. . . .
Man is the only animal that can remain on friendly terms with the victims he intends to eat until he eats them. . . .
Morality is the custom of one's country and the current feeling of one's peers. Cannibalism is moral in a cannibal country. . . .
There is a higher average of good cooking at Oxford and Cambridge than elsewhere. The dinners are better than the curriculum. But there is no chair of cookery; it is taught by apprenticeship in the kitchen. . . .
People are lucky and unlucky not according to what they get absolutely, but according to the rates between what they get and what they have been led to expect. . . .
Pain and pleasure are infectious. It depresses us to be much with those who have suffered long and are still suffering; it refreshes us to be with those who have suffered little and are enjoying themselves. But it is good for us to be depressed now and then.

From the writings of Samuel Butler

F. *Recognition of Pitch Level*

Now that your ear has grown accustomed to pitch designations, see whether or not you can judge the pitch levels of other speakers. A simple way to check yourself in practice is to listen to voices that have been recorded. Play a record as you match the note on the piano to that of the speaker. By now you will have developed ability to match pitch even when the pitch does not stay the same throughout the utterance. Fine discrimination and auditory memory make this matching possible. Your ear (and brain) will compute an average pitch (provided there are not too many wide fluctuations) as easily as a laboratory machine analyzes frequency. The result will be a more valid judgment of pitch than that of the machines, as machines can compute only frequency.

15.5. Pitch Level and Personality Estimate

Judge the average pitch of at least five speakers from their recordings. Use recordings only of people unknown to you. Indicate age, sex, and approximate size of each speaker. Compare your estimates with information about the speakers. You may be surprised at how far off your judgments are. The exercise may point up for you the fact that there is a wide distribution of appropriate pitch levels among people of the same age and sex. If each student in the class does this assignment for the same five students, you will realize too that the ability to discriminate pitch is not an evenly distributed skill. We remind you that the skill can be improved if you practice intelligently. If each student in the class, then, makes a judgment of five different speakers, you will have a large enough sample from which to draw some interesting conclusions.[5]

The population statistics of average pitch of various age levels and sex differences are based on extremely small samples. Although the finding may therefore be biased, they have set the stage for what many people expect a speaker to sound like. Wilbert Pronovost studied six male college students with superior voices and reported that they used an average pitch level comparable to *c* (132 cps). John Snidecor studied six female students with superior voices and reported that they used an average pitch level of *g* (212 cps). In an earlier study of six

[5] About thirty years ago a study of listeners' judgments of age, sex and occupation of speaker was made in England under the auspices of the British Broadcasting Company. The results were published in T. H. Pear, *Voice and Personality* (New York: John Wiley & Sons, Inc., 1931).

males who had a wide range of speaking ability, Lewis and Tiffin reported that the speaker whose voice was rated best used the highest average pitch level.[6] They concluded that, contrary to popular opinion, a high pitch level need not be a speech handicap.

We hope that your experience in class will provide you with sufficient evidence to recognize that it is more efficient for the user and more satisfactory to the listener when a speaker uses his optimum pitch. Neither masculinity nor femininity is transmitted through pitch. Quality is more likely to reveal some physical and physiological aspects of the speaker.

[6] Wilbert Pronovost, "An Experimental Study of the Habitual and Natural Pitch Levels of Superior Speakers," *Speech Monographs Research Annual*, 9 (1942), 111–23. John Snidecor, "Studies in the Pitch and Duration Characteristics of Superior Speakers," *Journal of Speech and Hearing Disorders*, 16 (1951), 44–53. Don Lewis and J. Tiffin, "A Psychophysical Study of Individual Differences in Speaking Ability," *Archives of Speech*, 1 (1934), 43–60.

chapter **16** *Loudness*

A SECOND DIMENSION of sound that we can perceive is loudness, the magnitude of the acoustic product. Loudness depends primarily on the intensity of the fundamental tone of the sound, which in turn is affected by the amount of force used to produce it. In speaking we achieve changes in loudness by applying different degrees of breath pressure to the vocal folds. When increased pressure is met by increased resistance at the vocal folds, the pitch of the voice is raised along with the loudness. In order to speak more loudly without raising the pitch, the speaker must be able to regulate the pitch mechanism to counterbalance the change in pressure. Shifts in loudness are easy for most speakers. The good speaker tries to modify loudness without always allowing an accompanying change of pitch.

16.1. Adequate Loudness

One of the problems that a speaker must solve is how loud to speak. Often he speaks more loudly than is necessary. We try to discourage the use of too much pressure on the vocal folds because we know that a constant use of considerable breath pressure may increase laryngeal stress and lead to changes in vocal quality and, if pursued long enough, to actual changes in the laryngeal tissues.

A. *Distance Between Speaker and Listener*

The perception of the intensity of a sound varies with the listener's distance from the source of the sound. It comes as no surprise to you that you must speak more loudly in an auditorium than in a living

237

room. One reason why some speakers find it difficult to regulate their levels of loudness satisfactorily is that they forget that they are as close to the sound source as is possible, whereas the listener is removed from it. Thus there is a difference in the level at which the sound comes to him.

B. *Competing Sounds*

The amount of other noise that exists between the speaker and the listener is a second element in determining what the intensity of the voice must be in order to reach the listener. The greater the rattling of dishes, cross-talk, moving traffic, blowing horns, and so forth the louder you must speak to be heard.

C. *The Listener's Judgment*

Because the distance between speaker and listener is so variable and because the interference (environmental noise) is not constant, you will need special alertness to determine how much voice to use. The difference between the auditory pathways from your voice to your ear and from your voice to the listener's ear accounts for the fact that your estimate of the loudness of your voice is not the same as his. As you speak, air-borne sound comes to your ears from your lips, and at the same time sound is carried to your ears through the bony structure of your head. Your listener must rely on the air-borne sound alone. What may seem inordinately loud to you may be just right for your listener. What may be too loud or unnecessarily loud to your listener may seem to you extremely soft. It is the listener's judgment of loudness that must govern the amount of force the speaker uses.

D. *The Reciprocal Effect of Loud Speech*

Too much vocal power is annoying. It can engender an increase in loudness when the listener becomes the speaker. You have heard that kind of reciprocal reaction when two people have an argument and each unwittingly retorts in a louder voice than the other to make his point seem the more important. Then one of the pair says "Don't shout at me!" which often ends the discussion but raises the emotional temperature of the other disputant.

16.2. Loudness and Breath Pressure

Control of the muscular activity of the thoracic cavity enables us to regulate the amount of air pressure that initiates vocalization. An increase in subglottal air pressure will increase the intensity of your voice, and the sound will be perceived as louder. The subglottal air pressure is derived from the air that is exhaled as part of the respiratory cycle. Whenever we speak or even get ready to do so, we impose our will on a mechanism that operates efficiently twenty-four hours a day without any voluntary help from us. A decision to speak changes the control of breathing from a chemical and involuntary act to a voluntary one during which chemical functions continue but do not set the pace.

When we control the respiratory cycle, we are able to take in air very rapidly and to extend the period of exhalation beyond that of involuntary respiration. The rapid intake of breath is facilitated by using the mouth instead of the nose as port of entry. The air supply is replenished during pauses between phrases.

A. *Breathing and Phrasing*

Failure to phrase material to allow for needed intake of air may result in unplanned interruptions of a thought unit, for the body's needs will not be delayed very long. The speaker who does not refill his lungs at the end of each phrase finds that he is forced to inhale at inappropriate times. Such involuntary inhalation may cause the intrusion of a noisy gasp for breath followed by a somewhat breathy voice quality. The break in rhythm may also interfere with the speaker's intended meaning. We rarely run into the problem of too little breath for the relatively short utterances in casual conversation. Platform speaking and reading are more likely to present difficulties.

Practice : Say the following sentences to someone about fifteen feet from you. Note the number of the sentence at which you begin to run short of breath before you have completed the phrase. Start your practice at this point. Use a vertical line to indicate appropriate places to pause. Then be sure to inhale wherever you have made a mark.

How are you?
I came too late.
When will Sophie start?
I telephoned you last night but your line was busy each time I tried.
The population of California exceeded that of New York during 1964.
Portofino is one of the most colorful towns on the Ligurian coast.

America's leadership must be guided by the lights of learning and reason— or else those who confuse rhetoric with reality and the plausible with the possible will gain the popular ascendancy.

—John F. Kennedy

Speak the speech, I pray you, as I pronounced it to you, trippingly on the tongue; but if you mouth it, as many of our players do, I had as lief the town crier spoke my lines.

Act III, Scene II, Hamlet
—William Shakespeare

I believe that in 99 cases out of a hundred, the American people will make the right decision—if and when they are in possession of the essential facts about any given issue.

—Adlai E. Stevenson

I think it is an universal truth that the people are much more dexterous at pulling down and setting up than at preserving what is fixed; and they are not fonder of seizing more than their own than they are of delivering it up again to the worst bidder, with their own into the bargain.

—Jonathan Swift

B. *Voluntary Control of Exhaled Air*

If you are able to focus attention on your breathing without causing unnatural or awkward movements when you do consciously what you have long done automatically, you will not need to do more than make a decision to use more or less breath when you wish to alter the loudness level of your voice.

For those of you who are not able to respond to the instruction "Breathe in" without raising your shoulders and pulling in at the waistline, we shall describe the movements that are essential for propelling air from the lungs and for replenishing the supply. In a medium loud voice give the command "To the rear, march!" You will observe a slow downward and inward movement of the lower ribs and chest, with perhaps an inward movement of at least the upper portion of the abdominal wall. When you breathe in after you have said the command, you will note a reversal of the process. The ribs will move upward and outward, and the abdominal wall will be relaxed after it returns to its forward position of rest. When you start to speak again, the abdominal muscles will begin to tense. They should remain contracted until you complete your phrase and are ready to take another breath.

C. *The Quantity of Breath Needed*

You need very little breath pressure to achieve a voice that can be heard in a relatively quiet room, for the speech mechanism is a remarkably efficient instrument. It can transform small puffs of breath into intense sound-pressure levels. As we know that we are able to create vocal sounds of considerable power with very little breath pressure, we can start our practice in modifying loudness levels without "breathing deeply." All we need to do then is to continue our breathing and to use the air we have breathed in as efficiently as we can.

THE MINIMUM LEVEL OF VOCAL INTENSITY

The supply of breath that you need in order to say even the loudest sound is not very great. It is only a fraction of what you have available every time you take a breath. Although the supply may not be enough to produce a phrase of exceptional length, it is more than enough for the usual utterance. What may come as a surprise to you is that you cannot reduce the air pressure to a point at which you can produce your voice at a lower level than can be clearly heard at a distance of three feet in quiet surroundings. Say as softly as you can, but do not whisper, the sentence, "A man jumped overboard." How far can you be heard?

TIME AND INTENSITY VARIABLES

The first step in our evaluation of breath pressure will be to estimate the supply of breath that is available for one utterance. To find out what is on tap for a given phrase, we measure the maximum duration of a prolonged vowel sound. If you can phonate a sound for X seconds at Y level of intensity, you can use X for comparisons with other levels of intensity and Y as a referent for loudness and softness. No healthy person lacks an adequate supply of breath for short utterances.

DURATION OF THE EXPIRATORY CYCLE AT AVERAGE INTENSITY

Intone the sound ⱷ at your optimum pitch loudly enough to be heard six to ten feet away. Try to keep the level of loudness constant throughout. Use a third ear to judge the constancy of the intensity. Count the number of seconds for which you can prolong the vowel on the one pitch at the selected level of intensity. You may need several trials to carry out these instructions. When you have succeeded in maintaining a specific loudness level at your pitch for the maximum period of time, record the number of seconds. Use your breath sparingly. Do not waste any breath by starting to exhale before you start to intone or by using more breath than you need to project your voice for the short distance. Your maximum duration of phonation may range from ten to thirty seconds or more. If you maintain the desired level for twenty seconds or more, you can count on an ample supply of breath without changing your depth of breathing. If you cannot maintain the sound for approximately eighteen seconds, you will have to improve the muscular control of the outgoing breath or increase the intake of breath prior to phonation or both.

VISUAL MONITORING OF EXHALED AIR

A VU meter or an electric eye on a tape recorder can aid your ear in monitoring fixed intensity if you have to practice without a listener. For the exercises that follow, the VU meter is an essential adjunct even in the presence of a listener. A VU meter is a device attached to an amplifier which provides a visual display of the volume changes of the sound carried from the microphone. It indicates relative intensity of the sound (see Figure 16.1). The movements of the needle of the VU

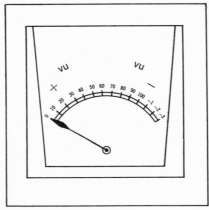

Figure 16.1. VU Meter Diagram.

meter can help you to locate the segments of your utterances at which control of breath pressure is inefficient. You may notice a brief maximum excursion of the needle at the initiation of vocalization followed by a marked reduction of movement to a level of about 25 per cent from the zero mark. The excess burst of breath at the start reduces the supply of breath on hand for the remainder of the voiced cycle. It is also a factor in the qualitative aspects of your voice.

KINESTHETIC MONITORING OF EXPIRATORY MOVEMENTS

Focusing attention on the abdominal musculature is one way to learn to control the pressure of the air stream. Concentrate on a steady, slow contraction of the abdominal muscles that move inward as you intone. Synchronize the flow of air with the contracting of the muscles that form the upper half of the abdominal wall. The compression of the abdominal wall can be sensed by you directly because of the presence of kinesthetic nerve endings in the abdominal muscles. (You are unaware of the diaphragm when it contracts during in-halation because it has no kinesthetic nerve endings.) With practice you will develop voluntary control of the abdominal muscular wall, and you will be able to maintain the needle at one level throughout the cycle. By then your ear will probably be able to direct the control of breath pressure, and you will no longer need to depend on kinesthetic cues from the abdominal muscles.

THE RELATIONSHIP BETWEEN PITCH AND BREATH PRESSURE

You can observe the relationship between the amount of breath required for different pitches by noting the length of time that the particular sound can be continued.

Practice : Intone the sound ⌀ at the same level of loudness that you achieved in the previous exercise but at a pitch one octave above your optimum. Again, record the duration of your longest trial. Repeat the prolongation of ⌀ at a third pitch either three notes above or below your optimum. In each case record the pitch used and the maximum prolongation on the chart in Figure 16.2.

	Comfortable level		Louder than usual		Minimal intensity	
	Pitch	No. of sec.	Pitch	No. of sec.	Pitch	No. of sec.
At optimum						
Octave above optimum						
3 notes above or below optimum						

Figure 16.2. Chart for Recording Maximum Duration of ⌀ at Varying Pitch and Loudness Levels. (Use musical scale notation to record pitch. See Figure 15.2.)

Now repeat the three exercises, using a louder voice. Ask your listener to move farther away from you. Check too to see whether or not you can maintain the VU meter at a higher level. Try to remember how this louder voice sounds to you. Record the length of intoning for each pitch level at increased intensity.

Repeat the exercises at the minimum level of intensity at which you can produce each of the three pitches. Record time for each exercise. Be sure to keep your mouth at a constant distance from the microphone for all VU meter readings. The listener may use a piano or pitch pipe to judge your pitch.

Now attempt to reproduce each of the nine sounds at random. Prolong them for three to five seconds. Check your judgment against the VU meter recordings and your listener's judgment of pitch.

We cannot predict the actual amount of time for each task because of the intricacies of muscular balance involved in phonation and the possible combinations of different muscles acting together that can produce the desired acoustic effects. The record of time offers a rough estimate of your proficiency in controlling the air stream at different levels of intensity at a number of pitches within your compass.

16.3. The Range of Vocal Intensity

An excess of breath pressure cannot produce infinitely louder sounds. There is a maximum level of intensity that you can reach at any pitch you can produce. At your lowest pitches your maximum intensity is less than at your highest pitches. At your optimum pitch you will produce sufficient intensity with a minimum of breath pressure. The limits of intensity cannot be changed by reduction of breath pressure below a fixed minimum or increase beyond a fixed maximum. We do not advise you to seek your limits of maximum vocal intensity. Its production puts an intolerable stress on the vocal folds. Phonation at minimum levels of intensity requires fine muscle coordination. Practice in precision control of voluntary respiratory musculature will lead to the development of muscular power. When increased intensity is desired, your muscles will be ready to respond to the demand for greater force.

Practice: Say the following short sentences loudly enough to be heard at a distance of ten feet. Use the VU meter to check the peak level for each syllable. Be sure that the last syllable can be heard as easily as the first. This exercise requires more effort than do those on monotones. Each time you shift the pitch you must make compensatory adjustments if you wish to maintain the same level of loudness. As you say the following sentences, your pitch will change within each syllable and from syllable to syllable.

How are you?
When did you go?
I rode four blocks.
Sue called Bob.
Sunshine melts ice.

Read the following excerpts in a voice loud enough to be heard at a distance of twenty feet.

Roll on thou deep and dark blue Ocean roll!
—George Gordon, Lord Byron

I was born an American; I will live an American; I will die an American.
—Daniel Webster

Ring out, wild bells, to the wild sky.
—Alfred, Lord Tennyson

I will speak daggers to her, but use none.
—William Shakespeare

My name is Ozymandias, king of kings:
Look on my works, ye Mighty, and despair!
—Percy Bysshe Shelley

Now reread the excerpts in a voice directed to a listener only ten feet from you. You can express the same intensity of feeling with a diminished loudness if you increase the antagonistic resistances of the muscles controlling the thorax, jaw, and lips.

Phonate the sounds of postvocalic /l/, /m/, /n/, and /ŋ/ at the same levels of loudness as those for the stressed vowels in the accompanying syllables.

re*mem*brance	*ling*er
*al*ternate	*sing*le
*cold*ness	*young*ster
*men*tor	*syn*thesis
*fan*tasy	*un*used

Read the following selection to a listener seated three feet from you. Read as quietly as you can without producing any whispered voice.

Note the size of the bird. It will be difficult to judge at first the size in inches, but you may compare it with certain common and well-known birds. You may have a scale of sizes, beginning with the Yellow Warbler or Chipping Sparrow, and reading like this: Chipping Sparrow, Song Sparrow, Bluebird, Catbird, Robin, Dove, Crow. Observe these birds well; note the size of each. Turn to your book, and get it in inches. Write it down; commit it to memory; have it always in mind. By making good use of such a scale, you may become expert in judging size and comparison.
Birds of America
—T. Gilbert Pearson, editor

The use of excess breath pressure on an initially stressed vowel is likely to result in a glottal stop. You can prevent its appearance by producing a crescendo of intensity rather than by starting out "full steam ahead."

Practice: Start the stressed vowel at an intensity loud enough to be heard 3 feet away and then increase the intensity rapidly. *Do not start with an aspirate sound.* For a stressed vowel syllable within the phrase, join the preceding consonant or vowel to it. Use a soft, clear tone when you begin the following sentences and do not pause before the end of the sentence.

Esther was Ahasuerus' queen and Haman's nemesis.
Arkansas's motto is "Let the People Rule"; her flower is the apple blossom.
I went East before I was eight.
In the National Archives Exhibition Hall are to be found the Declaration of Independence, the Constitution of the United States, and the Bill of Rights.
Ostriches are likely to bury their heads in the sand when a storm arises.

A. *Contrasting Levels of Loudness*

So far we have directed your attention to maintaining your voice at one degree of loudness throughout the period of phonation. The purpose of such practice has been to accustom your ear to recognize how your voice sounds at different levels of intensity and to develop the muscular control that is needed to regulate air pressure. In speaking, we do not produce all the syllables at an equal level of loudness. Unstressed syllables are not expected to be as loud as stressed ones. Contrasts in loudness are a distinguishing feature of our language. They require that a speaker produce succeeding syllables at louder or softer levels than the preceding syllables. The absolute magnitude of the difference is unimportant. The important consideration is that the difference be perceptible to the listener. It is equally important that the unstressed syllables, the softer ones, be loud enough to be heard by the listener.

Your practice in phonating the softest possible voice has revealed to you the fact that you cannot produce a clear voice at a level that cannot be heard by a listener in a relatively quiet room three feet from you. In other words, there is a minimum level of intensity at which your vocal mechanism can produce voice. If you supply less than the required amount of air pressure, you cannot overcome the resistance of the closed passage at the vocal folds. If you speak generally at a level only reasonably above the softest that you can produce you will be able to decrease or to increase intensity with little effort on your part.

B. *Avoidance of Vocal Abuse*

The high levels of noise that surround us much of the time are responsible for the use of habitually loud voices. When we try to speak above loud competing noise, we put intolerable amounts of stress on our vocal folds. The abuse does not cause pain, but it does cause changes in the tissue, which in turn reduces the efficiency of the vocal mechanism and further increases laryngeal stress. Although audibility is a minimal goal in speaking, we must understand that our voices cannot compete with noises from riveting, airplane motors, and steam engines. Nor can one voice overcome the cacophony of a large orchestra or of many voices talking simultaneously. In the presence of extremely loud noise, it is wise to refrain from speaking or to use an amplifier that might be able to increase the intensity of your voice above that of the surrounding noise. If you are at a party, get as close to your listener's ear as possible, and talk at your usual level. Your guide to adequate loudness in the presence of competing noise must be the reaction of the listener rather than your own auditory judgment at the moment.

LIMITATION OF INTENSITY IN THE PRESENCE OF NOISE

Practice in the effective use of voice at a low level of intensity in the presence of considerable noise may be obtained in the following manner.

Practice: Let all but two students in class talk to their neighbors simultaneously and continuously with medium loud voices. The talkers should surround one of the two who are not filibustering. The other should then see how close he must come to the first to have his question answered. He should not use more than minimum level of intensity. Be sure that he does not try to top the noise of the talkers.

Is the sound of rain dropping on the roof soothing or irritating to you?
When I talk softly in the presence of this noise do I speak more slowly or
   more quickly than usual?
What is the estimated population of Topeka, Kansas?
What is the altitude of Denver, Colorado?
Where is the geographic center of the North American continent?

USE OF AMPLIFICATION

Try the same exercise using a microphone and a public-address system. Change the order of the questions for each speaker's practice.

The necessity of talking to a member of the family who has impaired hearing often results in the habit of too loud speech. In such instances an amplifier, in the form of a hearing aid, should be part of the listener's responsibility. If a hearing aid cannot make your speech intelligible to the listener who is hard of hearing, neither can your increase in loudness.

16.4. Loudness and Communication of Feeling

Prevention of laryngeal damage is the major reason for avoiding phonation at the uppermost levels of intensity. There is, however, another important justification for encouraging people to speak at levels well below their maximums, that is, the effect of a loud voice on the listener. An overly loud voice may irritate the listener to the point that the loudness interferes with communication of the message and focuses attention on the listener. Stress and intensity of feeling must not be confused with loudness. Gradations of intense feelings are more easily conveyed in a voice that does not go beyond the listener's threshold of comfort.

Loud voices may be appropriate to the expression of anger. If we use loud voices when we are not angry and when the distance between us and our listeners warrants less loudness, we are likely to give the impression of anger, even though we may be completely unmoved and objective or loving. Misinterpretation of feelings can reduce the effectiveness of communication.

Remember what we have said: Loud voices beget still louder ones. The debater who shouts the loudest is not necessarily the most persuasive. The speaker who knows his subject can gain his point without assaulting the ears of his listeners. In the next discussion in which the barriers to communication provoke you to raise the level of your voice, try consciously to lower it instead. The effect will amaze you.

Practice: Read the following paragraph; then tell the class how the broadcasters can determine "suitable levels of loudness."

On July 12th, 1965, the Federal Communications Commission finally took a stand on the problem of loudness levels of recorded commercials. The decision to recommend regulation by the broadcaster of suitable levels of loudness came after several years of listener complaints and a prolonged study by the FCC of the issues involved. The stations will have the responsibility of making certain that the commercials they broadcast will not be "objectionably" loud.

chapter *17 Quality*

A PURE TONE is a single-frequency sound that has no identifying quality to it. It is a referent with which other qualities can be compared. All pure tones of the same frequency sound like all other pure tones of the same frequency. A 1,000-cycle tone produced by a tuning fork sounds just like a 1,000-cycle tone produced by an audio-oscillator. Sounds that have many frequencies are complex. All speech sounds are multiple-frequency, complex sounds.

17.1. Complex Tone

In Chapter 5, we classified speech sounds as tones, noises, and combinations of tone and noise. You will recall that each tone consists of a fundamental and harmonics or overtones. The harmonics are all integrally related to the fundamental. In other words, if the fundamental tone is 125 cps, then the overtones include 250 cps, 375 cps, 500 cps, 625 cps, and so forth but do not include 127 cps, 201 cps, 230 cps, 290 cps, 300 cps, and so forth. Noises, on the other hand, may include frequencies from any part of the sound spectrum. The tones of speech include the vowels, the nasals, and the semivowels. The speech sounds that are noises are the unvoiced consonants. The voiced consonants other than the nasals have both noise and tone characteristics. All speech sounds are differentiated from one another by the presence of a particular combination of frequencies. All speech sounds have identifying characteristics of quality.

250

A. *The Frequency Structure of Speech Sounds*

When we talk about quality of voice we often refer only to vowels. Strictly speaking, we should include the nasals and semivowels too. A descriptive analysis of the qualitative structure of vowels, nasals, and semivowels reports the specific frequencies that are present and the power or intensity of each. We do not list every frequency but only those that are most prominent. We usually refer to the more prominent frequencies or formants. When we describe speech-noise sounds, we refer to bands of frequencies, distribution of frequencies, or range of frequencies. Prominence of any portion of the range is less important than the width of the range. In Figures 5.1 and 5.2 you saw spectrograms of vowel-formant frequencies and consonant-frequency distribution.

B. *Resonance*

Voice quality is a combination of laryngeal pitch intensity and formant-frequency intensities. Pitch of voice is set by the rate of vibration of the vocal folds, which in turn have been set into motion by the force of breath from the lungs. The vibrating air continues to move through the vocal tract—pharynx and nose or pharynx and mouth—on its way out of the body. The tube-like passage affects the quality of the sound initiated in the larynx. Whenever we alter the size and or shape of any part of the vocal tract, we change the frequency structure of the sound by lessening the prominence of some frequencies and amplifying others. This is what we mean by "resonance." Resonance is the effect of the characteristics of the passage through which the sound waves travel. Often, when we talk about quality of voice we are limiting our description to the factor of resonance.

C. *Voice Quality*

The respective strengths of the overtones or harmonics give the particular character to a sound that enables us to distinguish a human voice from a violin or flute. Formant frequencies that vary from one vowel to another afford an identifiable quality for each vowel. The intensities of the overtones present in our voices depend upon the sizes, shapes, and textures of the vocal tracts, which are the resonators or filtering mechanisms through which the laryngeal tones must pass and by which they are inevitably modified.

D. *Range of Quality*

The range of qualitative changes that a speaker can produce is even greater than the range of pitch, for quality is altered by modification of the vocal tract, as well as by changes of pitch and breath pressure. The number of recognizable qualities that a speaker can produce is obviously greater than what can be produced by a single musical instrument. Although a piano can produce a wider range of pitch than can a human being, it cannot produce so many qualitatively distinctive sounds as can our laryngeal mechanisms.

LIMITATIONS OF PHYSICAL STRUCTURE

The range of qualities is ultimately bounded by our own physical structures. But within these limitations we have access to an abundance of qualities that we can draw upon at will if we have learned sufficient vocal control. Our voices can shift subtly from one quality to another to provide the nuances of meaning we wish to communicate.

LIMITS SET BY THE LINGUISTIC CODE

Quality is restricted by our own linguistic code. The vowels, the semivowels, and the nasals have their unique qualitative distinctions. Their compositions or acoustic spectrums are fairly well prescribed by the arbitrary nature of our language, and as you know, they vary from language to language. Among different speakers of English you expect more similarity of quality in /i/ than between a single speaker's /i/ and /l/ or /m/.

17.2. Identification of Qualitative Differences

You do, however, readily distinguish one speaker from another, despite the qualitative resemblance. One clue that you rely on is tempo. Other sources of identification come from the speaker's individual physical structure and from the way in which he uses his speech mechanism. The obvious difference in acoustic spectrums between your utterance of /i/ and your utterance of /u/ comes as no surprise to you because you can see the difference in mouth opening and you can feel the difference in the shape and posture of your tongue. The qualitative differences between an /i/, a vowel produced with oral resonance (actually oral and pharyngeal), and an /ĩ/, the same vowel produced with nasal and oral-pharyngeal resonance, may not be evident to you. These differences require greater discrimination on the part of the listener. And because they do not have phonemic values in English, they are likely to be overlooked by the linguistic scholar. They are of major importance in establishing good vocal quality.

A. *Recognition of Palatal Action*

The raising and the lowering of the velum are actions that you cannot readily see or feel kinesthetically, whereas the emission of air through the nose can be perceived by the sense of touch and by the sense of hearing.

THROUGH THE SENSE OF TOUCH

For tactile awareness, hold the palm of your hand or fingertips in front of your nose while you intone an /i/. If you feel air on your skin you know that the soft palate has not been raised sufficiently to block off the nasal passage. You would record your /i/ sound as [ī]. If you listen and at the same time use your skin as a gauge, you will soon be able to recognize the qualitative characteristics of insufficient palatal movement.

THROUGH THE SENSE OF HEARING

For auditory awareness, alternately occlude the nose with the thumb and forefinger, and then release it while you continue to phonate the vowel. If the palate is not raised sufficiently to block the flow of air to the nasal cavities, the sound quality will be radically altered when the nasal passages are occluded. When the palate functions normally, there is no appreciable qualitative difference between the vowel phonated during the period of occlusion and during the period when the passageways are open.

B. *Definitions of Terms*

At this point, it is well to clear up some misunderstandings that arise when simple words in our everyday vocabulary are used as part of a technical jargon. "Nasality," "nasal," "nasal quality," "nasal voice," and "denasality" refer to qualities that are not particularly desirable but are widely prevalent. The presence of these qualities may reflect inefficient use of the speech mechanism.

NASALITY, NASAL, NASAL QUALITY

An acoustic definition of "nasality," "nasal," "nasal voice," and "nasal quality" would specify the formant changes that may be perceived on a spectrogram. Nasal vowels are signaled by a reduction of the intensity of the first formant, as well as by an overall diminution of intensity, an increase in the band widths of the formants, and an additional band of frequencies just above the first formant.[1]

The articulatory mechanism for production of the nasal quality is the addition of the nasal cavities to the vocal tract by means of

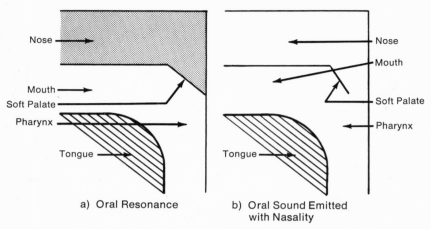

a) Oral Resonance b) Oral Sound Emitted
with Nasality

Figure 17.1. Schematic Diagrams of Vocal Tract for Emission of Oral Sounds.

lowering and relaxing the soft palate musculature. The resonator characteristics for nasal emission of vowels can be seen in Figure 17.1.

DENASALITY

As we all know, a severe cold that is accompanied by nasal congestion causes a change in the voice quality that is apparent to even the least discriminating ear. Our friends, in other words, know that we have nasal congestion by the sounds of our voices. They usually refer to this voice quality as "nasal." More often than not, the voice is *not* nasal; it is denasal when a small amount of air or no air at all is allowed to filter through the nose for the nasal consonants. The /m/, /n/, and /ŋ/ are likely to sound like their oral cognates /b/, /d/, and /g/. See Figure 17.2.

NASAL RESONANCE AND ORAL RESONANCE

"Nasal resonance" is the term we shall reserve for description of acceptable voice quality for the nasal consonants. Keep in mind that the nasal resonators become the ports of exit for only three English

[1] Arthur S. House and Kenneth N. Stevens, "Analog Studies of the Nasalization of Vowels," *Journal of Speech and Hearing Disorders*, 21 (June 1956), 218–32.

sounds. For all the others, we use the mouth as an exit and do not let air pass to the nasopharynx or the nasal cavities. We call the resulting quality "oral resonance." An acceptable voice is one in which *both* nasal and oral qualities exist, each in its appropriate place. Let us

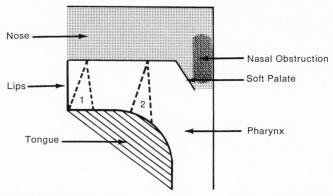

Figure 17.2. Schematic Diagram of Vocal Tract for /m/ with Little Nasal Resonance. (Dashed lines indicate point of closure in mouth at 1 for /n/ and 2 for /ŋ/.)

listen to these two qualities in our own speech, not perhaps as we habitually produce them, but as we can produce them if we make conscious efforts to follow instructions.

Practice: Start with your jaw, tongue, palate, and lips in the rest position (see Figure 17.3). Make a sound of medium intensity. Be sure to make no effort to have the sound heard at any distance from you. While you prolong this sound, try to develop an awareness of the feel of the lips, the tongue, the jaw muscles, the air passageway, and even the feel of the teeth as the uppers make contact with the lowers. You ought to be able to produce this sound with no movement of the face visible to your listeners. Because the qualitative goal for English nasal sounds requires adequate intensity and because the natural intensity is likely to be less than that of English vowels, we suggest that you add more force to the breath stream and listen to the louder sound. When you increase the breath pressure, you must do nothing that will diminish the size of the vocal tract or affect the texture of its surface. Can you increase the loudness and still maintain the feeling of rest that you had before you started to vocalize?

The nasal consonants are modifications of the sounds you have just produced. They are achieved by the addition to the vocal tract of a vestibule in the front of the pharynx where it joins the mouth. Keep your mouth closed (your lips together), lower your jaw, and allow your tongue to remain at rest and follow the jaw. You have now added an additional resonating space to the vocal tract. Can you hear the difference between your /m/ sound and the undifferentiated sound you started with? The difference may be very small, but with practice you will develop sufficient

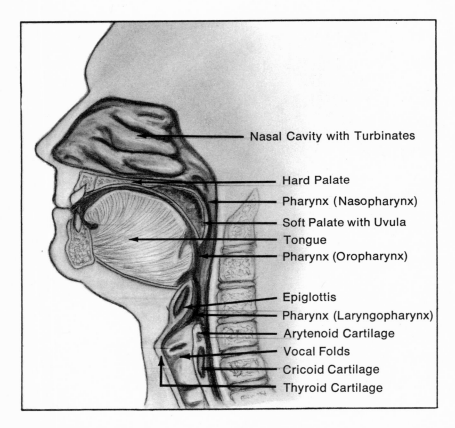

Nasal Cavity with Turbinates

Hard Palate
Pharynx (Nasopharynx)
Soft Palate with Uvula
Tongue
Pharynx (Oropharynx)

Epiglottis
Pharynx (Laryngopharynx)
Arytenoid Cartilage
Vocal Folds
Cricoid Cartilage
Thyroid Cartilage

Figure 17.3. Vocal Tract for Nasal Resonance.

auditory discrimination to recognize that the two sounds are not exactly the same. The sound you made without benefit of any oral movement can serve as the qualitative referent from which to take your bearing for the three English nasal sounds.

Start with the articulators at rest. Phonate a quiet sound. Increase its intensity so that it can be heard at a distance of about six feet. As you continue the sound, move your jaw and tongue into position for /n/. This time allow the lips to follow the movement of the jaw. The lips may be moved into this position, but they themselves do not take an active part. Now return to the rest position, and repeat the cycle again. Are you able to hear qualitative differences between the sound made with all of the articulators at rest and the sound of /n/?

Phonate a sound again while the articulators are at rest, and simultaneously lower the jaw, allow the lips to follow, and touch the back of the tongue to the front or middle of the soft palate. Can you hear a difference between the beginning and the end of the voiced utterance?

c. *Nasal Resonance*

There is a greater acoustic similarity among /m/, /n/, and /ŋ/ than between the unarticulated nasal voice and /m/ or /n/ or /ŋ/. The small magnitude of acoustic difference among the three English nasal consonants is demonstrated by the fact that, if you were to pronounce any of the sounds in isolation, a listener who was not looking at you would have great difficulty in selecting the particular phoneme you had uttered. Nevertheless, the distinctive qualities contribute to the voice quality, and they reveal their presence in the transitions to or from the vowels that they accompany.

The opening of the nasal port accompanied by a closure of the oral port at some place in the mouth cavity produces a distinctive vocal quality that we expect to hear at some moment during speech unless the phonetic content of the utterance contains no words with /m/, /n/, or /ŋ/ sounds. Nasal quality for nasal sounds constitutes a desirable voice quality. It is attained through the use of the nasal pharyngeal air channel with very slight modifications of the position of the oral port of the pharynx.

It is easy to achieve good nasal quality if the individual is in good health. It is even possible to achieve it if there is a minor obstruction in the nasal cavities. When the nasal cavities are reduced in size because of obstruction, we must increase the pressure behind the air stream to produce adequate vocal intensity. When the tissue lining the nose and or pharynx is inflamed, the acoustic effect is identifiable. Typically, it reduces nasal resonance and creates a denasal voice. Sometimes it changes the quality to something described as a "hollow" voice. When that happens to you, we advise you to keep quiet and go ome to rest.

Not only is nasal resonance a desirable vocal quality, but also the boost in intensity that accompanies its increase effects a remarkable improvement in intelligibility. It may require considerable practice to improve nasal resonance without upsetting accepted durational patterns or developing nasality on the vowels that precede or follow the nasals. Phonetic and semantic contexts govern the degree of prominence that can be given to any nasal phoneme. In the sentence "We had a wonderful time at the fair," the /n/ of *wonderful* can be prolonged and intensified more than the /m/ of *time*. But in the sentence "Time hangs heavy on my hands," the /m/ of *time* may be intensified but the /m/ of *my* would not be.

You would do well to work to increase nasal resonance if your voice has been described as light or thin, lacking in sufficient nasal reinforcement, or insufficiently intelligible.

Practice : When we increase the air pressure for the nasal, we inevitably prolong it. Be sure to *reduce* the duration pattern of the previous vowel, so that the time taken for the entire syllable is not increased unduly, thereby altering the stress pattern of the entire phrase.

Say the word *one* [wʌn] with a constant pressure for each phoneme Note how much louder the vowel sounds than the /w/ or the /n/. Now increase the loudness of /n/, in part by prolonging it [wʌn]. If you find it difficult to prolong the /n/ without also prolonging the vowel, we suggest that you try to lessen the intensity of the vowel. Try the same procedure on the words *time, charm, same, ring, strong,* and *English language.*

Say the following phrases first as you ordinarily would. Then repeat with additional energy on the italicized nasal sounds and shorter durations for the preceding vowels.

a war*m* personality	a gree*n* thumb
a fi*n*e point	a lo*ng* time

In the following sentences, increase the energy on the nasal sounds that are italicized. Practice reading the sentences aloud until you can say them without prolongation of the vowels.

Co*m*e ho*m*e.
That's plai*n* mu*m*bo-ju*m*bo.
I'd prefer wi*n*e rather than whiskey.
They stood in a si*ng*le li*n*e that stretched arou*n*d the block.
I*n* *n*o ti*m*e at all we'll have you ho*m*e again.
What was the na*m*e of the so*ng* that Maria*n* A*n*derso*n* sa*ng* on yesterday's
   progra*m*?

Tell it to the comma*n*der of the unit.

The stre*ng*th of the fabric was tested at the laboratory.

Do you know any of the me*m*bers of the You*ng* Republica*n* Club *on* campus?

Cotto*n* is Ki*ng*.

Unless the nasals are boosted, we are unlikely to recognize the distinctive quality of the liquid sounds that the poet often uses to produce a particular effect.

Read the following passages so that you give full expression to the poets' intentions.

> O what can ail thee, Knight-at-arms,
> Alone and palely loitering?
> The sedge has withered from the Lake
> And no birds sing.

> "La Belle Dame sans Merci"
> —John Keats

> When to the sessions of sweet silent thought
> I summon up remembrance of things past,
> I sigh the lack of many a thing I sought,
> And with old woes new wail my dear time's waste:
> Then can I drown an eye, unus'd to flow
> For precious friends laid in death's dateless night,
> And weep afresh love's long since cancell'd woe,
> And moan th' expense of many a vanish'd sight:
> Then can I grieve at grievances foregone,
> And heavily from woe to woe tell o'er
> The sad account of fore-bemoanèd moan,
> Which I new pay as if not paid before.
> But if the while I think on thee, dear friend,
> All losses are restor'd and sorrows end.

> *Sonnet XXX*
> —William Shakespeare

Perchance he for whom this Bell tolls, may be so ill, as that he knows not it tolls for him; And perchance I may thinke my self so much better than I am, as that they who are about me, and see my state, may have caused it to toll for me, and I know not that . . . .

> XVII *Devotions*
> —John Donne

One's-Self I sing—a
simple, separate Person;
Yet utter the word Democratic,
the word
    En-masse.
Of physiology from top to toe
I sing;
    Not physiognomy alone, nor
    brain alone, is worthy for
    the muse—I say the Form
    complete is worthier far;
The Female equally with the male I
sing.
Of Life immerse in passion, pulse,
and power,
Cheerful—for freest action formed,
under the laws divine,
The Modern Man I sing.

                "One's-Self I Sing"
                —Walt Whitman

D. *Oral Quality*

When the nasopharynx and the nasal cavities are blocked off from the vocal tract, the pharynx and the mouth act to filter the sound that has been produced in the larynx (see Figure 17.4). Sounds that pass through the oral and pharyngeal resonators are classified as oral. The label focuses attention on the feature that distinguishes such sounds from the nasals—the channel through which the air exits.

COMBINED ORAL-NASAL RESONANCE

All sounds in English are expected to be oral with the exception of /m/, /n/, and /ŋ/. Such pronouncements about speech sounds usually apply to the sounds in isolation. When we begin to study actual speech behavior as it exists in connected speech, we often find that we must modify our generalizations. For example, the statement that the plosive sounds /p, b, t, d, k, g/ are all emitted orally is true, except under special circumstances. When they are followed by nasals they, too, may be emitted nasally. No one is likely to quarrel with the original generalization, as long as the exceptions are recognized. Another generalization about speech production involves the necessity of velar closure for vowel sounds. Again there are exceptions to be noted. When the vowel sound is preceded or followed by a nasal

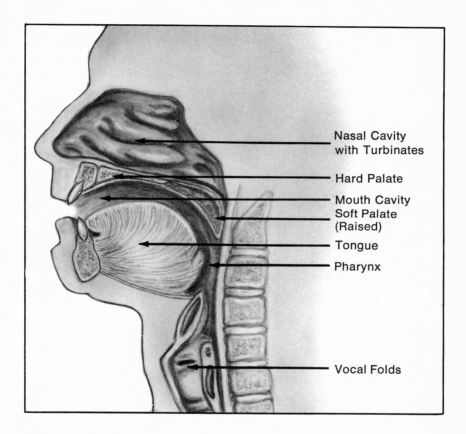

Figure 17.4. Vocal Tract for Oral Resonance.

consonant, there is a likelihood that the vowel quality (oral) will be colored or contaminated by the quality appropriate to /m/, /n/, or /ŋ/ (nasal). Such exceptions occur in relation to the phonetic contexts of vowels. There are, however, instances in which people allow the nasal coloring to remain on all vowel sounds—with more on some than on others.

There can be no denial that velar closure is not always absolute in the utterances of all speakers at all times.[2] But neither can one deny that the goal of the speaker should be absolute closure. The degree of openness that one can maintain without sounding nasal when saying "How did you like the apple pie?" depends on the relative size and shape of the individual's resonating cavities, as well as on the level of auditory tolerance of the listener.

The ability to maintain velopharyngeal closure requires a reasonable amount of muscular strength and a considerable amount of skill. Speed of action is essential. The faster you can move the palate into position, the shorter will be the samples of voice that are qualitatively neither completely oral nor completely nasal but are both oral and nasal. Keep in mind that intelligibility and power are likely to be reduced when the oral-nasal effect predominates.

IDENTIFICATION OF PALATAL ACTION

Oral quality can easily be distinguished from nasal quality and from oral-nasal quality. If your ear cannot perceive the differences in others, focus your attention first on changes in loudness level. Ask the speaker to say the following sentences aloud twice with equal efforts both times. For the first utterance, ask him to try to say each sentence with the soft palate at rest. For the second, ask him to make an effort to keep his palate raised throughout. You should be able to recognize the difference in vocal intensity. The qualitative difference that has accompanied the change in loudness is a change in the oral-nasal balance. After sufficient experience in hearing the sentences in paired sequences, you should be able to recognize the quality when either the oral or the oral-nasal emission is used by the speaker.

Practice : For perception of your own voice quality you may repeat the sentences while you hold your hand in front of your nose and mouth and listen to the sounds as you say them with your palate at rest and with your palate tensed and raised to a position of functional closure. The change in air pressure sensed through your hand offers a valid indicator of nasal emission and will help to reinforce the recognition of quality.

Hats off to the Greeks!
Youthful actors are expected to laugh.
Your voice expresses a great deal.

[2] In recent years, there have been a number of studies concerning the degrees of velar closure that are actually present when sounds are produced in connected speech. Authors have been at pains to demonstrate that speech may be perceived as oral and yet be produced with both nasal and oral emission. For a discussion of velar pharyngeal closure, see Charles Van Riper and John V. Irwin, *Voice and Articulation* (Englewood Cliffs, N.J.: Prentice-Hall, Inc., 1958), pp. 388–95, 411.

Why do you pay such a high salary?
That was her first vote.
They look like a pack of idiots.
The third rail exploded.
Brush your hair twice a day.

Now repeat the sentences with oral quality only. Use the ears of a listener, as well as your own, to judge quality. When there is a difference of opinion, use your hand to check. No breath should be discernible at the nares (nasal openings). Be sure to coordinate the movement of the soft palate with the onset of the breath stream immediately after inhalation.

If you have difficulty in producing oral quality and recognizing it you might try these conditioning exercises:

1. Look into a mirror as you say /ɑ/ with the palate at rest, pendant in the back of the mouth. Now gradually raise the palate. If you cannot do this voluntarily, watch your palate move up as you yawn. Once you see your palate move up during the yawn, try to duplicate the movement while you say /ɑ/. (One difference between a yawn and an utterance of /ɑ/ is the direction of the air stream. For a yawn we breathe in, and for /ɑ/ we breathe out. The similarity involves the raised position of the soft palate.)

2. Intone /ɑ/ for five seconds. Check for possible flow of breath through your nose. Work for complete closure of the nasopharynx.

3. Intone each of the following vowels for five seconds: /i/, /ɛ/, /æ/, /ʌ/, /u/, /ɔ/. Check for nasal emission. Try to eliminate all signs of nasal emission by recreating the feel (kinesthesia) of palatal muscles as they contract for a yawn. Whenever you have difficulty in achieving oral quality, contrast an obvious nasal form of the vowel with the oral form you are working toward. If you cannot recognize the qualitative difference, rely on the loudness difference. Follow the same instructions for the following words (do not intone them; try to achieve complete orality): *she, saw, paw, too, ask, is, fee, key, law, who, earth, off.*

17.3. The Pharynx and Quality

It may be necessary for you to turn your attention to the shape of the pharynx as you use your voice in connected discourse. If you keep the pharynx free of tension other than that needed for velopharyngeal closure and if you can prevent the tongue from moving back into the pharyngeal cavity, you will have a resonator that is uniquely suited to the transmission of the laryngeal sound. Injunctions to relax are of little value, as more often than not they produce body tensions. A helpful procedure for keeping muscles relaxed is to focus attention on an opposing set. In this instance, there are no antagonistic muscles to bring into action. Concentrate on the posture of the tongue that can change the shape of the oropharynx as well as the shape of the mouth. If you consciously try to keep your tongue from moving back into your throat, you may be able to engender the pharyngeal conditions for maximum amplification and minimum high-frequency distortions of voice quality.

Many investigators believe that pharyngeal resonance is of primary importance in overcoming vocal disorders associated with a cleft palate.[3] All students of voice agree that adequate pharyngeal resonance is an attribute of good voice quality. For the production of a clear voice, rich in overtones, the pharyngeal passageway should be maintained at its largest capacity. This position requires that you do not use the muscles encircling the open, pharyngeal portion of the vocal tract. Constriction of the walls of the tubular cavity diminishes the size of the pharynx, the resonator through which all laryngeal tone must pass. The reduction of the diameter of the pharynx, its caliber, renders the hollow structure sympathetic to the higher rather than to the lower frequencies in the laryngeal tone complex, thus affecting the quality of the voice before the articulators can act upon the sound. The less the low frequencies are filtered out, the "richer" or more resonant will be the voice quality. The low harmonic frequencies, those just above the fundamental tone of the voice, are needed for ample resonance.

Practice: In the following phrases and selections, try to achieve a balance of oral quality and nasal resonance, along with maximum pharyngeal resonance. Project your voice to a speaker seated no more than six feet away from you. Be sure that you are familiar with the articulatory information about sounds presented in Part Three of this text.

When I was one and twenty . . .
Come into the garden . . .
Now to the sessions of sweet, silent thought . . .
I remember, I remember the house where I was born.
Old time is still a-flying . . .
Ye gentlemen of England/That live at home at ease, . . .

[3] Dr. Eleanor Luse discussed the function of pharyngeal resonance and cleft-palate speech at a meeting of the Speech Association of the Eastern States, New York, April 1963. For further discussion, see Margaret C. L. Greene, *The Voice and Its Disorders* (London: Pitman Medical Publishing Company, Ltd., 1957), p. 41; and Henry M. Truby, "Contribution of the Pharyngeal Cavity to Vowel Resonance and in General," *Journal of the Acoustical Society*, 34 (1962), 1978.

Shall I, wasting in despair,/Die because a woman's fair?
I strove with none, for none was worth my strife, . . .

> Little Fly
> Thy summer's play,
> My thoughtless hand
> Has brush'd away.
> Am not I
> A fly like thee?
> Or art not thou
> A man like me?
> For I dance
> And drink and sing:
> Till some blind hand
> Shall brush my wing.
> If thought is life
> And strength and breath:
> And the want
> Of thought is death;
> Then am I
> A happy fly,
> If I live,
> Or if I die.

"The Fly"
—William Blake

LXXXV

Thus, usually when he was asked to sing,
    He gave the different nations something national;
'Twas all the same to him—'God save the King,'
    Or 'Ca ira,' according to the fashion all:
His muse made increment of anything,
    From high lyric down to the low national:
If Pindar sang horse-races, what should hinder himself from being as
    pliable as Pindar?

LXXXVI

In France, for instance, he would write a chanson;
    In England a six canto quarto tale;
In Spain, he'd make a ballad or romance on the last war—much the same
    in Portugal;
In Germany, the Pegasus he'd prance on
    Would be old Goethe's—(See what says DeStaël);
In Italy he'd ape the 'Treceentisti';
In Greece, he'd sing some sort of hymn like this t'ye:

The isles of Greece, The isles of Greece!
    Where burning Sappho loved and sung,
Where grew the arts of war and peace—,
    Where Delos rose, and Phoebus sprung!
Eternal summer gilds them yet,
    But all, except their sun, is set.

"Don Juan"
—George Gordon, Lord Byron

To thee, old Cause!
Thou peerless, passionate, good cause;
Thou stern, remorseless sweet Idea!
Deathless throughout the ages, races, lands!
After a strange, sad war—great war for thee,
(I think all war through time was really fought, and ever will be really
    fought for thee;)
These chants for thee—the eternal march of thee.
Thou orb of many orbs!
Thou seething principle! Thou well-kept, latent germ! Thou centre!
Around the idea of the strange sad war revolving,
With all its angry, and vehement play of causes,
(With yet unknown results to come, for thrice a thousand years.)
These recitatives for thee—my Book and the War are one,
Merged in its spirit I and mine—as the contest hinged on thee,
As a wheel on its axis turns, This Book, unwitting to itself,
Around The Idea of thee.

"To Thee, Old Cause"
—Walt Whitman

    But as for certain truth, no man has known it,
    Nor will he know it; neither of the gods,
    Nor yet of all the things of which I speak.
    And even if by chance he were to utter
    Finality, he would himself not know it:
    For all is but a woven web of guesses.

—Xenophanes

"Well, I do begin to understand your broken English better than I did; but no wonder I could not make it out very well at first, as you come from London; for everybody knows that London slang is the most dreadful in the world. How queer it is now, that all people that live in London should put the *h* where it is not, and never put it where it is."

    I was egotistical enough to ask the lady who said this, if she found that I did so.

"No; you do not," was the reply; but she added, with a complacent smile, "it is easy enough to see the pains you take about it: I expect you have heard how we Americans laugh at you all for it, and so you are trying to learn our way of pronouncing."

Domestic Manners of the Americans
—Frances Trollope

17.4. Quality and Laryngeal Resistance

At the beginning of this chapter, we mentioned that qualitative changes can be initiated at the larynx itself. A clear tone, which is one of the acoustic goals that we set for ourselves, must be present in the laryngeal pitch before it passes through the vocal resonating cavity. As long as you remain within the limits of optimum pitch and optimum pressure, the laryngeal tone will be clear. Exceeding the limits will cause either a breathy or a harsh quality. Focus on pitch and loudness should be sufficient to rid the voice of noisy accompaniments of breathiness or harshness. With enough practice you will habitually produce a voice that remains within the clear area but moves from one particular part of that area to another because of the changes demanded by the phonetic, semantic, and emotional contexts.

There is another perceptible attribute of quality that is worth trying to develop. It is the result of ever-changing forces that work in opposition to and in sympathy with one another. It is the result of muscular interplay, of resistance and counterresistance, of pressure and counterpressure. It is evidence of the continuous movement of structure that is necessary to produce voice. It is the dynamic quality we associate with abundance of energy. And it comes from the use of a generous amount of energy, albeit not too much. It is to be heard in a continuing modulation of pitch. It is as different from the static pitch that is the hallmark of the voice of the deaf as it is from the alternating pitch cycles of the adolescent boy. It is to be heard when the muscular system is in good physical condition, when the muscles essential to speech contract and nonessential ones remain in repose. In short, it is an attribute that develops out of the need to balance forces that never stay the same for more than a fraction of a second.

17.5. Quality Changes and Mood

In Chapter 2, we made reference to emotional and vocal habits acquired concurrently at an early age but not related to one another causally. Now we are ready to make a statement that may at first glance seem to contradict what we have asked you to accept. Changes in quality of voice may easily be observed in speakers as their moods change. This statement does not mean that mood determines voice quality. Anger may alter voice quality. But anger is not endowed with a particular quality of voice. There is no absolute vocal quality that represents anger for all speakers or even for all speakers of the same age and sex or even for two speakers of the same household. The voice quality you use when you are at ease is likely to change as anger is aroused. The change may be an increase in loudness, a higher pitch, a sharper quality, a more rapid pace, or a combination of them, or it may be exactly the opposite. The increased release of energy can effect changes, but what the specific changes will be are not always predictable. At the opposite pole of feeling, that of love, the quality may become softer, the loudness may diminish, and the pitch may drop. If you habitually use a soft, low-pitched, mellow voice or a very high, loud, shrill voice, changes of mood will be noticed only by those who are very familiar with your voice.

Although most of us are quick to make judgments about personality based solely on voice characteristics, we know we are in error as often as we are right. The facts, which we rarely have access to or which we don't want to have access to, do not always support our first vocal impressions. Recognition of this fact does not stop us from predicating personality on voice. But neither should it stop us from changing our voices for fear that others will misinterpret the changes. An habitually clear voice of adequate carrying power and ample overtones is a powerful instrument through which we can express our feelings. As long as the voice is not limited by constraints from past habits or by excessive muscular tension in its production, it will be free to reflect current feelings.

Any noticeable change in voice quality—whether an improvement or an impediment—will be perceived and even commented on by your closest friends. People who have grown accustomed to your voice may be startled when a new quality displaces the old one. Their verbal behavior often reflects their attitudes toward change rather than evaluations of the quality of your new vocal habits. If their remarks disconcert you, remind them that skillful use of muscles is not "unnatural" or "putting on airs" or "giving up the real you"; it is simply the most sensible goal for a healthy, vigorous, well-adjusted young adult who wishes to communicate effectively with his friends, his fellow students, and whatever audiences will lend him an ear.

Practice : Study the following passage. Jot down your reaction to each sentence. Then read the passage aloud to the class at the same time that you make a recording. When you have finished the reading, ask the class to list the *feelings* you expressed. Then analyze each sentence as it sounds on tape. Are there acoustic changes in voice pattern that can be identified with feelings? Are there noticeable changes in pitch contours, in loudness, in quality, or in timing? Do your feelings expressed on paper match the feelings recognized by the listeners? Repeat the assignment until your intention and your performance are in keeping with each other. If your feelings are not transmitted by acoustic changes, concentrate, as you read aloud, on particular instances in your own experience associated with the feelings to be expressed. Recalling such events may enhance the feeling to such a degree that you will convey it through your voice.

> A CULTURE is a conglomeration of the
> values, goals, habits, traditions of
> a human social group.
> Parents are people who build a culture.
> A culture is always a product of people.
> People affect a culture, a culture
> affects people.
> AMERICAN CULTURE is marked by many
> contradictions;
> PARENTS incorporate the contradictions.
> Contradictions cause trouble when they
> block action, when parents want approval
> from all factions.
> Parents transmit the culture to their
> children to prepare them for a way of
> life.
> We are a free people,
> But Public opinion is our
> authority.
> The Family is our basic institution,
> But Business is paramount.
> Children are priceless,
> But The price is too high.
> All men are created equal,
> But Some are "equaler."
> Love thy neighbor
> But Get ahead.
> Be a rugged individualist
> But Conform.

Quality is what counts
> But Quantity counts more.

Patience is a virtue
> But We want immediate results.

Hurry to save time
> But There's plenty of time to
> kill.

New ideas are fine
> But Things should remain the
> same.

A Child's Guide to a Parent's Mind
—Sally Liberman[4]

[4] From *A Child's Guide to a Parent's Mind*, by Sally Liberman, illustrated by Kiriki, with a postscript by Mary and Lawrence K. Frank (New York: Henry Schuman Company [Abelard-Schuman Press], 1951), pp. 78–101. Copyright © 1951 by Sally Liberman. Reprinted by permission of Sally Liberman Smith.

chapter **18** *Time and Durational Considerations*

PITCH, LOUDNESS, and quality of sound are characteristics of an acoustic event that exist for a certain period of time. The amount of time they cover is a factor that affects our perception of frequency, intensity, and quality. Time is therefore an important aspect of pitch, loudness, and quality.

18.1. The Duration of Phonemes

The duration of any segment of speech influences the listener's impression of the sound. If the exposure time is too brief, the listener may not hear it. There is, therefore, a minimum period of time that we use to sound distinctive elements of speech. Beyond the minimum time requirement, we have a fairly wide range of duration patterns from which we can select. Like our selection of pitch and loudness, selection of timing sequences becomes habitual in our speech. It is often as difficult to change our rate of speaking as it is to change our pitch and loudness. This difficulty may arise from the fact that exposure time is muscle-bound. An underestimate of the concentration that is necessary to alter habits of timing dooms the result at the outset. The patterns of contrasting duration are important cues to intelligibility of speech. In addition, the tempo of our speech offers significant clues to connotations. In the letter to a deaf boy on page 279, you will find a detailed explanation of the relationship between length of phoneme and meaning.

A. *Effects of Extremes of Rate*

Timing of speech warrants attention beyond general advice not to speak too quickly or too slowly. Your instructor's judgment of your rate is a more valid yardstick of tempo acceptability than is the frequently used average of number of words per minute. Listener evaluation determines the speed limits at both extremes. Speak no more quickly than your articulatory skill permits and no more slowly than your listener will tolerate. A too-rapid rate decreases intelligibility. At the other end of the scale, too slow a pace decreases credibility. When we attempt to speak more slowly than usual, we must be sure to maintain the appropriate syllabic time contrasts.

B. *Rate and Precision*

A vowel that is produced for too short a time decreases the listener's awareness of voice quality and at the same time decreases the ease with which the message is comprehended. Short exposure time of vowels must be compensated for by extraordinary precision and rapidity of articulation. If your articulation is especially crisp, you may be able to read as many as 220 or more words a minute. If your speech lacks sharpness, 200 words a minute may be your maximum rate. The number of words you say in a minute, however, does not give adequate information about rate, for it does not include the periods of silence that occur in a minute's speech. Furthermore, sudden starts, abrupt endings of vocal patterns, and lengthy pauses tend to disconcert the listener. Speech with many and long pauses and brief sound exposures can add up to the same number of words per minute as does speech with few and short pauses and long sound exposures. The former gives the impression of rapid speech more often than does speech in which the voice patterns seem to flow together. Rapid, jerky speech patterns may give the impression that the message is trivial or of little worth.

C. *Limited Exposure Time*

The tempo of your speech is a factor in the total impression your voice makes on listeners. As the exposure time of any quality (vowel) is increased, your voice itself makes a more noticeable impression on the listener. When the exposure time of stressed syllables is too long, the listener becomes aware of the quality of the voice. Whether the quality is clear or hoarse, the speaker's message is interfered with. It is true that the nature of interference for a clear voice is different from that for a raucous one. Nevertheless, we strongly advise against presenting a particular quality for too long a time. Excessive elongation of speech sounds may give the listener the impression that the speaker is pompous.

18.2. Reading—Words per Minute

Despite the fact that a particular number of words expressed in a minute is not a valid index of acceptable tempo, we shall use the device as an introduction to our discussion of tempo.

Practice : We suggest that you record the time that it takes you to read this passage:

You must be able to show your permit in order to pass through the iron gates that guard Moscow University. If you have left your identification card at home you can probably get by the kerchiefed old grandmothers who guard the gates from 6 A.M. to 2 A.M., if you plead with poise and vigor. The university maintains four research institutes, two hundred and fifty laboratories, eight scientific stations, four observatories, a library of six million volumes and an Institute of Oriental Languages. It is not a place for a casual scholar. The nationwide extrance examinations are roughly equivalent to American College Boards. (105 words)

Note the number of seconds it took you to read the passage. Check it on the first line of the scale in Figure 18.1. Read the number on the line below

Reading time for 105 words: (seconds)	60	55	50		45		40		35			30
Reading rate: (words per minute)	100	110	120	130	140	150	160	170	180	190	200	210
Listener acceptance:			Satisfactory					Unsatisfactory				

Figure 18.1. Scale for Determining Reading Rate (words per minute).

for reading rate (words per minute). Indicate class reaction to that reading rate. To calculate your average reading speed, divide the total number of words read by the number of seconds it takes you to read the passage aloud; then multiply the result by 60.

A. *The Optimum Rate*

It is likely that your speaking rate and your reading-aloud rate differ. Do not be surprised if your reading rate is faster. If the rates are significantly different, you would do well to explore the causes for the difference. Keep in mind that an exceedingly slow rate of speech, which may be warranted in situations that require deliberateness, may in other circumstances be intolerable to the listener. Remember, too, that at the other extreme rapid speech gives an impression of frenetic excitement that is out of keeping with most speaking situations.

Practice : Read the following passage as slowly as you can. Record your speed. Read the next paragraph as quickly as you can. Record your speed. What is the difference between your fastest and your slowest rate? Is it as much as 60 words per minute? It could be.

It would be a great misunderstanding of this doctrine to suppose that it is one of selfish indifference which pretends that human beings have no business with each other's conduct in life, and that they should not concern themselves about the well-doing or well-being of one another, unless their own interest is involved. Instead of any diminution, there is need of a great increase of disinterested exertion to promote the good of others. But disinterested benevolence can find other instruments to persuade people to their good than whips and scourges, either of the literal or the metaphorical sort. I am the last person to undervalue the self-regarding virtues; they are only second in importance to the social. It is equally the business of education to cultivate both. But even education works by conviction and persuasion as well as by compulsion, and it is by the former only that, when the period of education is passed, the self-regarding virtues should be inculcated. Human beings owe to each other help to distinguish the better from the worse, and encouragement to choose the former and avoid the latter. (185 words)

On Liberty
—John Stuart Mill

It is somewhat disturbing to one who visits the west for the first time with the purpose of writing about it, to read on the back of a railroad map, before he reaches Harrisburg, that "Texas is one hundred thousand square miles larger than all the Eastern and Middle States, including Maryland and Delaware." It gives him a sharp sensation of loneliness, a wish to apologize to some one, and he is moved with a sudden desire to get out at the first station and take the next train back, before his presumption is discovered. He might possibly feel equal to the fact that Texas is larger than all of the Eastern and Middle States, but this easy addition of one hundred thousand square miles, and the casual throwing in of Maryland and Delaware like potatoes on a basket for good measure, and just as though one or two states more or less did not matter, make him wish he had sensibly confined his observations to that part of the world bounded by Harlem and the Battery. (177 words)

West from a Car Window
—Richard Harding Davis

B. *Factors Affecting Rate*

When we read simple material to an audience that is familiar with the vocabulary, we read faster than when we read complex material that includes vocabulary with which our audience has had only brief acquaintance. The listeners' ability to comprehend is the key factor in the selection of the appropriate rate. So far we have estimated the tempo of speech on the basis of units per minute. If we expect to change our habitual patterns of timing, we have to work with shorter segments of speech. The average speed of syllables or words uttered in single breath groups or in phrases gives a more valid index of time exposure than do average words per minute, because in the former case the results are not contaminated by extended periods of silence.

It takes a certain amount of practice for a listener to record the times of short speech samples. But measurements are extremely useful to speakers who habitually speak too slowly or too quickly and who have very little range of tempo. A stop watch and a listener with a quick reaction time are helpful for such time measurements. A timepiece with a second hand and your own efforts are sufficient, however.

Practice : Start your utterance when the second hand reaches a quarter interval, 12, 3, 6, or 9. Then record the number of seconds it takes you to say each phrase. Do not pause before you complete the phrase. The only silence periods that will be included will be those necessitated by the periods of closure for the plosive sounds. Record the number of seconds in the parentheses to the right of each utterance. The number of syllables in each is shown in brackets following the end of the sentence.

	Seconds	Syllable rate
The sea is calm tonight. [6]	( )	( )
At what time will the curtain rise? [8]	( )	( )
I won't take "no" for an answer. [8]	( )	( )
When is the jetliner from Chicago due? [11]	( )	( )
Floods are not uncommon in the spring of the year. [12]	( )	( )
Do you live in Portland, Oregon, or in Portland, Maine? [13]	( )	( )
Television has influenced presidential campaigns. [14]	( )	( )
In Shakespeare's day a man was counted old by the time he had reached fifty years. [19]	( )	( )
Today we reckon a man of fifty years old only when we ourselves are twenty. [21]	( )	( )

	Seconds	*Syllable rate*
You should be punished for scaring me so as I am very sick and very likely to succumb to fear. [24]	( )	( )

To compute the number of syllables per second divide the number of syllables by the number of seconds.

$$\frac{\text{Number of syllables}}{\text{Time in seconds}} = \text{Syllable rate per second}$$

Does your average time per syllable change significantly as the length of phrase increases? If your listeners think that your rate of utterance is too rapid or that you speak in a jerky, staccato manner, try to slow down with each utterance proportionately, or keep the breath moving continuously from syllable to syllable throughout the entire phrase.

18.3. Speaking Rates

Now you may wish to know the average number of words you usually say in a minute. The easiest way to find out is to set up a tape recorder in a room while you are having a conversation. After you have talked continuously for a 30-second period, stop the recorder and count the number of words as you play back your speech. The same equation that you used to determine reading rate can be applied again.

$$\frac{\text{Number of words said}}{30} \times 60 = \text{Speaking rate}$$

If you wish to determine your rate of extemporaneous speaking, let your speech be recorded, and count off the words you say in a 60-second period. You will need no computation. The actual count will be your word rate per minute.

A. *Precise Measurement of Rate*

An accurate measure of syllabic vocalization time is provided by the visual display of acoustic characteristics that can be recorded on a spectrogram. If you cannot control your tempo easily because of poor auditory discrimination of time, you may find the detailed visual display useful. Most universities have such equipment in their speech department laboratories or in their departments of physical science. For a segment of speech that lasts 2.4 sec., durational patterns can be studied objectively. We can read the duration time of a

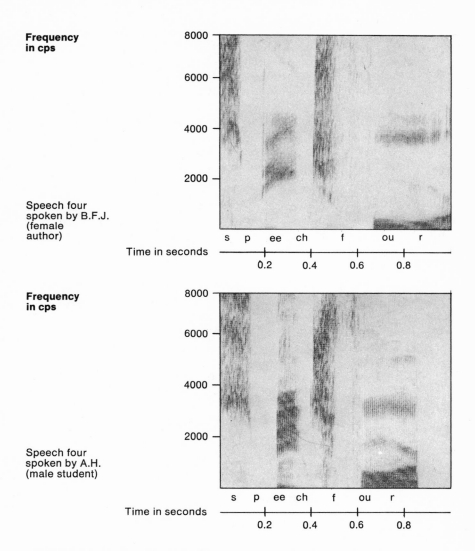

Figure 18.2. Spectrograms of Two Utterances of *Speech Four.*

Note: Frequency analysis of spectrum up to 8,000 cps. Time is indicated on horizontal axis, frequency on vertical axis, and intensity by darkness.

syllable from the photograph, which usually has a time marker in tenths of seconds below it.

B. *Comparative Rates of Two Speakers*

Using Figure 18.2, you can measure the time of each phoneme, the time taken for each syllable, and the total elasped time for each word. The phrase "speech four" was spoken by one of the authors and by one of her students. The first utterance lasted for just under one second or 0.95 sec. It may surprise you to discover that the /s/ and the silent period for the implosion of /p/ are of equal length (0.12 sec. each). The vowel /i/ is slightly longer than either of them (0.15 sec.), but the vowel /ɔ/ in the following syllable is twice as long (0.32 sec.). Both /i/ and /ɔ/ are long vowels. If you compare the duration of the student's speech with that of the author you will note that the former took only 0.75 sec. for the two-word utterance. The consensus on campus, however, is that the author speaks more rapidly than the student speaks. Although the vowel sounds are longer in her speech, she gives the impression of speed because the consonants are articulated very rapidly. The short and infrequent pauses in her speech (which are not included in the sample shown) further support the impression of speed, in spite of the increased exposure time of the voice.

C. *Rate and Stress*

Time contrasts afford an effective technique for emphasis. They are easily recognized by the average listener, even when unaccompanied by obvious shifts in loudness. Durational stress is particularly useful to the speaker who has a tendency to speak in a too-loud voice.

D. *Rate and Intelligibility*

The recognition of words rests to a large degree on syllabic timing. Nonnative speakers of English often find that they are not easily understood in spite of their accurate production of English phonemes. Their intelligibility improves when they learn to use the appropriately timed allophones. An example of extreme distortion of timing can be heard in the speech of the deaf. Their speech is difficult to understand because of the uniformly prolonged syllables and the absence of time contrasts that we expect to hear and that we rely on for quick comprehension. Specific instructions on timing appear in the following letter.[1]

---

[1] Excerpt from a letter to a young deaf boy written by B.F.J.

In preparing to read aloud the practice material for this week, I thought it might be helpful for you to consider the factor of duration or length of sound. The following notes are pertinent.

In general, the first time you read a sentence aloud, *you* take about twice as long to say it as *I* do. After you have repeated the sentence several times, you are able to speed up the utterance. However, the total time of utterance is not the significant difference between your rate and mine. The important difference lies in the distribution of time units within the utterance.

Consider each sound as a separate unit. Some sounds must be twice as long as the shortest sound, some sounds must be three times as long as the shortest sound and some sounds must be four times as long as the shortest one. Or you can reverse the statement and say that some sounds are 1/4 as long as others, some 1/3 as long, and some 1/2 as long.

But REMEMBER that the shortest sounds must last long enough for them to be recognized by the listener.

The major problem with the timing of your speech is that very often the short sounds are too long, and the long sounds are too short. Since last year, you have made CONSIDERABLE progress on shortening the short sounds. Now you would do well to concentrate on lengthening the long ones.

You have already learned when to use long vowels or short vowels /i/ or /ɪ/ and when to use a long form of a short vowel or a short form of a short vowel (/ɪ/ as in hid and /ɪ/ as in hit). You have learned this by looking and by prescription (descriptive rule).

Changes in consonant length are equally important in identifying word groups. They can be perceived by the ear very easily. But they cannot be perceived by the eye in the normal rhythmic speech. They can be perceived by the eye only if the acoustic patterns are recorded on devices such as the oscilloscope or the spectrograph.

As a result of auditory analysis by the ear and visual analysis via the spectrogram, linguists (speech scientists) have evolved a number of rules about lengthening. They have noted a correlation between *length* of sound and the meaningful position of the word in the word group. For example,

1. That's his.
2. That's his book, not mine.
3. His name is on the tip of my tongue.

In the first sentence the /z/ is the longest sound. *His* the loudest word in the sentence.

In the second sentence the /z/ is long, but not as long as in the first sentence, and the /ɪ/ is the longest sound. *His* is the loudest word in the sentence.

In the third sentence the /ɪ/ in *his* is shorter than the /ɪ/ in *is* and both of them are shorter than the /n/ and /m/ in *name* and the /ʌ/ and /ŋ/ in *tongue*. *His* is now one of the softest words in the sentence.

E. *Duration and Pitch*

Extended prolongation of stressed syllables is accompanied by an increase in pitch modulation. The changes in pitch offer significant clues to the interpretation of the words. With the lengthening of the vowels, an effort must be made to widen the pitch contour or to provide a greater number of pitch intervals. The maintenance of a uniform pitch throughout the extended syllables results in a quality more appropriate to singing than to speaking, and it should therefore be avoided.

F. *Increased Exposure Time*

Most students' speech improves considerably when they decrease their rates of speaking. In order to speak more slowly, they must stress syllables for longer times; the unstressed syllables must be continued only proportionately. The lengthening of all the syllables must be accompanied by appropriate changes in pitch and intensity. The unstressed syllables require less energy than do the stressed ones. The stressed syllables require increases in pitch modulation. When you try to speak more slowly than usual, be certain to keep the flow of breath moving throughout the clause or sentence. Pausing after each word within the group results in a staccato rhythm. Although such breaks increase the total time spent in speaking, they interfere with stress patterns and thereby distort the intent of the message. For initial practice in speaking slowly, start with short phrases.

Practice : After you can say the words in each column slowly and with appropriate time contrasts, read the last two columns as phrases. Be sure to maintain the duration contrasts imposed by the linguistic code. Check Part Three for information about the timing of individual phonemes. If you have difficulty in slowing down your speech, use lines of varying length to help you visualize syllabic length and a stop watch to measure the total time of the sounding of the phrase.

queenly	a mean man	in Aberdeen
labor	ancient times	a blaze of light
iceboat	a high wind	dry as a bone
gruesome	beautiful	choose another
hardly	far above	lethargic state

Say each of the following sentences on a single breath group. Try not to pause between words in any sentence. Strive for maximum intelligibility but do not neglect to put across the intent of the message.

Aberdeen Angus is a breed of hornless beef cattle.
The fame of Rome spread throughout the world.
You must try the electric typewriter.
The monsoon is a seasonal wind accompanied by heavy rains.
They arrived at a partial agreement.
Industrial production has reached a new high.
We need to remember the past but not to repeat it.
They gave us a most generous reception.
To preserve the freedom of our society, we must obey the laws.
It is from this point of view that I urge you to support the campaign.
A high government official made the announcement at a special press conference.
In addition to taking pictures, they made recordings of the speakers.
A course in the theory of economics is offered on Wednesday evenings.
The greatest challenge confronting young people today is a moral one that concerns personal values.

As you say each of the following phrases, think of an occasion where you might be likely to use it.

Four, zero, one . . .
From the mountains to the plains . . .
In the whole, wide world . . .
By the year two thousand and two . . .
At the sound of the bell, start.
As the crowd watched him go . . .
In the final analysis . . .
Once more into the valley . . .
For the first time in a decade . . .
From Florida to California . . .

When you are able to pronounce the phrases at a satisfactory rate, add your own words to complete each sentence. Try to maintain the slow tempo throughout the entire sentence.

G. *Monitoring*

Continuous self-monitoring of the acoustic aspects of speech is suitable for exercise purposes only. Adequate practice in the voluntary manipulation of the speech mechanism will lead to new vocal habits. Once these new patterns have become automatic, we no longer have to concentrate on pitch, loudness, quality, and duration of sounds. We can then give our attention to the meanings of the sounds.

index*

Abel, James, 130n
Abdomen, muscles of, 72–73, 240, 243
Abramson, Arthur S., vii, 130n
Accent, 40–42
  and information, 41, 42
  and pitch change, 41, 42
  defined, 41
  of clause or sentence, 54
Added glides, 139, 140
Affricates, 126–27
Allen, Harold B., vi, 10n
Allophone, defined, 82, 278
Alternative pronunciations, 38
Amplitude, 69
Arnold, G. F., v, 30n
Aspirated plosives, 101–02
Aspiration, defined, 92
Atwood, E. Bagby, 9n
Auditory discrimination, 222, 228, 230,
  235, 252

Back and central checked vowels,
  162–76
  before fricatives and affricates, 164
  before nasals and laterals, 164
  compared in prevoiceless and prevocal positions, 163–64

in stressed and less stressed syllables,
  165
  see also Vowels
Back checked, vowels, 162–76
  defined, 91
  shapes of resonators during formation of, 163
Berger, Marshall D., vii, 41n
Berry, Mildred F., 223n
Bilabial fricative, 115–16
Black, John W., vi
Bolinger, Dwight L., v, 41n, 46n
Breath pressure, 72, 75, 79, 223, 227
  and flow of air, 224
  and laryngeal tension, 223
  and loudness, 238
  and quality, 225, 252
  and pitch, 243
  and simultaneous emission, 224
  and sound pressure level, 225, 240
  increase for nasals, 257
Breathy quality, 267
Brodnitz, Friedrich, 223n
Bronstein, A. J., 10n, 88n, 100n, 118n,
  143n, 149n, 155n, 163n, 164n, 169n,
  178n, 179n, 188n, 196n
Bryant, Donald C., 172n
Bryant, Margaret M., 13n

* Special information about vowels, diphthongs, and consonant sounds is listed separately in an *Index of Symbols* following the subject index. Symbols are indexed in the order
in which they appear in the text. A special *Index of Practice Material* follows the *Index
of Symbols*.

index *of Symbols*

index *of Practice Material*

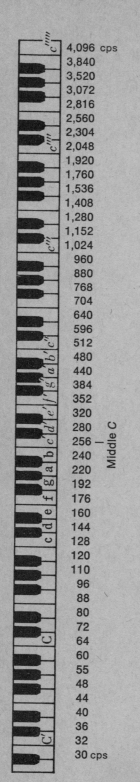

c''''	4,096 cps
	3,840
	3,520
	3,072
	2,816
	2,560
	2,304
c'''	2,048
	1,920
	1,760
	1,536
	1,408
	1,280
	1,152
c''	1,024
	960
	880
	768
	704
	640
	596
	512
	480
	440
	384
	352
	320
	280
Middle C	256
	240
	220
	192
	176
	160
	144
	128
	120
	110
	96
	88
	80
	72
	64
	60
	55
	48
	44
	40
	36
	32
	30 cps

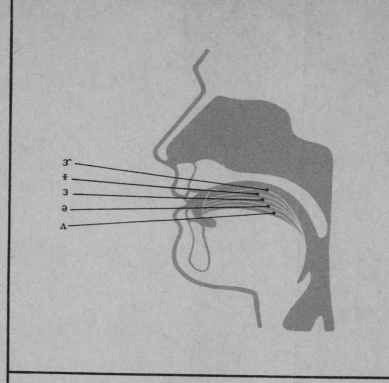

ɝ
ɨ
ɜ
ə
ʌ

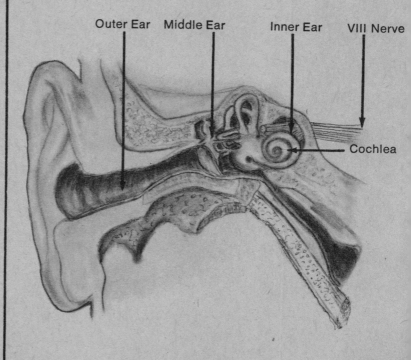

Outer Ear Middle Ear Inner Ear VIII Nerve

Cochlea